THE NEW YOUTH ARTS & CRAFTS BOOK

ALAN DEARLING
HOWIE ARMSTRONG
ILLUSTRATIONS BY GUBBY

THE NEW YOUTH ARTS AND CRAFTS BOOK

First published in May 1996 by
Russell House Publishing Limited
38 Silver Street
Lyme Regis
Dorset DT7 3HS

Cartoons by Gubby

Diagrams by Gubby, Willy Langlands, Ian Hamilton, Jerry Neville and Alan Dearling
Design by Alan Dearling

British Library Catologuing-in-Publication Data:
A catalogue record for this book is available from the British Library.

ISBN 1-898924-75-9
Printed by Hobbs the Printers
Totton
Hants.

CONTENTS FOR THE *NEW YOUTH ARTS AND CRAFTS BOOK*

ACKNOWLEDGEMENTS

This is a new book, but it is also a development of the *Youth Arts and Craft Book* published in 1982. Over the intervening years, both of us have continued to work with young people in a diverse range of settings, including youth clubs, youth social work groups, playschemes, Travellers' sites and festivals, and, of course, in our families. Arts and crafts have been a part of this work, along with group work, individual work, residential projects, use of games and policy development work with both statutory and voluntary agencies. There is no way in which we can honestly remember to thank **all** the individuals, agencies and youth groups who have in some way contributed to this collection.

However, accepting our own limitations, we would like to offer especial thanks to certain groups and individuals. We'd particularly like to thank all the young people in Scotland and England who participated in our 'trial' sessions. Everyone, young and old alike, had lots of fun, even when not every aspect of our artistic endeavours went exactly to plan! Over the years we have also worked with a number of outstanding adult staff, notably, Kate, George, Linda, John, Donald, Charley, Gilly, Jack and others who were part of the original practical skills 'Roadshow' which took arts and games activities to youth and social work organisations throughout every region of Scotland. George Symington from Glasgow has contributed a 'guest' section on DJ culture and mixing for the Music section – thanks George! We'd also like to thank Bob Stead and Simon Jacquet for their contributions to the section on the creative use of Questionnaires, Russell House Publishing and Phil Bayliss (who proofed it!)

We are very grateful to Gubby for his patience with us while we have sent him a seemingly interminable flow of sections to illustrate. His humour and skill with the pen make this a much more enjoyable book to use. Whilst we were compiling the activities for the book, we consulted with a number of suppliers of arts and crafts materials and equipment. These are all listed in the Suppliers'section and many offer special discounts to youth organisations. We would especially like to thank Paul Crick and Rob Jones at Specialist Crafts, formerly Dryad; Tim Bean at NES Arnold; John Tiranti, even if we couldn't include that many of Tiranti's sculpting and casting materials; Sue Morse and friends at the London Emblem Company; Stuart Hails at Le Prevo Leathers and staff at the Big Top and Jugglemania.

Finally, our thanks to our families and friends for putting up with us while we've been searching out, testing (playing with) activities for yet another book.

Alan and Howie

I knew that I should never work with children or animals!

INTRODUCTION

The aim of this collection of arts and craft activities is to provide anyone who works or spends time with young people with activities which are:

- exciting
- creative
- lively
- practical
- and flexible.

Neither of us are artists or 'experts' in this field of work. We are like the majority of youth workers, playworkers and staff involved in social education – we are more than willing to have a go, and participate in arts activities with young people. Most of the activities included do not require 'specialist' tutor skills, but many do require preparation, planning and careful consideration of appropriateness for particular groups, ages, abilities and, of great importance, safety.

The examples we have included of what goes wrong, as well as the descriptions of 'how-to-do' various activities should seem familiar. They are taken from the daily lives of adults working with young people, not the pages of Craft Encyclopaedias. Most importantly, we have tried to stress the importance of adopting a flexible approach to activities which encourage individual young people to develop their personal style and interests. There is no adherence to a curriculum involved in this collection, even though art teachers may well find useful information and ideas; rather it is designed as a hands-on guide to successful participation in the fullest range of arts activities possible.

Who is it for?

In each section, we have tried to give a certain amount of information, both about how to approach a particular activity (the gathering together and preparation of tools and materials) and the running of the activity session in different settings, with varying types and ages of young person. It can be very different operating a papier mache session with eight year olds in a Junior Youth Club in rural Sussex, to organising the same activity with a Youth Treatment group on the outskirts of Glasgow. Although this is stating the obvious, many books which are presently available to those working with young people, do not always take account of the pitfalls which can occur in organising an arts activity with 'real' kids. You try hot air ballooning in a Force 10 gale, or hot enamelling with a bunch of amateur tattoo artists!

We have also tried to remain flexible in our presentation of the various arts and activities mentioned. What is suitable for silk-screen printing as a style, i.e. hard, factual information on how to build a screen and stencil, is not required in the presentation music-related work. Music is such a broad area that a thick book would be needed to cover the scope of the subject, as it might be applied to working with young people. So, we have tried to indicate how we, and some of our colleagues in a variety of UK work situations, have used music-related activities as a creative tool.

Within this approach then, the information offered in this book will vary, depending upon the subject under discussion. For some, we have offered only 'tasters', giving a few ideas for how a particular activity may be incorporated into a youth programme. Scraperboard, building bogies and circus skills are pretty typical of this pared-down presentation. On the other hand, the sections on video, papier mache and murals all offer a wealth of knowledge on some of the most popular youth activities.

All about 'doing'

The anecdotal style of the book, we think, makes the subjects come alive. Arts and crafts are hardly a 'book' subject; they are about 'doing'. We hope that this comes over in the descriptions of each activity as they might be used in your club, play centre, festival or organisation. What we and our colleagues have done wrong, as well as correctly, will help you to plan some new arts and crafts sessions with the young people in your area.

The main thing about arts and crafts is that they can be used to introduce young people to a wide range of new skills, yet at the same time can be fun to be involved in. If you are at all like us, you will find that in using arts activities, you will also be enjoying the satisfaction of being able to produce articles which you would not have thought possible. This element of 'success' is crucial to building up the self-image of many youngsters, and it is the key to using the arts and crafts activities described in this book, positively.

Getting prepared

For each activity, we have tried to offer:

- how-to-do-it information;
- information on what can be produced and how it might be used;
- details of materials, tools and often suppliers;
- an idea about space, time, safety and staffing considerations;
- commentary on working with young people of differing ages and abilities and backgrounds;
- problems, pitfalls and how to avoid them.

It is impossible to make suggestions which can be applied to all the situations in which you will be working. Some youngsters will need an especially high level of support in attempting many of the activities – we think here of people with learning difficulties or impairments with whom we have worked. For them, you will probably have to adapt our directions to suit individual requirements. In other instances, it may be particularly necessary to keep a weather-eye open to dangers which may become apparent as you are organising a particular session. For instance, the woodworking skills needed for making a bogie may be imaginatively transformed by your youth group, ending with you being nailed into the resources cupboard!

As you can see from the style of the book, it is about getting involved. Young people you are involved in spending time with will frequently show you artwork or crafts they have experimented with, as well as vice versa. As a reader/user, you can be involved too. If you find any mistakes in the text, or you would like to tell us about the arts and crafts which you use with your youth group, do contact us through Russell House Publishing.

Both of us still do get involved with practical skills training, often in the form of a travelling 'Roadshow', demonstrating a selection of arts, crafts, games and group work sequences – if your organisation would like details, let us know. We hope that you enjoy using this book!

Alan + Howie

Alan and Howie.

ORGANISATION OF MATERIALS

If arts and crafts activities are to be a regular feature of your work with young people, then it is pretty obvious that some thought has to be given to the way you organise and store the necessary materials. Simply chucking everything into one corner of a room is not to be recommended!

For those lucky enough to have a workshop with storage facilities there should be no real problem; others may have to make special arrangements, like building cupboards, storage boxes, etc.. We have used a lot of the plastic storage boxes, which stack neatly into one another and are easy to label. Material that is well stored is easy to organise and use and means that people don't have to spend ages looking for the scissors which were with the comics which were thrown in a box which was put...?

Messy or dangerous materials (paints, adhesives, chemicals, modelling knives, turps, etc.) should be carefully stored and kept under lock and key if you think that necessary. Other things can be grouped together for storage, e.g. paper and cardboard, crayons, pens and pencils, findings for jewellery making, enamelling and leatherwork, printing materials, etc.. As well as organising your material carefully, you will have to consider the security of materials and tools. Especially vulnerable are photographic and video equipment, bicycles and some 'popular' arts materials such as mouldable candle wax. Youth premises are notorious for having vast quantities of items 'walking'. Padlocks and locked cupboards are a virtual necessity.

Things like Scrap Boxes and Dressing up Boxes are useful to have around, as they keep things tidy and can offer valuable inspiration to bored kids.

Scrap Box

Many of the arts and crafts which you are likely to use with groups depend on a ready supply of suitable materials. Often these materials are commonplace and easily obtainable for free, or next to nothing. Having a good supply, readily available, makes sense, not just from the economic point of view, but because you will never be short of ideas or a suitable activity if you have a wide selection of 'bits and bobs' available.

Your should consider collecting:

> Wallpaper; milk bottle tops; newspaper; colour supplements and magazines; egg cartons; milk cartons; yoghurt cartons; match sticks; ice lolly sticks; wood offcuts; corks; matchboxes; tins; buttons; shells; string; pebbles; wine bottles; coat hangers; boxes; washing up liquid bottles; soap; wool; fabric; eggshells; silver paper; old posters; and comics.

Virtually anything can be collected (as long as it doesn't go off or smell) and young people can easily be involved in gathering and searching for material. You could, for example, consider organising a trip to the beach to collect shells and small and interesting looking pieces of driftwood. It can also be worthwhile contacting local businesses for 'end-runs' that they don't need. Wooden offcuts, ceramic tiles, wallpaper, newsprint and printing ink can often be obtained in this way.

Bear in mind that shops you give custom to are likely to be sympathetic to an occasional request for materials. For example, the thin plastic bags used in corner shops are perfect for making 'delta' kites (if you get a pile of new bags you can use a template to cut out masses of kite shapes at one go.

Dressing Up Box

Any kind of clothing – shoes, hats, dresses, trousers, feather boas, skirts, scarves, waistcoats – can be chucked in the Dressing Up Box. These items can be gathered by young people themselves, or you may be able to get hold of a good selection of interesting clothing at the local jumble sale or charity shop. This can be used to hilarious effect at special occasions such as parties, open days, etc.. 'Dressing up' complements other activities like face painting, drama, and role play particularly well. And, after all that effort, it would be a great pity not to record the event for posterity, wouldn't it? Still photographs, or video films can be great fun to shoot when everyone is dressed and made up. A good time can be guaranteed at the subsequent viewing session!

Foraging

Autumn is an excellent time for collecting materials out of doors. Vibrantly coloured leaves are a must and it is easy to find a range of different sized cones which can, for example, be sprayed lightly with gold or silver paint to use in Christmas displays and decorations. We've also mentioned a number of activities which require 'found materials', such as: stone painting; eco costumes; flowercraft; and certain types of collage work.

AIRBRUSHES

A lot of commercial artwork, especially where it is produced for advertisements features the use of an airbrush. Futuristic landscape artists like Giger, famous for the 'Alien' film sets, and many poster and rock cover designers, work almost entirely with very fine airbrushes. Likewise, airbrush work features in most car and motor-bike customising – you know the sort of thing – featuring three dimensional figures and scenes. The airbrush is also a very popular tool with modelmakers, animators and cartoonists. Airbrush painting particularly appeals to young people, because, in the right hands an airbrush can be used to produce immaculately textured results of near 3-D quality, and photographic look-alikes. In youth group work, it is probably only appropriate for the adolescent age range and then only in very small groups, or for individual, supervised art work. A skilled supervisor is pretty much a necessity, because of the delicacy of the work and patience required from the potential students.

The main trouble is that the airbrush itself is:

- relatively expensive;
- requires a good deal of patience, and
- can be easily wrecked.

So, if you are thinking of buying one or two airbrushes for your youth group work, you have been warned! Make sure that a reasonably watchful eye is kept on the equipment.

The basic principle of the airbrush is used in a very simple piece of equipment called a 'diffuser'. This utilises the fact that air pressure can be used to extract paint out of a paint and blow a spray of paint onto another surface. A diffuser costs very little and can produce some interesting, simple textures onto a surface. However, it does take quite a lot of puff and the results are a bit uncontrollable.

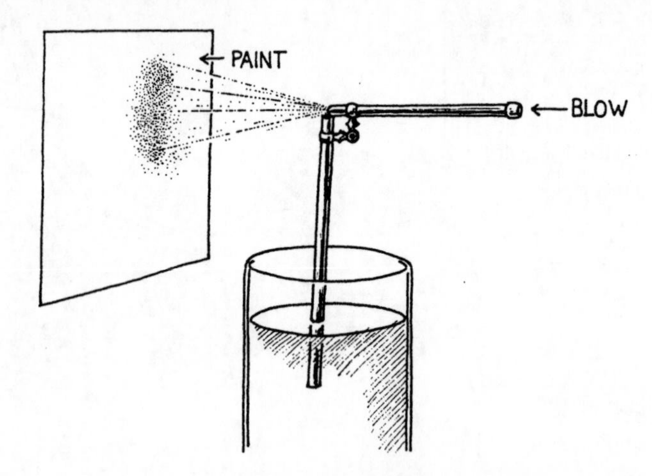

Proper airbrushes are a development on the aerosol paint can, and come in an almost bewildering range of styles and types. The old adage, 'you pays your money and takes your choice' is very apt. The more you pay, the more control the artist will have over the range of possible effects. The degree of control over the paintflow and airflow is usually managed by pressing a finger lever on the top of the airbrush using a single or double action. The button may move forwards, backwards and downwards. Unfortunately, the greater the level of independent control, the harder the airbrush is to learn to use!

The second area of expense is buying the source of the air, which will propel the paint through the instrument. A small compressor from a well known airbrush manufacturer such as DeVilbliss costs about the same as twenty disposable cans of air. For larger scale work, such as car-customising, a larger compressor will be required. If your youth group develops a great interest or aptitude for airbrush work, it will be necessary to have a compressor which includes a pressure gauge and a moisture filter. Without these sophistications, the flow of air will always be slightly variable, which will make very intricate, fine line work impossible.

The 'medium' used – the proper word for the type of ink or paint being sprayed, can be fed through the airbrush by gravity, or from underneath using suction. However, with all airbrushes it is best for young people to learn how to use the airbrush using a relatively light medium such as ink, starting with a dark colour so as to easily judge results. Whenever a new colour is introduced it is necessary to empty the airbrush and completely clean it. This helps to prevent the nozzle becoming clogged up; a frequent and often frustrating experience for younger airbrush artist. Later on, as people develop a mastery of the instrument, thicker paints can be used, but these may require passing through a filter to remove lumps.

A few hints

To get young airbrush users started, it is important that they practice some basic techniques. The airbrush has a different 'feel' to any other art instrument they are likely to have used.

1. It is vital to start and stop the airbrush while on the move, otherwise you will end up with uneven, splodges of paint.
2. To produce a fine line, the nozzle of the airbrush will be almost touching the paper and the brush must be moved quite quickly, but smoothly, above the surface. The pressure on the button must also be decreased which is quite hard to do without a lot of perseverance and practice!
3. To produce an even tone of ink across a wider area, the airbrush should be held further from the paper, usually about six inches, and more air and ink must be fed through.
4. Much airbrush work depends on adding a number of layers of colour. This builds up an image and creates the impression of shape and depth, which is so characteristic of airbrush work. Being 'slow and careful' are basic requirements of this type of art work.
5. Masking is another basic feature of airbrushing. Pre-cut or shaped card is the simplest form of mask, but masking film is the most accurate form. It is cut to shape, usually using a surgical scalpel. The film is then stuck lightly onto the surface being sprayed. Masking film is clear, and therefore, with care, can be cut 'in situ' whilst stuck over the surface.

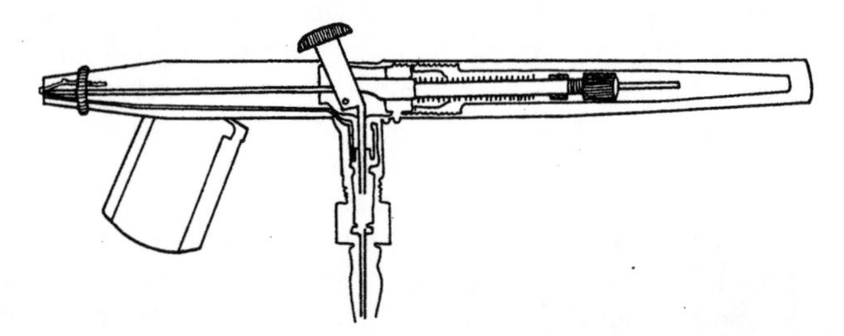

Overall, the airbrush has its merits, but is probably a risky extravagance for most youth groups, unless there is a skilled tutor and one or more highly motivated pupils. The benefits can include some very polished mural work for a building or complex design work on vehicles, leather jackets, denims or whatever.

BADGE MAKING

Most young people enjoy wearing badges. They are often used to stress individuality, identification with styles and cultures, as well as and sporting and music groups. Helping young people to design and make their own badges makes the process even more personal. In this section we look briefly at some of the ways in which you can organise a badge-making session with a small group of youngsters.

Tin Badges

Metal button badges of various sizes from 25mm to 77mm, round or square in shape, can be made using a badge-making machine. These machines are heavy duty presses, which are used to bend a thin clear sheet of plastic film over a drawing, cartoon, pre-printed picture or whatever and attach that permanently onto a metal badge, to which a pin is attached at the rear. A number of companies including Enterprise Products, Badge-a-Minit and the London Emblem Company (see Suppliers' Addresses at end of book) can supply the equipment:

- a circular cutter for cutting out the artwork
- the badge-making machine
- components
- pre-printed artwork.

Badges are cheap to make and when used in group-work or for fundraising can provide a popular and profitable activity, even with very young groups. The badge machines are relatively expensive, with robust models like those from London Emblem costing upwards of £250 – quite a large, capital outlay.

Getting youngsters started can often be the most difficult stage in any artistic endeavour, so, plan what you are going to try and produce and have the necessary materials prepared. You'll need plenty of paper, circles of paper already cut out, pencils, rubbers and a variety of felt pens, including some fine-tipped black pens.

If you are lucky, your group will be full of ideas for the badges and raring to go. If not, you'll have to motivate them. For instance, provide copies of old cartoon books and comics for copying or even tracing. London Emblem and others also produce pre-printed sheets of artwork, ranging from wildlife pics through to Drugs Awareness captions.

If your youthful artists are designing their own artwork, you must remember to tell them that they should not draw too close to the edge of the paper circles, otherwise their masterpiece will be curled up round the edge or back of the badge.
Another dodge is to prepare some samples of cartoons drawn simply on A4 sheets of paper, spaced out for cutting into circular badge shapes. These sheets can then be photocopied and this then supplies a re-useable resource for groups. The individual line drawings can be coloured, modified and personalised with names, story-balloons etc.. For younger groups, just get them to produce brightly coloured doodles to which staff can add clearly printed names. These make surprisingly professional looking badges. After the artwork has been completed, each badge can be produced in less than a minute on the more sophisticated machines.

Other ideas for what to put on badges are fairly obvious. Names, slogans, pop groups, football teams are typical examples. London Emblem have also been marketing Berol Cromar paints along with their badge/keyring/magnet and mirror backs. This paint stays liquid under the seal of the plastic cover sheet of the badge. The result is a coloured painting which can be squeezed and which can change effect.

Our experience has shown that it is best to have only older, perhaps fourteen plus, young people actually operating the badge machine. This saves on wastage and ensures that the badge machine remains operational for as long as possible! Whilst they are not difficult to operate, each badge requires a sequence of operations and getting used to that sequence needs a bit of practice, which can prove expensive!

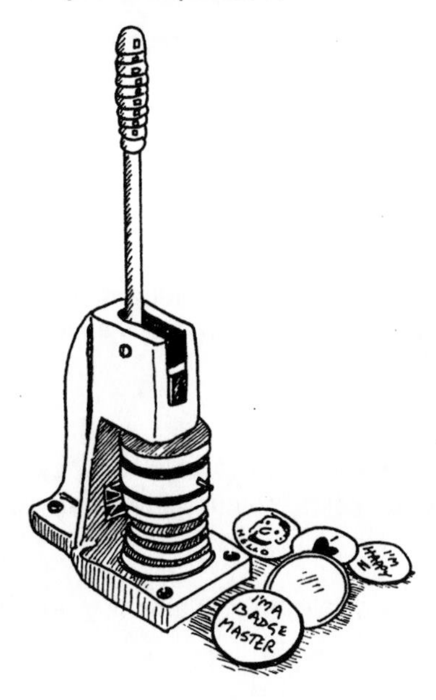

The badge-making machine can always be used to help pay for itself at fairs, festivals, open-days, carnivals, fetes and fundraising events. The machine can also be used for semi-commercial work producing runs of badges for sports teams, community groups etc., especially if you commission good quality art work.

Wooden Badges

Before we discovered the electric fret saw, 'Shaper Saw', or similar make, we used to use a coping saw for cutting out shapes from thin plywood. Although it is not the quickest way to make a badge, some unusual and striking results can be obtained. The method involves drawing a simple shape on the wood, cutting this out with the saw, cleaning it up with a fine file or sandpaper, then painting and varnishing the shape, finishing it off with a badge pin at the back of the wood. Such wondrous items as bright yellow Teddy bears, menacing Dennis's, Power Rangers and Oor Wullie's (a Scottish character) can be manufactured without too much difficulty.

The two main skills involved are:

(a) cutting out the wooden shape using an electric fret or coping saw, and
(b) painting a design on the badge.

These skills can easily be mastered by most young people aged about ten to twelve years or over. Part of the attraction of this kind of badge making is that the creative element is very high, but it does require a fair investment of time and commitment from the participants to produce the finished article.

We hear you asking, how dangerous is all this sawing?, we hear you asking. The answer is hardly at all. The Shaper Saw does tend to break blades quite quickly and it takes some getting used to pushing the wood into the blade, rather than the other way round. But despite being noisy and a little frightening at first because of the vibrations, we've never seen anyone hurt themselves. A coping saw is slower, perhaps more fiddly, but easier to control.

Wooden badge making itself is most likely to appeal to those who are already acquainted with arts and crafts activities and who can concentrate for a good half hour or longer on one activity. It is best treated as a small group activity, with one 'instructor' to every four or five young people.

How to do it

Materials and other requirements:

A workshop is virtually essential for wooden badge making, involving as it does, wood cutting, paint, glue etc.. Minimum requirements are as follows:

- Vice
- Plywood
- Tracing paper, pencils and comics
- Electric fret saw or coping saw(s) and spare blades, sandpaper
- Enamel paints and brushes, poster colour pens or acrylic paints
- Glue and varnish
- Badge/brooch pins

Specialist Crafts of Leicester stock just about anything you could require for this activity, except the plywood.

STEP 1: prepare space and materials.

Create sufficient space for yourself and the young people in the workshop area, and then lay out tools and materials, checking that vices and coping saws are properly set up.

STEP 2: brief the group.

Make sure the young people know what's involved by showing them examples of wooden badges, and briefly outlining the processes to be involved.

STEP 3: choose and cut out your shapes.

Unless anyone is particularly good at freehand drawing, designs should be transferred from comics to a piece of plywood, either by careful copying or by using tracing paper and carbon. Encourage young people to choose a shape which does not have complicated contours and is therefore easy to cut out. Shapes should be traced towards the edge of the plywood, so that they can be easily cut out.

The coping saw or Shaper Saw should be handled gently, so that the thin blade does not break. When the blade needs to be withdrawn from the wood, the sawing motion should be continued and the blade 'reversed' back the way it came. Once shapes have been cut out, any rough edges should be sandpapered.

STEP 4: paint your shape.
This can be done using tins of enamel paint and fine brushes, making sure that the paint is well stirred before use. Painting can be done freehand, or following the traced image. The painting process is critical to the whole sequence, as it is on this that the final appearance of the badge will depend. Young people should be given every encouragement at this stage to ensure that the badge shape is well painted. Helpful hints can include using only one or two 'blocks' of colour so that a contrasting effect is obtained. If enamel paints are too fiddly or slow in drying, use acrylic paints or permanent poster pens, such as the Posca range from Mitsubishi. A permanent black fine liner pen is useful for finishing off the outlines.

STEP 5: turn it into a badge.
Once the enamel paint has dried (up to three-quarters of an hour), a badge pin can be glued on, and the shape varnished to provide a protective coat. With poster pens, you can move quickly to this stage.

Staffing

Although some artistic ability can be an advantage to those intending to run a wooden badge making session, it is in no way essential. The process of tracing out shapes and designs is adequate and gives good results. The cutting out of shapes requires little more than patience and a respect for the tools being used.

It is, however, crucial that the staff member is confident in passing on badge making skills to the young people. To this end, it is important to be fully acquainted with the tools, materials and skills required; this can easily be acquired by doing a 'dry run' and making badges, possibly with other members of staff. This is a useful way of ironing out any potential difficulties relating to premises, tools or materials.

Other Badges

Badges can be made in many different ways. You can, for example, use self-hardening modelling clays (like Das, Newclay or Darwi Roc) to make badge shapes which can be painted and varnished. Tiranti's, Specialist Crafts and Arnold's all offer a range of useful products. Oven-hardening Fimo is another useful product. it comes in a good range of colours, which can be blended and mixed in unusual ways. Once baked and varnished the results are very professional. A badge pin can be added to any of these creations.

Shapes can also be cut out using pastry cutters or a craft knife. You can even (believe it or not) make badges out of an extra hard biscuit mix! Once they have been baked in the oven or even in a microwave oven (using staged cooking times; often five minutes on medium – stand; five minutes medium – stand; one minute medium – stand; one minute on low power. They can be painted and finished as above.

Plain copper shapes (used for hot enamelling, not microwaving!) can be decorated using an engraving drill, or by burnishing with a blow torch. A coat of varnish and a badge pin should be used to finish. (see Hot Enamelling section)

BAKING AND COOKING

As well as having 'survived' a variety of youth projects which have included cooking as one of their activities, we have occasionally dabbled in the kitchen ourselves! However, don't be put off, as the comments and suggestions in this section come from more able folk than ourselves. Pilton Youth Programme in Edinburgh, West Sussex Youth and Community Service and a number of our colleagues from around the UK all provided us with useful material. While it is not exactly the youth work equivalent of Mrs Beeton's, we hope that it will provide a useful starting point for groups who want to use baking and cooking as an activity with young people.

In this section we have tried to offer something of an idealised set of ground-rules. We realise that you may have to battle with problems like lack of space, resources and money. Hopefully though, you can move towards these safety standards, even if they are unattainable in the short term. The recipes, which form the bulk of the section are mostly nice and simple, and should offer some unusual alternatives for the young people you are working with.

In the Kitchen

If you are going to work with a group of between six and eight in number, the kitchen should be large enough to allow young people to spread themselves about, without adding danger to the activity. For this reason, it is vital that the space is left uncluttered. Working with this size of group, an extra large oven is really essential, if everyone is to be fully involved. Similarly, bowls, trays, measuring jugs, pans, scales etc. should be large sized. Often in youth work, it is the paid or volunteer member of staff who provides equipment, so you will have to adopt an adaptable and flexible approach to 'making-do'.

In social education groups, and in some of the drop-in centres and playcentres, the provision of meals is crucial to the identity of the groups. Meals and their preparation, in such circumstances, take on an important role as a central part of the group provision, rather than a peripheral activity. The 'main meal' experience can provide a very useful platform for relationship building, and used supportively, it is a good shared activity which encourages co-operation between adult and youth group members. It is worth remembering that if you use cooking as a regular part of your youth programme, it is likely that you will suffer far less hassle when you go for camping and self-catering residential holidays. The same equally applies in the family home, where the adult members are fed up being unpaid galley slaves!

Group rules

Safety and cleanliness are central to this activity. To help ensure that the activity does not turn into a health and safety nightmare, it is worth agreeing certain basic rules, such as:

- everyone should wash hands and dry them thoroughly on a clean towel before starting;
- everyone should take a share in food preparation, cooking and washing up;
- there should be no poking of fingers into food, pies etc., while in preparation;
- once cooked, the food should be divided up fairly;
- cultural and religious traditions must be considered(for instance, many young people will come from families which do not eat meat; most Muslims and Jews do not eat pork; many Muslims fast during the daylight hours of the Ramadan; Hindus do not eat beef – many are vegetarian; many Jews do not eat dairy products and meat at the same meal);
- have a first aid kit handy and try to organise some first aid lessons for staff and young people;
- a fire blanket and appropriate fire extinguishers are important for safety in the kitchen in case of fire;
- once a cooker is on, it should not be left unsupervised;
- be aware that matches, scalding water and hot containers can all cause serious injuries.

The Main Meal

In quite a number of youth projects, children come straight to the facilities from school and may stay on quite late into the evening. At holiday times and weekends, they may be present for the whole day. For this reason it is important that children get a wholesome meal. Regrettably, there are also many children known to youth workers who are poorly provided for in the way of food. A diet solely of fish and chips is hardly a stimulating, balanced guide to healthful living! In offering the opportunity to prepare and eat a main meal, a youth programme can:

- offer children the opportunity to acquire new skills, in the areas of food preparation, cooking, and diet;
- provide the meal as an exercise in mutual co-operation between members of the group;
- provide a 'social learning' experience, in sitting down as a group and eating a meal together.

To quote the Pilton Youth Programme: "We have found it to be frustrating, chaotic and sometimes onerous. However, it can also be productive, pleasant and cohesive for the group. At any rate, a meal is always prepared and leftovers are a rarity. It is, nevertheless, hard work to organise."

With those cautionary words, it is hopefully a model which other workers will want to copy. In the setting up facilities such as drop-in coffee bars, where there are multi-cultural groups, it affords the opportunity for youngsters to engage in a down-to-earth experiment with their own culinary traditions. A West Indian coffee bar in Acton called NOCTA used to run disco evenings (called 'Sounds') where goat curry was the staple food. The other staple additive – the 'herb' was mostly prevented from being put into this Rastafarian dish!

Try to give the young people as much responsibility as they can handle. It is worth getting suggestions for menus from the young people themselves. Pilton use a loose-leaf folder as a group cook book, which is kept handy for easy reference. With groups in fairly deprived areas, it is best to avoid being too ambitious or too experimental. Spaghetti with too many 'raj' vegetables (Pilton term to describe disliked items such as: peppers, celery, garlic, courgettes etc.) was a disaster. On the other hand, spaghetti along with a simple sauce (mince, onions, tomatoes, mushrooms) has proved a great success. Needless to say, it is usually lots of fun to watch it being eaten! As prejudices are broken down, the menu can become more ambitious.

A number of groups in the social education field have used 'going out for a meal' as an enjoyable, shared experience towards the end of a group's life. Alternatively, this can always be adapted to a 'cook-in' at the centre. Pilton used the concept of a 'Chinese evening' with the 14 to 16 year old group – they are now quite expert at stir-frying in a wok and eating with chopsticks!

Baking and Snacks

Youth clubs from the Junior variety upwards, can concoct quick snacks and baked items at little expense. Care may be needed using hot ovens and some workers would suggest avoiding recipes involving frying. Most young people like to produce items which look nice, e.g. coloured sweets and fancy biscuits, but the speed of production is also of primary importance. Pilton's favourite for instant gratification is popping corn. It's great value and the kids love making it. You can make either sweet popcorn using a small amount of golden syrup to sweeten it, or season the corn with salt. It takes only a few minutes to make – but it gets eaten just as quickly, so you may need a shift system at the stove.

Always use recipes when working with young people, and prepare for a cooking session by making sure that you have the necessary ingredients and cooking implements to hand. A stock of the 'basics' such as flour, sugar, dried fruits, spices etc., is useful; fresh items such as eggs and milk can be bought on the day. There are plenty of simple recipes in most cookery books, but we would suggest a few well tried and tested favourites which are worth looking for in the books:

> simple biscuits; flapjacks; chocolate cookies; chocolate crispies; peppermint creams, ginger bread.

With a number of baking recipes, it may be worth starting with pre-prepared packet kits. They are available in the cake section of all supermarkets. These are useful with low ability groups and give almost guaranteed results. If your group is organising fetes, gala days or the like, baked goods can be sold to the visitors to raise some funds. Finally, we offer a few recipe ideas of our own. We have tried to move away from 'traditional' British recipes, and offer instead some simple snacks which may be slightly unfamiliar, but use familiar ingredients.

Snack recipes for children and young people

French Toast

Quick, tasty, easy to make and relatively hassle free! Mix two tablespoons of milk with one large egg, a small amount of sugar, salt (and pepper and herbs according to preference). This mix produces enough for about three slices of bread, about enough for a snack tea for one person.

Cut the slices of bread into two, or into fingers, then dip them into the egg mix. Meantime, heat a mix of one ounce of butter with a tablespoon of oil in a frying pan. As soon as the oil starts to 'foam', put as many pieces of soaked bread into the pan as are required (or will fit!). When the bread is brown on the underside, turn over and when that side is also brown, serve while hot. Obviously, when frying with hot oil, an extra amount of care must be taken in the cooking area.

Cheese steaks

These are quick to prepare and are tasty. The following recipe produces enough for between one and two young people, depending upon their appetites. Whisk one egg until frothy, then add to a quarter pound of cottage or cream cheese, one big tablespoon of self-raising flour and half a teaspoon of salt and sugar. Mix well.

In a frying pan, heat two tablespoons of butter with one tablespoon of oil. When it begins to bubble, add a tablespoon of the cheese mix and fry on each side until nicely browned all over. Serve hot.

Swiss eggs

This produces enough for a snack for four. Pre-heat the oven at gas mark 5 or 375° f (190° c). Spread a thick layer of butter over the bottom of an oven proof dish. Cover this with thin slices of Edam, Gouda or Mozzarella cheese. Carefully break eight eggs and pour them one at a time onto the cheese. Add ten ounces of single cream and sprinkle with salt, pepper, nutmeg and your choice of herbs. Sprinkle grated cheese over the top. Bake for ten minutes, then place under a very hot grill to brown. This is an unusual egg and cheese dish.

Bacon cakes

You need a mincer for this recipe! Take any odds and ends of bacon, the end of a bacon joint or gammon steak and mince it until it's quite fine. Mix up a packet of sage and onion stuffing with the required amount of boiling water. When it cools a bit, mix in the shredded bacon. Mould the mixture into flattish rissoles, dust with flour and fry in shallow oil in a frying pan for four minutes per side, until golden brown. Most youngsters love these served with a healthful mountain of baked beans.

Basic cakes

Cakes are easy to divide up, and quite easy to prepare and cook. Extra ingredients such as sultanas and fruit peel can be add if required. Heat up the oven to 350° f (180° c). In a bowl, mix three and a half ounces of margarine or butter with the same quantity of sugar, beat in two eggs and sieve in five ounces of self-raising flour. Add about one or two dessertspoons full of milk and mix well. The mix should be put into a well greased baking tin or poured into individual paper baking cases. A tempting cake will be ready in between 15 and 20 minutes, depending upon the size of the cake(s) and the particular oven.

BOGIES

This is one of those activities which are part of street culture. Young people build and play with 'bogies', 'box-carts' or 'go-carts' on estates, derelict sites, etc. without much help from adults. However, that is not an argument for avoiding the use of this activity with youth groups, rather it is meant as a memory jogger for professionals who are getting forgetful of their own youth.

Since a box-cart is built from available resources, it fits into the area of junk or found art, which is mentioned elsewhere in this book. No two carts are identical and that, indeed, is part of the charm and attraction for young people. The bogie is seen as a scaled-down version of the car by many youngsters, and as long as this does not lead directly to staff encouraging auto-crime, it can be a pleasant, lively exercise, building and then racing the carts. As a group activity it has different stages.

1. *Planning and foraging for materials.* This includes assembling the required tools for the job (probably screwdrivers; saw; spanners; drill; sandpaper; nails; screws; two-and-a-half inch bolts; paint and the necessary wood and pram wheels with axles).

2. *Building.* This is a good activity to be done using volunteers and perhaps even parents. Some 'DIY' type help can be very useful at this stage – a trawl of your volunteers or local parents will usually uncover the necessary skills. With this kind of help the building process is fairly straightforward. The basic design we offer here can be tailor-made to suit your own group's preferences.

3. *Finishing.* If possible, allow time to paint/varnish/decorate the vehicles. Personalising/customising is fun! When building the carts, a decision should be taken, early

on, as to whether the finished items belong to the individual builders or the establishment. Our advice is that it is better to encourage a wee bit of private ownership (and pride) in the creation of these mini-vehicles.

4. *Racing.* Young people will quickly organise their own fantasy world around their carts. This can be encouraged, if you wish, by using events, races, downhill trials or team competitions as part of the activity.

Overall, the activity will probably be most acceptable to the younger age group. *As with adventure playgrounds, workers might be advised to check insurance liability, in case of mishaps.* We have seen carts used by youth organisations as part of their contribution to community events, such as fetes, carnivals and gala days. This is worth a thought, as a different style of contribution to the local neighbourhood. With children over twelve, the fascination with engines, motor-bikes, cars etc. is likely to have taken over. If you are working with this older age group and want further advice on motor vehicle projects with young people, contact the National Youth Agency, 17-23 Albion Street, Leicester LE1 6GD.

Materials required

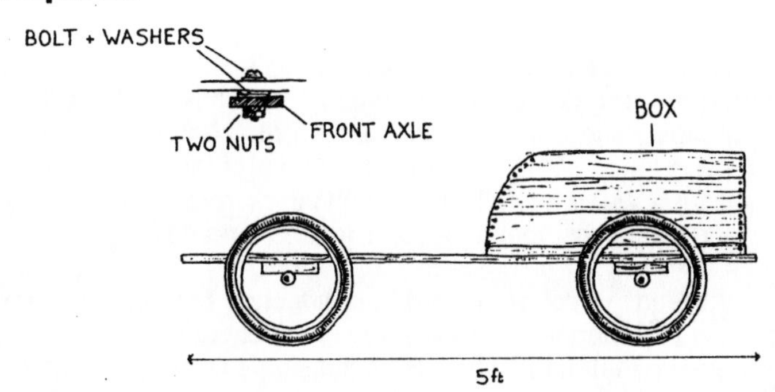

The baseboard should be prepared to the approximate dimensions in the diagram. Be flexible about this, because it has to fit the youngsters **you** are working with. The cut out front sections ensure that the front axle has freedom of movement, to enable tight turns to be made.

The front axle is bolted to the front frame, the rear axle is preferably screwed to the base plate. The box section, with front removed should be bolted to the base plate. It will take a lot of pressure! Make sure that any sharp bolts and screws are cut/filed/covered, before embarking into the world of racing. The hand held rope loop is an additional form of steering, which uses the feet as well as the hands. With more elaborate carts, we have seen steering wheels and turning gear fitted and also braking devices. Brakes are usually pads attached to pivoted 2 x 1 inch wood, which can be swung onto the rubber of the rear wheels. We haven't seen them being very effective. One design which **was** very impressive was built by two thirteen year olds. This used rear motor cycle wheels, on the back of a cart, utilising hub brakes and cables. The front wheels were from the old Moulton/RSW 16 cycles. The eventual product was rather in the style of U.S. of A. chopper-bogies. All it lacked was the high-level handle-bars!

BRAIDING AND PLAITING

We'd like to thank Tanya and Kirsty down in Lyme Regis for their help with this section. Since then, Alan, despite nine fingers and three thumbs, has made his first couple of friendship bracelets, so it can't be that difficult! Braiding and plaiting, especially, around hair have become incredibly popular. At first it was a 'crusty' fashion only copied by the envious or faithful, but it has since blossomed and grown into a popular hobby and a mainstream fashion accessory. Go almost anywhere on holiday, and you'll probably encounter a youthful entrepreneur or three, sitting on a rug plaiting other people's hair for anything up to a tenner a time. Who said crafts can't be profitable? As a youth activity, it is possible to accomplish reasonable results with youngsters from about ten upwards, but expect a few knots and the occasional naughty words as threads get 'dropped'!

Plaiting and braiding threads of cotton around hair, attached to hair, or to make items such as chokers, headbands and friendship bracelets is relatively easy to learn. The basis of the craft is the simple weaving technique which links the single or double strands of cotton thread together. These can stand alone, as in bracelets, or can be intertwined around a person's hair.

Friendship bracelets

To start off, choose three colours for the bracelet, then you need to measure one thread around a suitable wrist. Double this length and then add four or five inches to allow for the tying off at one end and any fiddly bits. Measure the other two coloured threads against the first and cut to a similar length. The very process of plaiting naturally shortens the overall length of the threads.

We have found that cup hooks screwed into a wall or plastic hooks with suction pads are useful to assist the process of plaiting. Now take each of the three threads and double them over so that loop at the top is over a separate hook (see next diagram).

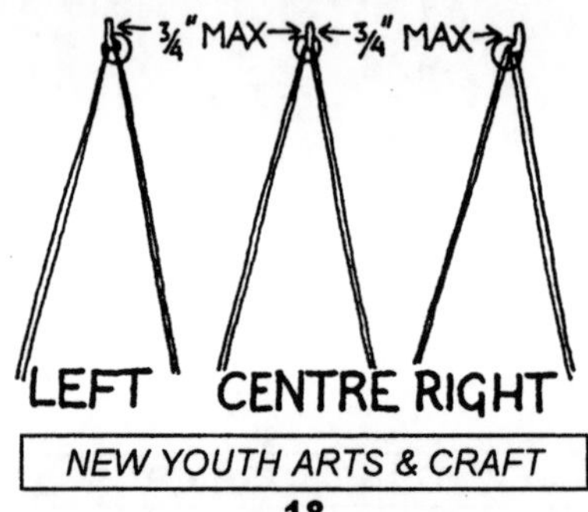

Next comes the first encounter with simple plaiting. Using the pair of threads to the right of central pair, fold them over and under the central pair. Repeat this with the left hand pair, wrapping the pair over and under the central pair. The braider (person doing the braiding) must try to keep all three pairs of threads tensioned and get a plaiting-rhythm going.

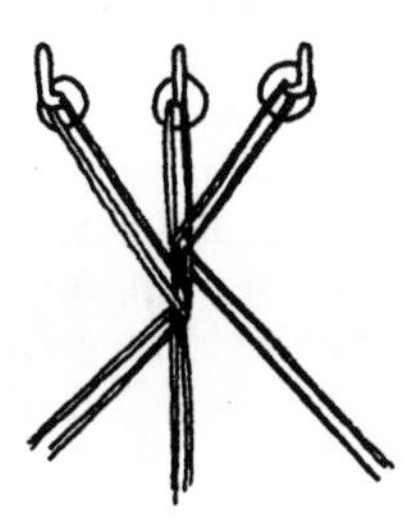

To finish off, tie a knot at the end of the plaiting, about two inches from the end of the loose threads. Similarly, tie a knot below the loop at the top of the plaiting at the other end of the bracelet. By pulling the knot through the loop, the bracelet has a natural fastener.

Hair braiding

The simplest and much less permanent way to add a hair braid to someone's hair is to use the above method to make a length of braiding, then to use the loop to tie it to the hair. However, it's not the proper method! With younger children it may be best to check out whether parents mind having their kids with braids before you embark on the following, since it can be a bit fiddly to take apart. Some schools are also distinctly 'iffy' about pupils with hair braids in their classes.

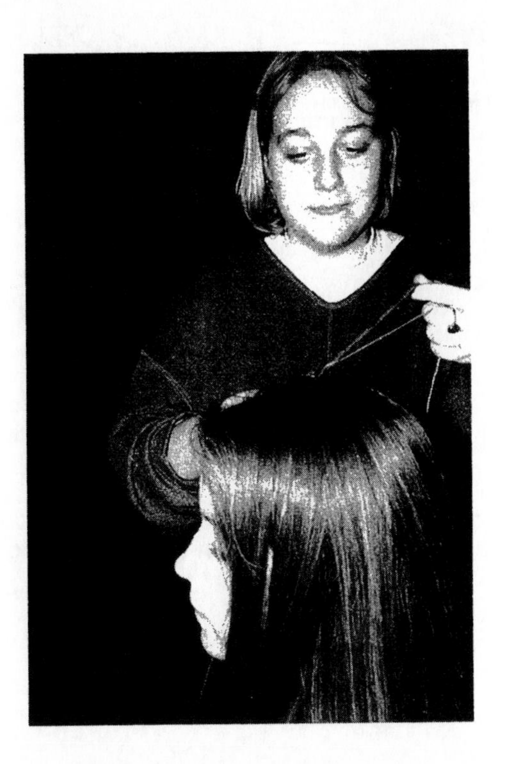

Unlike in the bracelet example, hair braiding (rather naturally) requires someone acting as braider and a second person as model. The model should be sitting at a lower level than the braider – it's easier to work this way. The stages for the method we want to describe are as follows, but, hair braiding lends itself to experimentation. There are no single right and wrong ways, and all sorts of unusual results are obtainable. Our method, based (we hope accurately) on what Tanya showed us, works as follows, with instructions aimed at the braider:

1. Plait the model's hair, (using the same technique as described in the bracelet example) separating a length of hair into three bunched strands.
2. Tie off the plait at the bottom with a piece of thread.
3. The braider may, with the model's permission, use a pair of scissors to tidy up any split ends sticking out of the plaited hair. Otherwise these stick out of the braided hair.
4. Take two or three lengths of thread all cut to similar lengths. Usually, at least twice the length of the hair plait.
5. We'd suggest tying these together neatly at one end.
6. Getting started with the braiding is the most difficult bit, because you are trying to keep the braids and the plait away from the rest of the hair. Here we go! Choosing one colour thread and starting at the top of the hair plait nearest to the scalp, wind that thread around the plait for between one quarter to one half inches worth of turns. Make sure that the other one or two threads are held taut together with the hair plait and under the thread being twisted round the hair plait.
7. Continue to repeat the process with the second and third colours of threads until you begin to run out of thread towards the bottom of the plait.
8. Knot the threads together and neatly cut off any loose ends of cotton.

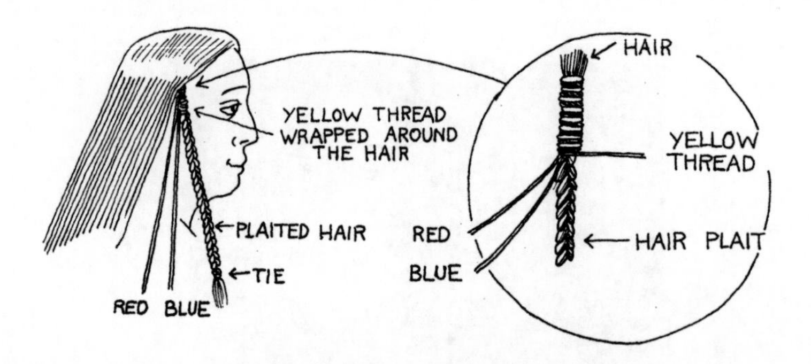

For an addition to simple hair braiding, add a criss cross pattern around the hair plait, by tying one or two threads together, and then wind them tightly around the hair plait and the original braiding in two, overlapping spirals. Finish the pattern by tying off neatly at the bottom.

A further interesting, but obvious variant, is to take three single or double stranded lengths of thread and plait them around the entire length of the hair, working in the same way from top to bottom.

BUBBLES

Blowing bubbles holds a fascination for children, but have you ever watched the poor souls trying to make bubbles with washing up liquid? Right – it doesn't work at all well.

We don't know why British washing up liquid doesn't blow good bubbles – nor do we have any evidence of an anti-fun conspiracy on the part of detergent manufacturers! Although it sounds utterly ludicrous, the only way to make good bubbles is to use *American* washing up liquid. Luckily, suppliers like The Big Top in Glasgow (see Suppliers Guide) import the stuff, so all you need to do is buy it off the shelf. Inevitably it's expensive, but if you avoid using it for washing up dishes it will keep you in bubbles for a fair length of time!

The good news is that bubble making has been transformed by the arrival of 'bubble wands.' Even better, they cost a fraction of the cost of a big bottle of 'Joy' or 'Dawn' (the American stuff you need to get hold of).

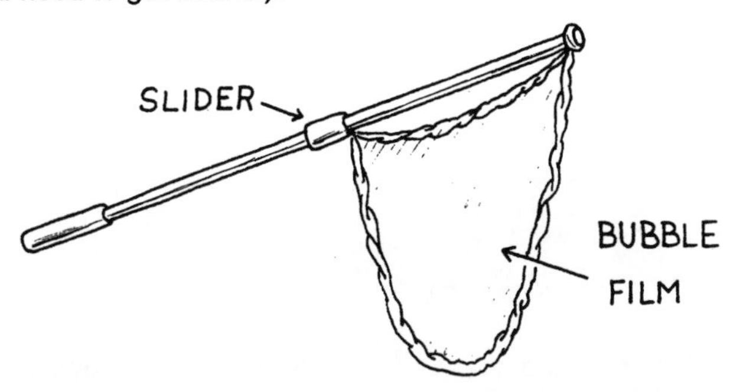

The bubble wand is a pole and slider arrangement. Two loops of fabric are connected to the end of the pole and to the slider. From this simple contraption, gigantic bubbles can be made to appear – it's a magical and addictive process.

Bubble Solution

First you need to make up some bubble solution. Follow these directions carefully (Howie didn't first time around and discovered that warm water kills the solution!)

- Measure 10 cups of water (and one or two extra cups on a hot, dry day) into a clean bucket followed by one cup of Joy or Dawn. We recommend that you add three or four tablespoons of glycerine at this stage to make the bubbles more durable (now you know how TV 'bubble magicians' do their tricks – lots of glycerine!)
- Stir the mixture very gently to avoid frothing it, and leave it to settle.

Precautions

Gigantic bubbles produce copious amounts of slippery liquid, particularly around the solution buckets, so avoid smooth surfaces like worn pavements, metal grilles and covers etc.. Wash away spillages with clean water when you're finished.

This is an outdoor activity which should be kept well away from roads to avoid distracting drivers. Bear in mind that children like to chase bubbles to burst them so make sure that your downwind playing area is safe. In any event, anything above a light breeze will make bubble blowing difficult so you may have to find a sheltered spot.

Remember that these detergents are powerful – excessive contact can do horrible things to your skin – make sure that children rinse their hands often, so have plenty of clean water nearby. Have some disposable gloves with you for children with sensitive skin or allergies and for the staff member on bubble duty! Avoid suds in the eyes.

Gigantic Bubbles

Make sure you have a bubble wand for each person, unless you want to referee arguments about who gets them first! If you can, provide a solution bucket for every four or five people. There is a simple technique for using the wand and this should be demonstrated to the group. You can pick it up yourself by following these instructions.

- Skim away any froth from the surface of the solution – froth stops bubbles from forming properly on the wand.
- Make sure that the fabric loops of the wand aren't tangled and move the slider to the bottom of the wand, i.e. all the fabric hangs from the end of the wand.
- Now immerse the loops in the solution and leave the soaking for a few seconds. make sure that all of the fabric is coated with solution but do **not** stir!
- Raise the wand until the loops are out of the solution, but keep the wand over the bucket to catch the drips. Open the loops a little by pulling the slider and look for a film of solution between the loops. If it's not there, soak the fabric in the solution again for a few seconds.
- This is the bit that needs some hand/eye co-ordination! Blow a gigantic bubble by pulling the slider along the wand towards you – as you wave the wand to create enough draught to form the bubble – then almost immediately push the slider back to the end of the wand to close off the bubble.

If you leave the wand 'open' for too long, you'll create a long sausage shaped bubble – fun, but they don't last very long. With practice, you'll learn how to control the size and shape of the bubbles by varying the distance you pull the slider towards you, how quickly you wave the wand, and when you close it. During your session, keep the wands and buckets 'froth free' for best effect. You can get several bubbles from each 'dipping.'

Other Bubbles

You can easily find smaller scale bubble blowing 'gizmos' in toy shops and department stores (often sold as part of a kit). These can be fun to use to make, e.g. different shapes, masses of tiny bubbles etc.. We didn't find any of them particularly easy to use – they are typically made of plastic and the solution sometimes doesn't adhere to them too well.

Clearly, the manufacturers of the bubble wand knew what they were doing when they used a fabric loop! If you can incorporate a covering of fabric or cloth tape on your bubble blowing implements you will achieve outstanding results. Big Al found a fabric and wire coat hanger in a junk shop and it works a treat – as long as you pull it out to a circular or oval shape! The tricky bit is removing the kink where the wires twist together; you may need to use pliers for this.

In fact, many 'found' objects can be used to make bubbles. Remember that you'll need to find a suitably shaped container for your gizmos, e.g. a large dish or frying pan for the coat hanger. Baking trays come in handy for items like:

- Plastic 'six pack' can holders.
- Two straws and a loop – thread a piece of string through two straws and tie off to make a squarish frame. Dip in the solution, carefully lift it out and pull it towards you to make the bubble. The knack is in flipping the frame to close off the bubble.
- Kiddie's fishing net frame.

You can blow loads of bubbles into the baking tray itself to create interesting effects. Do this using a straw which is first dipped in the solution (to create a film on the end). Now hold the tip of the straw just above the bubble solution and blow a bubble directly onto the solution. Blow it to a fair old size if you can and then carefully withdraw the straw and repeat the process as often as you like.

The most impressive bubble blowing feat we've heard of (at a Fair Play for Children in Scotland annual event) is life sized bubbles. Unfortunately we did not see this demonstrated, but we are assured that it works very well. To try it for yourself, apart from plenty of bubble solution, you will need a large tyre (lorry or tractor) and a Hula Hoop. The tyre is sliced in two laterally to make two containers for the bubble solution (although you may only want to use one of them.) The Hula Hoop should be covered in fabric or cloth tape, and is placed into the solution in the tyre and allowed to soak for a minute.

A volunteer can now stand in the middle of the tyre and be encased in a bubble created by a couple of people lifting the hoop out of the solution and over the volunteer's head to create a bubble. Again the knack is in how you flip the hoop to close off the bubble.

CALLIGRAPHY

This is the 'proper' name for the art of handwriting and lettering. Calligraphy is the technique used for creating italicised and script lettering. Many of us probably saw it for the first time when looking at old manuscripts and books now preserved in museums. As a creative art form for use with young people, you need to inject fun into the activity. For instance, with a younger group you might suggest that they design a 'Treasure map'. With an older group it could be design a 'Handbill,' 'Certificate' or 'Poster'.

The materials needed for calligraphy are cheap which is a bonus. To begin, all that is needed are a small selection of pens with different widths of nibs, paper, ink, and some way of creating lined paper. The pens are principally sold in three forms:

1. A pen holder with a selection of broad lettering nibs, and reservoirs which fit on the back of the nibs to provide enough ink for a few letters at a time.
2. A fountain pen, again with a range of interchangeable nibs.
3. Single nib width italic felt pens.

A number of manufacturers make these pens and you will probably find a range of each kind in your local art shop. Strangely, perhaps, calligraphy materials are one of the art materials which can be obtained from almost all art suppliers! The very largest interchangeable nibs are about one inch wide and from personal experience can take a little practice to get used to. The ink channel is so large that there is definite tendency for the ink to spill out in unwanted blobs – not a good recipe for providing young people with a successful artistic experience. William Mitchell, Dryad (Specialist Crafts), Gillot, Pentel, Shaeffer and Nikko are among the main manufacturers of pens for squared, left-oblique, italic and poster nibs. The best inks are permanent, waterproof and non-clogging. Black is still the most popular colour, but inks are available in crimson, emerald and other striking, bold colours.

Getting started

You'll definitely need one of the cheap sets of sample alphabets or calligraphy books, which offer both instruction and examples to copy if you are going to really get to grips with the range of calligraphic possibilities. To keep the lettering straight it is usually best to use a grid sheet underneath the lettering parchment/paper, or to lightly pencil rule lines with three elements:

This is a sample

These offer guides for where the tops and bottoms of most letters should be placed. The difficulty for young people, especially, is to have the patience to spend time practising each letter. The most important aspects of calligraphic lettering are:

- to hold the pen at a 45 degree angle on both vertical and horizontal strokes(both strokes should be equally wide);
- to consider how tall and wide each letter should be relative to its alphabetic companions;
- to learn how many individual nib strokes are required for each letter. For instance, many calligraphic masters would argue that a capital 'S' is constructed from three strokes:

Our illustrator and cartoonist, Gubby, writes all his letters to us in calligraphic form, so here we've let him loose with a bit of space to offer examples of how he constructs one particular style of script. With upper case on its own, there is no real problem with spacing between letters. When using lower case lettering, there should always be enough space to avoid the upstrokes of letters (called ascenders) colliding with the downstrokes (called descenders).

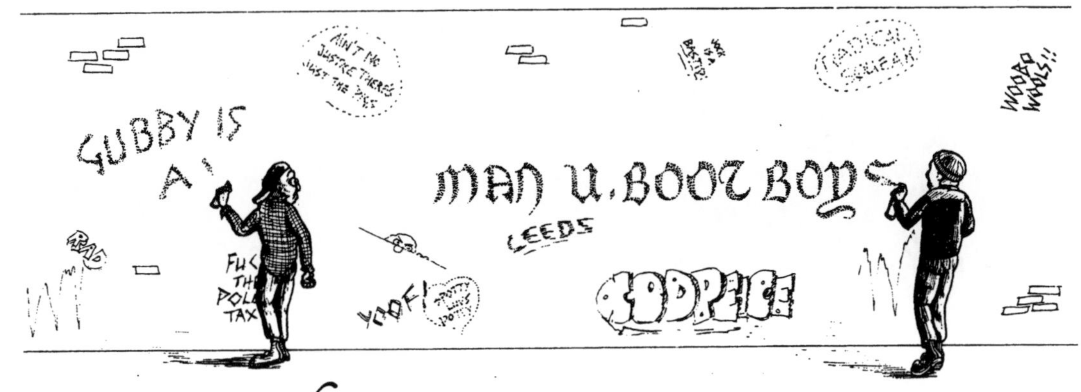

Calligraphy, I must explain,
is a damn fine thing to do;
'Cos when Xmas or a birthday comes,
& granny sends to you,
some bright green socks or a horrid tie,
that makes you want to spew,

You write her back to thank her
& say how do you do,
In a cursive script that's beautiful,
& regular & true,
Then she will barely note the fact,
that she got nowt from you!!
So now you see, this script can help,
when pounds & pence are few!

Gubby

Many young people will not be tempted to get involved with calligraphy, purely because it smacks of school and being told to 'improve handwriting'. For those who do try it out, making letters into art forms and experimenting with inventing new styles of lettering can be fun and can even earn the proficient calligrapher a few spare pounds, helping design things such as certificates and posters.

CANDLE MAKING

Wax is a versatile material (witness Madame Tussaud's!) which can be used to make an incredible range of differently shaped, textured and coloured candles. At its simplest, the craft involves melting wax, dyeing it, pouring it into a mould and allowing it to set. It is important to prepare your work area well, as wax can be unbelievably messy – a few minutes spent covering working surfaces and the floor with old newspapers is time well spent. Wax is well nigh impossible to remove from carpets – plush youth centres beware! And, without putting you off, overheated wax can ignite, just like cooking fat – so, always heat wax and stearin very, very slowly!

Apart from slabs of paraffin wax (the cheapest way of buying it) or pellets of wax (easier to use), you will need:

- Stearin (helps the wax set, intensifies colours, and makes it easier to remove from moulds).
- Candle dye (disc form is easiest to use).
- Candle wicks (of varying length and thickness).
- Wicking or knitting needle.
- Skewers.
- Kitchen thermometer.
- Double boiler (or two saucepans – one to fit inside t'other. It should be either an old pan, or one which will be kept for use with wax). A thermostatically electric wax pot is also available but costs £80+.
- White spirit or turpentine.
- Blowtorch (optional).
- Moulds.
- Vybar, used instead of stearin when using flexible moulds.
- Bucket of sand (to make sand candles)
- Wax perfume or fragrance discs(optional).
- There are also non-heated options for younger children using coloured beeswax sheets, a new mouldable, coloured candle wax, or candle sand.

If your budget stretches to it, you can buy bags of wax ready mixed with stearin. This is certainly easier to use, but you will pay a premium. Flexiwax is a specially blended wax for use with flexible moulds. All the above and more are available through Specialist Crafts.

As we've already mentioned, wax can burn very fiercely, so care is needed when melting it down. A double boiler is safest, but you can use a saucepan sitting in another pan of boiling water. One Scottish I.T. worker we know (who shall remain nameless!) confided that he heats the wax directly in a saucepan, as this greatly speeds up the process. His inference was that the danger from burning wax was substantially less than that from a bunch of impatient, frustrated I.T. kids! If you do not mind using this method (we cannot recommend it) a thermometer can be used to keep a check on the temperature. Smoking wax is the danger signal to look out for. In case of fire, have a tight fitting lid to hand – this will take care of the problem more quickly and safely than a fire blanket or wet dish cloth. For most purposes, the wax should be heated to between 57 – 92 degrees C, (see maker's instructions) depending on the specific wax type and the strength of the mould, although sand candles may need hotter wax.

Method: Tapers, Moulded Candles, Layered Candles

Slabs of wax should be broken up into chunks for melting. Try wrapping it up in an old sheet and setting someone loose on it with a hammer – that usually does the trick! Approximately 10% stearin should be added to the wax – this should be heated up separately along with the dye and the perfume, if required, before mixing with the wax.

Simple candles, or tapers, are easily made by repeatedly dipping a wick into a deep container of dyed wax. The wax should be allowed to harden between dips (doesn't take long) and should be pulled taut after the first dipping. Interesting effects can be obtained by dipping in different colours. Once the candle has set it can be scooped back with a hot spoon to expose multi-coloured layers. Remember to use a thick or thin wick, depending on whether you want to dip a thick or thin candle! This can be a time-consuming process, and you may want to start your group off with something that produces a quicker result, by using commercial or 'found' moulds like milk cartons, yoghurt tubs, plastic balls, empty eggshells, wine bottles, etc.

These moulds should be cleaned before use and the inside treated with silicone spray or washing up liquid to help the candle slide out of the mould easily. The candle can be wicked before or after the wax is poured. Commercial moulds tend to be designed to be wicked beforehand (i.e. they are provided with a hole to take the wick) so it is just as well to prepare them this way. Knot the wick (selecting the correct thickness of wick) and pass it through the hole in the bottom of the mould, tying it to a skewer placed across the other (open) end of the mould.

Plastic Mould

The wick should be arranged centrally in the mould and should be quite taut; the knot at the bottom should be sealed with Blu-tak or candle sealing compound.
The molten wax can now be poured smoothly down the centre of the mould; the mould should then be tapped gently to release air bubbles. The candle should be left in a cool place to set, or if you want a quicker result it can be immersed in water (taking care to match the depth of water with the depth of wax in the mould), or put in a fridge. The quicker you cool the candle, the more difficult it will be to remove from the mould; you will also get a frosty effect on the surface due to thermal cracking. You can get rid of this by first dipping the candle in very hot water and then cold to glaze the surface. Alternatively, the surface can be rubbed with white spirit or heated gently with a blowtorch. Because wax contracts as it cools, a well is formed in the centre of the candle which will need topping up – poke holes in the surface crust to provide a 'key' and carefully pour in the new layer of wax. A candle should only be removed from its mould once it is perfectly cold and set hard. Remember to cut off the wick knot first and then to trim it down to a quarter inch. Polish with a pair of old tights for a high-gloss finish.

Wicking a candle after it has set is relatively easy, and is recommended for most found moulds as they are often fragile. A hole needs to be bored in the candle once it has been removed from the mould. A heated wicking needle, knitting needle or skewer can be used for this. The inventive among you can try attaching a knitting needle or similar to an electric drill – this greatly speeds up the process. (This **may** be dangerous. Ed.). Alternatively, you can insert a metal wire when the wax is still soft and remove it once the candle has set. The wick should be pre-waxed by dipping, inserted into the hole, sealed with a blowlamp at the top and bottom, and trimmed. We'd suggest keeping the blowtorch in adult hands, unless you are sure of your young people.

When using found moulds like bottles, light bulbs, eggshells, etc. you will have to carefully break the mould once the candle has set hard. The 'dipping' technique can be used to colour part of your candle and you may find that some commercial moulds are designed with this in mind.

A variation on this kind of candle is to make it with different coloured layers. Each layer should be allowed to set a little before poking holes in it to form an anchor and pouring in the next layer. It is possible to produce diagonal layers by supporting the mould so that it is set at an angle. The angle can be changed between pourings to produce even weirder results!

Chunk or Carved Candles

So called because these candles use chunks of pre-dyed wax which are bonded together with fresh wax and then carved back to produce a rock-like effect. First of all break up a block of pre-dyed wax into small chunks and put into a prepared mould or other suitable receptacle (e.g. pint or half pint tankard). Now pour in hot wax of a contrasting colour and allow to set. Once set, the candle can be wicked and carved back with a craft knife to expose the original chunks or cross-sections of contrasting colours. You may like the rough effect created by carving but you can smooth it out by using a blowtorch or dipping the candle into white wax for five seconds.

Sand Candles

These got their name because (yes! you've guessed it) sand is used as a mould for the wax. Making a candle in this way bonds sand to the outside of it creating a nicely textured terra cotta effect. The sand you use should be damp (but not too damp as the result will be a poor coating of sand on the candle) and should be put in a bucket or other suitable container. The next step is to make a mould by pushing a suitably shaped object e.g. bowl or block of wood into the sand to create a recess. The recess itself can be indented with e.g. a spoon or small block of wood to create surface patterns. Hot wax can now be poured into the recess to create the candle; you may wish to experiment a few times to get the effect that you want, as a thicker coat of sand can be formed by using hotter wax or drier sand.

Once the candle has set it can be removed from the sand and wicked. The sand should be trimmed back to an even thickness with a craft knife – vivid patterns can be made by cutting through the sand crust to create coloured 'windows' in the candle. Also, the top of a rectangular candle can be pared down to create a conical shape if desired – use a craft knife and an old electric iron (set at warm) to smooth the wax.

If you want to try something spectacular, make three identical moulds in the sand and link them with channels. This will create three linked candles suitable for use as a table centrepiece. Small sand candles set relatively quickly and can usually be completed within one, two to three hour session. Another advantage of these candles is that once they have burned down the sandholder which is left can simply be topped up with fresh wax and re-wicked.

Other Candles and Waxy Ideas

Balloon Candles: fill a small balloon with cold water and tie the neck. Dip it carefully into hot wax several times to build up layers, taking great care not to let the balloon touch the bottom of the pan (it will burst if you do and may propel hot wax all over the place). Once enough layers have been built up for it to remain rigid, carefully cut the top off it, pour out the water and remove the balloon. The wax holder thus created can now be filled up with hot wax, a little at a time, swilling it around until it sets. Once all the wax has set the balloon candle can be wicked, sealed and trimmed.

Ice Candles: put a ready made commercial candle into a mould and pack with ice. Pour in hot wax to create a cratered, cave-like effect.

Candle Modelling: warm wax is nice to handle and can easily be modelled and sculpted into unusual shapes.

Decoration: plain candles that you make can be decorated in many different ways. They can be carved with craft knives or painted with acrylic paint or hot coloured wax. You can apply transfers to them or indent the surface repeatedly with a hard object to create a pattern. Chunks of discarded wax or strips of modelling wax can be glued onto them, and the artists among you can use modelling wax to create intricate patterns or artificial flowers to attach to the candles.

Face Masks: pour hot wax onto a large plate or tray and allow to become cool and pliable. It can then be peeled off and carefully placed over someone's face, care being taken to leave a breathing hole and to smooth in all the details. Once removed it can be hardened in cold water and painted.

Gory Hands: the wax specialists at Dundee's Clubbie assured us that you get a realistic gory effect if you drip warm multi-coloured wax onto your hands and arms. This was apparently an accidental discovery (we are not surprised!) which seems to have a lot of potential, particularly for those interested in making horror videos. The idea of meeting a pair of gory hands **and** a painted wax face mask on a dark night hardly bears thinking about!

Shell Candles: these are some of the nicest effects we have seen. If you are unable to collect large shells at your local beach, you can buy them from suppliers. You will need shells with a deep, wide opening so that you can pour the wax in easily. A large opening also means that they will shed a good amount of light. Conch and bonnet shells are particularly suitable.

If your chosen shell will not stand upright of its own accord, fix some modelling clay under the base. As with any other 'stand alone' candles, you should really place them on a saucer when burning to avoid spillages on your favourite table!

Shell candles must be wicked before pouring the wax. Hang a wick of correct length and thickness from a rod or pencil placed over the top of the shell. Use a thin wick for openings of up to one inch, medium for up to three inches and thick for openings larger than this. Make sure the wick is hanging straight down and gently pour the wax in until it is almost at the top of the shell. Finally (once the wax has set) remove the rod and trim the wick.

Beeswax sheet candles: These are used cold, by hand-wrapping around a wick in tightly formed cylinder shape. They come in 40 cm x 20 cm sheets in a range of colours. Ideal for younger groups.

Mouldable candles: This is rather like making candles out of plasticine! The trays of mouldable wax can be cut from the container with a knife and then moulded by hand. It is safe, easy to use and requires no stearin, dyes or melting. It comes in six basic colours which can be mixed.
Candle sand: This is not the same as Sand candles! Candle sand is simple for any age group to use. The sand is poured in any thickness into a suitable container, then a wick is inserted and the candle can be lit. It also floats, which can give stunning effects with the silver, gold and purple star mixes. Not cheap, but fun and definitely less messy!

Candle making is an excellent activity to use with small groups (4 or 5 at a time) of young people for several reasons. If you plan properly, some candles can be completed within one session, enabling them to be taken home immediately. Candles are always useful and can be used straight away, while the process of making and decorating them allows for individual creativity and experimentation. Although it is a good all year round activity, candles become 'extra-special' if made in the autumn leading up to Christmas and New Year. They make good Christmas gifts or first-footing presents, and generally add to the festive atmosphere.

CARDS, CALENDARS AND CARTOONS (including Stencilling)

Cards

Young people are often keen to produce designs for cards, notelets, calendars and all manner of greetings missives. These may be linked to special occasions, and especially the festive seasons celebrated by different religions. There are many different techniques which can be applied, some of which are covered elsewhere in this book. For instance, lino and screen printing, collage, airbrush techniques and photography can all be used to make interesting designs for cards. When working in monochrome – black and white – designs can easily be enlarged, reduced or multiply copied on a photocopier. This can be an impressive way for kids both to show off their own developing skills and to obtain good results for relatively little labour.

Design

In the collage section we mention cutting and pasting photos. A professional looking greeting card can be produced by pasting a photo onto card on its own, or with a 'bubble' or some other sort of caption. This can be very effective and is easily produced using only card, photo images, scissors, paper and glue. Old cards can be recycled this way. The more environmentally-conscious, or perhaps miserly, will use this technique to return a Christmas robin to Great Aunt Jane!

Young groups still enjoy making cards which abound with glitter and all things silver and gold. Pilton Youth Programme recommend the purchase of quite expensive gold and silver pens which are oil based as: "Well worth the trouble and expense". Posca pens by Mitsubishi are the best we've encountered and come in a vibrant range of colours as well as metallic finishes. Specialist Crafts market Edding metallic markers and the Zig professional marker range, which can be refilled. Paper, glue, glitter and coloured sheets of tissue come in useful in this method of card or calendar design.

Drawing and painting are still, happily, popular with youngsters. The youth worker may be required to brainstorm a few ideas to determine suitable subjects. This can then avoid the constant flowing chorus of youthful voices saying: "What shall we draw?" Tracing is another way in which accurate representations can be realised. It is not 'cheating' in the way youngsters see it – graphic artists do it all the time! The ideas described in the rubbings section could also be considered for pasting up onto card. As with collage, a drawback of some glues is that as artwork dries out, bubbles tend to form and in extreme cases, central heating can cause almost total destruction of home produced artwork. If you can afford it, and provide a well ventilated area, 3M's Spraymount range is very reliable, and Pritt-type stick glue is non-toxic and fairly effective.

Lettering

It can be a good idea to encourage young people to produce lettering, often referred to as *typography* on a computer. They might either use a word processing package such as Word 6, or a design application like Corel Draw; also there are a number of CD packages offering literally thousands of different type founts and clip art. The danger lies less in their use, but in the potential to overload the computer's memory. For instance, the words 'Happy Birthday' look very different in different typefaces:

HAPPY BIRTHDAY

HAPPY BIRTHDAY

Happy Birthday

Happy Birthday

HAPPY BIRTHDAY

Happy Birthday

Most young people will have had some experience of using different type styles at school or home and experimenting with lettering can be a very creative exercise. An alternative, is to use sheets of *dry transfer lettering* such as those manufactured by Letraset or Edding. To use these it is necessary to draw a light pencil line on the paper. The letters are then lined up with their base against the pencil line. Rounded letters tend to be slightly larger, therefore line up with the lower curve just below the pencil line. Once the lettering is finished, tell the budding graphic artists to carefully and lightly, rub out the pencil line. When trying to make photos into cards, a good dodge for lettering, which has been used by youth groups trying to produce cards for fund-raising, is as follows. Letraset, as above, onto the clear film directly over the paper. The result will give accurate, professional, white lettering contrasting against a darker background. One last comment (for the moment) on the use of dry transfer lettering: the spacing between letters **can** be proportionally worked out. With youth groups, especially under-twelves, this normally gives untidy results. An easier answer is to line up each letter as close as possible to its predecessor, whilst still leaving a very minimal amount of space.

Other forms of lettering which can be considered include:

1. stencilled letters;
2. cut-out letters from magazines and newspapers;
3. italic or handwritten (calligraphic) headings.

*Stencils: t*hese are OK for use with youngsters, although since it's a slow process it may use up the kids' patience rather quickly. If you buy stencils you will often be offered a stencil brush which can be used with water colour/poster paint. The stencil must be held firmly onto the paper of card, otherwise an untidy image is produced. Really, for hand producing cards, it is a bit laborious. One useful dodge for work with younger groups is to use special stencils with prepared messages, such as 'Thank You' or 'Happy Christmas' already cut out as a complete image.

Stencil sheets of single letters are more suitable for producing lettering onto T-shirts etc., used in conjunction with fabric pens made by reputable firms such as Dylon, Berol and Pebeo. A quick look through the Arnolds' and Specialist Crafts' catalogues will provide plenty of ideas.

If you are feeling very masochistic, you might follow our example and occasionally make your own stencils, with lettering already spaced and perhaps included within an overall design. To do this, use at least 120gsm paper and preferably heavier weight card. Mark out the design as accurately as possible, then cut out sections of the letters with a designer's knife/scalpel. When used for calendars or T-shirts, this can, if you are careful, produce a good primitive lettering style which can be repeated a number of times. It's still time consuming, but less than stencilling individual letters. Only older young people will have the skill and patience to use this technique, but younger children would be able to use stencils already prepared for them. For use on cards, unless they are quite big, or require only a few letters, this lettering system will be too fiddly. Yet another word of warning! Watch out when you are cutting out the letters, otherwise you will be left with rather odd letters, for instance, a big round hole, as opposed to an 'O'.

*Cut out letters: s*ince blackmail letters and later punk rock became cults, youngsters have enjoyed experimenting with their own forms of typographical layout. The idea is simple. Collect various printed material. (If you are planning for a group, think ahead and ask them to bring old newspapers and magazines on a specific day). Individual letters and words can then be cut and pasted onto the card or paper. It if is a 'one-off' design, youngsters can, in this way, add colour to their artwork. If it is for photocopying, it is safer to stick to black letters. Some photocopiers dislike particular colours and they are reproduced in a very faint form.

Calligraphic headings: you might like to refer to our short calligraphy section for more technical advice on this form of lettering. Some young people will welcome the opportunity of sitting down and painstakingly writing headings and lettering by hand. As a youth worker, the job is to encourage, and offer alternatives to youngsters who do not have this skill, or perhaps confidence. Plenty of useful books on calligraphy are usually available from the local library. In Lothian Region in Scotland, one of our staff team at the Longniddry Youth Centre successfully used calligraphy as the basis for a popular and well attended group.

Cartoons

Cartoon animation work with youth groups is covered elsewhere, but popular cartoon characters can be copied by a lot of youngsters, if you have done your homework and brought along a goodly stock of cartoon books. Depending upon the age group, Hagar, Simpsons, Viz, Beavis and Butthead, Flintstones, Peanuts; Asterix; Tom and Jerry; Marvel Comix (Superman etc.); the Brooms etc., should add a bit of inspiration to a drawing session. From experience, it would seem quite useful to pull tables together and attempt to give a stock of books and felt pens, paper and tracing paper to each small group. This makes the session easier to supervise.

There is sometimes a temptation for talented members of staff to end up doing all the designs for youngsters. This is hardly the purpose of the exercise, though it's a good idea to involve members of staff in this activity who have a genuine interest and are willing to get fully involved. You may also find that some of the youngsters you are working with are able to invent and develop their own cartoon characters and story lines. Using cartoons in this way can lead to the development of cartoon strips and even little books. Our artist, Gubby, started this way and has produced a number of irreverent little A5 cartoon books.

Using cartoons to illustrate cards, a personalised bubble caption can radically alter a cartoon into a personal message. So, when Bart from the Simpsons starts to say rude things about **you** in a Christmas card from a hulking sixteen year old, you will know you've made it! If you still make the effort and facilitate the activity to take place, there is a good chance that you may be able to mobilise a range of hidden talents in your youth group. If you find yourself as a youth worker with a number of talented cartoonists, this may be very useful if you plan to start a youth magazine or similar. (see magazines, zines and publications section) The organisation of a competition or a non-competitive show/display could also be a way to generate increased enthusiasm for the activity.

Calendars

Not a lot needs to be said about these. There are (at least) three ways of producing calendars which are accessible to youngsters:

1. The simplest is to produce a design on a card and glue or tape a pre-printed calendar block on to the bottom of the card.
2. This involves drawing out the months of the year by hand into month-by-month sheets. These could also be the printed sheets from a calendar block, pasted onto separate sheets for each month. Seasonal photos, cartoons or some such item could complete the presentation.
3. Another method is to draw out a wall calendar for the whole year. Rather a mammoth task, but we have seen A3 or A2 size versions constructed by youthful artists. In one case, a youngster produced a calendar based on the theme of Tolkien's 'Lord of the Rings', dragons and all!

CARNIVALS, FESTIVALS AND PERFORMANCE ARTS

We honestly weren't sure what to call this section. For youth clubs, playschemes, community groups and the like, performance arts and street arts have become a form of celebration. These activities may be organised for friends and parents or may be part of a community event such as a festival, fete, street party or carnival. One of the most noticeable developments of the late 1980s and 1990s has been the proliferation of such participation events, whether they are 'traditional', as in the local church fete, multi-cultural, such as the Notting Hill Carnival and its many offshoots, or counter-cultural such as the Tree Fayre and the Rainbow Circle camps and workshops. What is true of them all is that they can provide a unifying influence on communities in the planning and organisation of such events. They also offer the opportunity to present 'arts activities' to audiences who might normally run for cover to try and avoid anything 'cultural' or 'arty'.

Working with young people, the key aspects of **performance arts** are that they provide opportunities for:

- learning new skills;
- gaining confidence to perform in front of other people;
- participation by the audience;
- interaction with other people;
- having fun.

A number of the activities featured in this book can have a part to play in performance arts. Along with obvious ones such as circus skills, there are bubbles, masks, papier mâché, face painting and make-up, puppets, kites, film and video making, and murals which may also have an important part to play in any arts or community event. They are also easy to transfer from the confines of the playscheme or community centre out into the street or the local playing field.

In the individual sections of the book dealing with these subjects, we have tried to make it clear which activities require skilled instruction and lots of practise, such as juggling and unicycling, and are therefore, best tackled with young people in workshop sessions. Others such as face-painting, murals, hair braiding and video-making can produce attractive results without a long learning curve. And, most importantly, every one has fun!

Carnivals, festivals and street events

Nearly all youth-related organisations are likely at some time to participate in street celebrations and community events. Some may build a float on the back of a lorry or trailer, others will design and dress walking displays. The reasons for taking part can include:

- gaining publicity for the group and good public relations;
- the chance for winning prizes;
- a co-operative undertaking involving adults and young people working together;
- raising money for charities or the organisation itself;
- making a contribution to the community;
- practically learning arts and performance skills.

Design of floats

Young people can be encouraged to help with, or entirely design a float, or a costume. An event may have a theme or entrants may be invited to produce the most colourful, humorous or dramatic display. When designing a float, for instance it is important to consider all of the following:

- safety for those taking part and those watching, and, potentially insurance;
- cost and ease of construction;
- how many people need to fit on the float and what they will be doing;
- what type of vehicle is carrying the design/people and its overall dimensions;
- types of materials to be used;
- need for power for music/sounds.

As a general rule, the materials used may depend on whether the float is to be used only once or at a number of events. For instance, in the south-west of England there is a bustling carnival season each autumn, with floats sometimes appearing at three or four venues in different towns each week. Hardboard and plywood can make useful frames for float designs and are often covered with stretched cloth which is painted in a similar way to theatre stage 'flats'. Cardboard and strong paper are easier for children to work with, but can rip easily on the back of a moving vehicle. For costumes and floats, there are three stages of preparation:

1. design
2. manufacture
3. assembly (onto the vehicle, on the day or soon before).

Many of the most successful floats combine strong visual images, constructed into imaginative and unusual shapes. Some employ movement such as a mobile dragon's head at the front. Slogans on the float can offer humour, whilst the people on the float should be colourfully dressed and present an active spectacle to their street audience. The themes of many floats use songs, music and dance as a major part of the moving presentation. Among many unusual floats we have seen were: Sinderella (we'll leave that to your imagination!); The Batgirls; The Sounds of Music and How the West was Lost. Frequently, the images and actions portrayed on the float are enhanced by walking participants in an array of costumes. The carnival streetwalkers will often employ circus skills: clowning, juggling, stilt-walking, uni-cycling, to increase their visual impact. If you are briefing walking performers or those on floats, it is important to tell them that they must continue to 'act' all the time they are in a procession. Masks, as described in the special section of the book, have a special place in fiestas, carnivals and community arts, and this even spills over into street demonstrations and protest. Television has broadcast many images of larger than life world leaders involved in anti-road rallies and protests against the Criminal Justice Act.

Multi-cultural

In recent years, carnivals have taken on a much more international dimension which can make them a useful part of multi-cultural education for children and young people. For example, in Alan's current area of Lyme Regis in Dorset, the annual summer Street Party organised by Ayvin from the Fuego South American shop, always features music, dance and artists from a variety of cultures – Caribbean, South America, Africa etc.. Percussion is particularly popular with street audiences, and steel drums, bongos, bodhrans, mancalas, tablas, whistles and rattles can bring a carnival or street event to life.

Walkabout performers

Increasingly, there are more anarchic walkabout acts, which often can abuse as well as amuse audiences. How far this is relevant to *your* youth work depends a great deal on your politics and the views of your organisation. Typical examples include dressing up as police, penguins, escaped convicts, a troupe of Scottish bagpipe players, aliens, or an entire squadron of red arrows' pilots, pushing wheel-barrow planes in earthbound aerobatics! Confrontation can be part of the act, and young people like dressing up as outcast sub-cultural groups like Hell's Angels or Punks. Unusual behaviour and quirky dress like gay police, walking hand in hand, complete with handbags over their shoulders are typical ploys of walkabout, street performance. This is very much the territory where carnival crosses over into street theatre.

Planning and safety

For the organisers of most events there are a number of things to consider:

- To start with, publicity is important.
- A good show with no audience, isn't much good! Think of ways which will give the local media the chance to 'tell a good story' about your event.
- Try and get bunting, flags and banners erected around the route or event site.
- Seek permission from the police for the route you intend to use. You may also need to work closely with the local council and other public authorities.
- It is wise to take out public liability insurance.
- Check the safety of the vehicles and constructions on floats. You don't want either performers or spectators to get injured.
- Look out for temporary or permanent obstructions and inconveniences like: wind, rain, tight bends, low bridges and erratic drivers.
- Heat can also pose a problem for performers on very hot days, especially where they are wearing heavy costumes, masks or big heads.
- Have adequate first aid assistance on hand.
- Try not to block access to shops for any longer than necessary.
- Brief participants and vehicle drivers in particular. Tell them that patience and good humour are vital to make the event a great success.
- If the police require co-operation, try to be as helpful as possible.

CIRCUS SKILLS

Historically and culturally it may be argued that most circus skills are popular developments from the traditional skills of the magic men – the shamans. These were the people in a tribe who conjured up spirits and whose stock skills were magic, acrobatics and the skills of the fakirs, such as levitation, sword swallowing and sitting on a bed of nails. The 'fools' of the medieval court often employed juggling and clowning skills. Nowadays, the UK's newer Travellers are among the most recent group to continue in the tradition of the ancient buskers and showmen using juggling, street music, fire-eating and occasional buffoonery. What has made them, and many European anarchic circus acts such as Archaos, Royale de Luxe, Malabar and Generik Vapeur particularly exciting for young audiences, is the confrontational nature of many of the acts. This type of circus uses no animals and the performers bring street skills and values of skateboarding, motor cycling, punk and rave cultures, radical theatre, loud music and pyrotechnics along with the more usual skills of acrobatics, clowning and juggling.

This book does not allow the space for a full scale introduction to circus and juggling skills. Dave Finnegan's 'The Complete Juggler' is about the most practical guide to juggling and

the associated skills required for balancing, diablos, plate and ball spinning, and using devil sticks. In the same Butterfinger's series is Sebastian Hoher's 'Unicycling from beginner to expert'. A good book on circus skills with youth and community groups is Reg Bolton's 'Circus in a Suitcase'. His book is particularly good on clowning and community participation. He also offers the following **checklist for street circus/busking**:

- Don't obstruct the street or sidewalk.
- Don't block access to shops, which would turn the shopkeeper's goodwill into bad.
- Be sure the ground is safe for stilts and unicycles – not wet or slippery.
- Don't plan an acrobatic *rolling* sequence, unless you have a mat or grass.
- Don't use bouncy juggling balls unless you're an excellent juggler.
- Take a length of bunting for the front row of the audience to hold, if it is necessary to keep them back (from the performance area).
- Don't take a lot of loose props, and keep an eye on those you have. The public is generally kind to street performers, but you should avoid providing the temptation to steal your gear.

One of our advisors who runs a London-based juggling shop and teaches circus skills, confided with us, "Juggling is basically a very boring activity." However, it is still a skill which is not too hard to learn at a basic level, and children and young people seem to love both its repetition and the almost infinite variety of items which can be juggled or manipulated: balls, beanbags, rings, clubs, cigar boxes, scarves etc.. Special juggling scarves are particularly suitable to learn with because they fall more slowly through the air than balls. As Dave Finnegan says:

> "Another characteristic of juggling is its rhythmic, almost mystical nature. It can have the same calming effects on your spirit as playing or listening to good music. For many, juggling is a form of meditation, of integrating mind, body and spirit."

It sounds pretty good to us!

Having attended a couple of circus skills workshops ourselves and quizzed the instructors, we'd like to emphasise that juggling and circus related skills are not like a lot of the other arts activities described in this book. They do take a good deal of practice to become proficient, and they cannot be learned in one practice session by adults, who can then teach them or pass them on to groups of young people. We would recommend that nearly all circus skills are best learned in workshops run by experienced practitioners. Young people often learn more quickly than adults, and learning by 'seeing and doing' is the most effective way to learn.

In the last couple of years the use of devil sticks, two sticks held in either hand and used for tossing and flipping a centre-stick have, together with the use of diablos and plate-spinning, greatly increased in popularity alongside juggling.

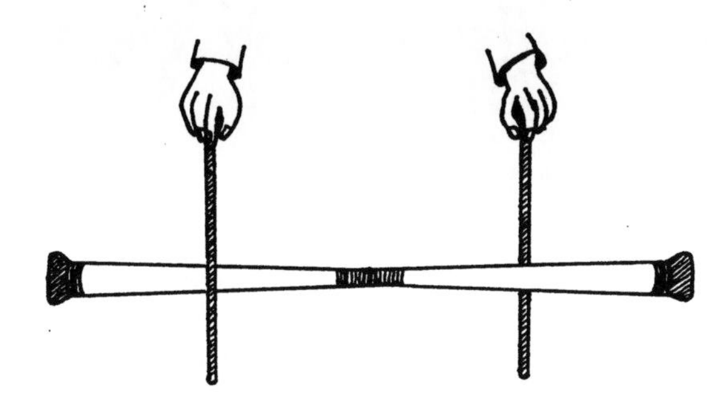

Many young street performers now mix juggling with the use of diablo spinning and throwing and devil sticks, and may even combine this with:

- unicycling
- stilt walking
- clowning
- acrobatics.

Putting on a show

Whilst it is easy to accomplish basic moves, the juggling arts, acrobatics and balancing take practise and more practise to achieve real skill which can be used to entertain an audience. From Aikido, performers may learn to 'stay with the experience' – the more you practise, the better the focus of attention. Showmanship is also something which has to be learned. For young people, it is worth getting them used to thinking in terms of:

- how they are dressed and made up;
- what they say;
- how they move;
- how they can involve an audience;
- good links to use between sequences and stunts;
- the development of their own personal, unique style of presentation.

For playschemes and similar, a 'circus' performance for families, friends and other members of the very localised community can form a good focus for an event. There can be lots of different types of performance including BMX/mountain bike riding, dance and skateboarding and roller or blade skating. Plate-spinning and diablo manipulation are easier to learn up to a rudimentary level for a lot of young people than juggling, and offer a useful introduction to circus skills. Use of a 'Play-go' which is a bit like a pedal skateboard, can be a good way to learn the balancing skills and co-ordination necessary to ride a unicycle. Combined in a show with a compere, music, acrobatics and plenty of colourful costumes, lack of highly developed skills don't matter much. Enthusiasm and energy count for a lot!

There are also a lot of myths and secrets surrounding circus skills; for instance, many young people can learn to stilt walk in under two hours! If you are stumped for contacts in the circus/juggling worlds, you could try to get help from the people listed in the suppliers' section at the end of the book. As well as supplying circus and other equipment (such as training videos, books, earthballs and parachutes) to buy and hire, often at discount prices they also have a lot of experience in running kids' workshops and circus shows.

COLLAGE, MOSAICS AND MARBLING

Actually, this section is quite 'arty', with a number of suggested methods for using art techniques which are best suited to a setting which is at least somewhat structured. Otherwise, it is perhaps only too easy to picture the scene of flying shreds of paper wafting not so delicately through the space of the temporary craft room. After the section on collage, there are sections on mosaic and marbling, which will provide a starting point for enterprising adults who wish to brighten up the premises where youth work is carried out, or perhaps add some new, youth art work to the local neighbourhood.

Collage

For most youth groups, there are two distinct memories of collage. One involves the primary school technique which sounds like,

> "One group should paint a background scene onto a large sheet of paper or wallpaper. The main group work must work individually to paint/colour/draw objects, people, animals etc. which can be pasted onto the background."

The second, and oft-prepared collage is a scissors and paste job. This turns sections of colour supplements and similar into a mass of dissected images which can then be re-positioned and pasted to form a new work of art. The process can be carried out individually or as a group activity, and no artistic skill as such is required. Usually the more bizarre the collage is, the more successful the image. A Dali-montage or surrealist images can be constructed in this way by even the most uncompromising GBH specialist! It is also particularly successful and enjoyable with younger groups, aged between eight and twelve.

Collage, almost by definition, is concerned with turning discards and disposables into art forms. A base onto which items can be attached must first be prepared. The question, is it to be permanent or disposable?, should be asked early on since it affects what sort of materials to consider using. If participants are new to collage work it is best to start with fairly small designs first. As mentioned in our section on organising and gathering materials, it is important to amass a collection of 'FOUND OBJECTS'. The list below might give a guide to the sort of things which can be used:

> corrugated paper, bottle tops, old posters, sacking, rice, string and rope, milk bottle tops, watch parts, colour supplements, pop newspapers, women's papers, pasta shapes, tissues, photos, herbs, cellophane, coffee beans, dried leaves, seeds and pods, feathers, fabric/cloth, sequins, and film negatives.

Some of the items will give a two-dimensional image, similar to the wall displays used in a number of popular restaurants and pubs, where montages of photos, posters, stamps and bank notes and now a common decoration. These are the easiest form of collage and if used directly onto a wall, they can be varnished into a permanent state. In the club or centre it can prove an impressive and professional form of decoration. The youth club in Tranent, East Lothian has an entire stairwell adorned in this fashion. It has a hallucinatory effect on the eye, but at the same time is stunning. One word of warning: you may, as a youth 'leader' find yourself out of favour with mums and dads, when the youngsters practice their new found skills on the bedroom at home! Some of the images produced by youthful collagers may be discriminatory, so it is important to prepare for a bit of lively social education on images, stereotyping and why they might be hurtful to others.

Three-dimensional collages rely on the sense of form and texture which can be achieved using this medium. It is not a subject which should be learned or taught. Experimentation will show the range of art forms which can be produced. However, when organising this sort of group, enthusiasm may have to be generated. One way of doing this is through the employment of the old teaching adage of 'structure'. Suggest themes for the exercise, i.e. advertising, people, animals, or alternatively stress contrast, texture or impact.

With regard to adhesives, one almost feels hesitant to make recommendations given the current anxiety concerning solvent abuse. However, here are a few types of adhesives which have been used effectively. Which you choose will depend upon both the nature of the materials used (some glues can only adhere to paper) and where the end product is to be a temporary or permanent creation.

> Cow gum; Berol Marvin medium and other PVA adhesives (polyvinyl acetate adhesive); Spray mount (various); Pritt stick and Evostick have all been successfully used in different circumstances. NES Arnold, Galt and Specialist Crafts all market a good range.

Application can be made using a knife, brush, aerosol, a piece of card, or, as will probably occur, fingers (!). Be careful, since some of the adhesives are dangerous to inhale in a confined space – so, window open!

Other techniques which might be combined into collages or murals are offered below:

Mosaics

The simplest mosaics are made using gummed paper shapes which are stuck onto sheets of paper in imaginative combinations. There are also various sets of tessellated shapes made of card or wood which schools use for maths teaching. These offer a variety of shapes and colours which can be joined together to make mosaic style patterns and pictures. Galt's offer a useful range of these.

When starting with a new group, especially with younger children or people with learning difficulties, it is important to show some examples of what sort of thing might be produced. Mosaics are easier to understand by looking and doing, than through description. A simple exercise involves each participant having their own sheet of card, at least A4 in size. Get them to cut or tear up lots of pieces of different coloured papers. Old wrapping paper, sweet papers, metallic foils or newspaper can all be effective. Using wallpaper paste, or slightly diluted PVA adhesive, these shapes can be stuck either adjacent to one another, or in slightly overlapping sequence. Using lots of varied types of paper can produce nice textural effects. Once the picture is completed, a further coat of PVA will give it a shiny, varnish-like finish.

Specialist Crafts and others market colour beads, which are small plastic beads that come in a nice variety of colours and which can be pressed into place on peg-boards to form mosaic pictures. These are popular with younger groups, up to about thirteen and with therapeutic groups of various kinds.

Traditional mosaics do not use overlapping pieces. The designs tend to be geometric and are part of Indian, Greek and Roman cultures. It is still possible to purchase from Specialist Crafts, the glass enamel and glass pieces, known as 'Smalti', which can be cut to shape using a special set of nippers. Bonded with tile cement and tidied up with a palette knife, squeegee and sponge, this is all (apart from a lot of patience) that is required to produce either authentic or modern mosaics.

Marbling techniques

There are a variety of techniques which can be used to produce unusual marbling techniques on paper, fabric or other surfaces.

1. *Wet paper.* Wet a sheet of colour supplement thoroughly, crush it into a ball and squeeze hard. Open and place on a newspaper to dry. The result is a cracked image. A similar result can be achieved by crushing paper while dry and then running water over the surface. Coloured tissue papers are worth experimenting with if you have some funds for materials. The colours run and when glued together, the sheets can combine elements of collage and origami.

2. *Oil in Water/Marbling. Method One.* We found this technique popular with youth groups of most ages, though it may have been over-used in some schools. Using a tray of water about an inch deep as a base, add different quantities of oil paint which has been diluted with a small quantity of oil thinners. Stir or splash the water around (not too vigorously!) and when the pattern on the surface of the water is interesting, place a sheet of white or coloured paper onto the surface. It takes only a few seconds and unusual, almost psychedelic results abound. If you are using a smooth surface card or cartridge paper, you can try floating pools of water directly on the surface of the card and then adding the oils. By rocking the card, swirling patterns of colour can be achieved. The end result is similar, but **feels** slightly more like an act of creation as opposed to spontaneous luck!

3. *Oil in Water/Marbling. Method Two.* This process enables multi-coloured images to be made on plain paper or fabric. It can be used for collage work, wall displays, fabric design, end papers for hand made books, or pasted onto greetings cards. Marbling relies on the fact that oil and water don't mix and is a quick way of making highly individual designs without the necessity of being artistically gifted.

All these collage techniques have been used with people with learning difficulties and young people of all ages. The end products are both unusual and professional looking, and do not require any degree of technical or artistic skills, which makes them ideal in a wide range of settings.

Most of the necessary materials can be prepared in advance, leaving you free to nurture the kids' creative talents!

You will need:

A shallow container like a photographic dish, or the kind of tray butchers use.
Artist's oil paints, or specialist fashion marbling colours, seaweed colours or Marblin inks.
Oil thinners/turpentine/white spirit if using oil colours.
Things to stir with, particularly a marbling comb.
Small jars or pots.
Old newspapers.
Sheets of plain paper (as long as it's not too soft, thin or porous) that are slightly smaller than the container.
A packet of powdered gelatine size, or marbling ground.

Prepare the size by mixing one dessertspoon of gelatine with a little boiling water in the container, or the ground following the instructions. Mix well and make up to the quantity required with cold water. Ideally, the container should be about three-quarters full and be allowed to stand until it reaches room temperature.

Oil colours are prepared by mixing a small amount of each colour with turps, oil thinners or white spirit in a separate pot. These should be well stirred until they reach a runny consistency. Special marbling inks and colours are pre-mixed to the correct consistencies.

The size and colours must now be tested to obtain a good match. Before using any colours, use some strips of newspaper to break the surface tension in the container of size. Then, drop a spot of each colour onto the surface and spread out till each is one or two inches across. If the droplets spread out too much, the paint is too thin, and vice versa. If the droplets stay at the bottom, then the size needs thinning, and if they expand and then contract, it should be allowed to stand a little longer to reach room temperature.

COMPUTERS, VIDEO-GAMES AND RADIO-CONTROLLED MODELS

Lots of things electrical with plenty of likelihood of blowing-up or going wrong have crept into the repertoire of work with young people. Computers, in particular, have had a dramatic effect on almost everyone's lives in the past ten years. Video games machines were really a forerunner of the multi-megabyte powered computers. In both cases though, they have provided an entertaining source of fun and a means of improving dexterity. The computer has taken this a stage further with the development of software with a high educational value.

Computers

The current generation of multimedia machines, with their capacity to run e.g. interactive encyclopaedias such as Encarta and complex games, have brought the computer into many living rooms. An impressively powerful computer can now be purchased for well under £1,000, although you will have to pay a little more for a complete multimedia machine, which includes full sound, music and video capabilities.

Youth workers, teachers, social workers and the like mostly now take for granted the computer's capacity to act as a word processor, saving time and effort in re-drafting letters and reports; as a data-base for keeping records; and an accountancy package for monitoring finances. It can also be a valuable learning tool for work with young people. Computer obsolescence has become less of a problem, as most new machines are easily upgradeable.

Powerful new software packages have transformed the capability of home computers over the past decade. As long as you can afford the software, you can have a 'home office' (this software is often bundled free with new computers), digital recording and mixing capability, graphic and design studio or desktop publishing outfit.

Some of the most useful software to use in creative work with young people is of the graphics/desktop publishing type. Commercially obtainable images on disk (called 'clip art') can be combined with photographic images, animation and video to produce unique results. The processes involved offer endless possibilities, and of course you can manipulate the images as much as you like with specialist software.

Hand held 'scanners' are very cheap and enable you to introduce line art and greyscale or colour photographs. You can edit these images pixel by pixel (dot by dot) on screen. However, unless you have access to a 1,000 dpi (dots per inch) printer the output quality of line art and photographs will be degraded.

We strongly recommend that you use computers in this kind of creative way with young people. Other specialist software programmes can be used to create sound mixing facilities or to publish newsletters, magazines and fanzines. You'll find that several graphics programmes, e.g. Corel Draw, include founts (type styles) which kids love to use.

Many programmes allow you to stretch and otherwise manipulate text to produce special effects. We especially liked the 'Banner' software which is very easy to use and can produce some very fine poster designs.

Available Software

The following list comprises the types of games software currently available:

- Quizzes and competition programs ranging from hangman to trivial pursuits.
- Decision-making games and role playing adventures, which may involve a sequence of puzzle solving, similar to the 'Crystal Maze' on the TV.
- Personal assessment programs on behaviour and attitudes. Aggression, drugs, alcohol and crime are all covered by specialist programs.
- Computer versions of commercial games such as Scrabble, Monopoly and chess.
- 'Intelligent' action games based on settings such as wars, sports and activities such as flying, driving etc..
- Simulations which try to recreate a real situation where choices can be made which affect outcomes.
- Learning programs which teach keyboard, computing, language, literacy, numeracy and music skills.
- Questionnaires on a variety of subjects.
- Virtual reality games which put the players in the centre of 3-D action, sometimes using headsets.

This list is not a comprehensive one, but it does highlight the usefulness of the computer in working with young people.

Video Games

'Dedicated' video games machines remain very popular with today's youth. As these machines can *only* play games you need to give careful consideration to forking out £300 or £400 for the most powerful versions. The received wisdom is that a good computer is better value, as it will run leading edge games and is upgradeable.

The ubiquitous Sega MegaDrive was selling for around £100 in early 1996; it is enormously popular, there is an excellent range of software available and a healthy second hand market. Interactive CD machines, or CDi's, were around £400 and competing directly with multimedia computers. The Sony Playstation was the newest machine around. Costing around £300 the graphics quality is excellent, but it still does not win out over a decent PC or Mac.

It is still the case that many games are not well enough designed to retain their interest value beyond the first few playings. Some are of little use at all. Others, however, can be ideal group work tools providing the basis for thought-provoking discussions and valuable insights into how individuals think. Some of the specialist organisations listed in the

Supplier's Guide may be able to help you with advice and information on the most up-to-date programs and where to obtain material which most nearly meets your particular needs.

Radio-Controlled Models

Planes, boats, cars and tanks are just part of a growing range of model transport which is appealing both to the eye and the brain. But, they can be expensive and their popularity may be short-lived relative to the financial outlay. Where we have been involved with the use of these vehicles, the regular availability of space for the activity has been a necessity. When no accessible indoor space is available, or outdoor for planes, tanks etc., the activity tended to fall flat.

The nature of the activity requires both money and a reasonable technical dexterity. The best models require attention on a regular basis and this puts the activity into the fifteen plus age range – much older than might be thought at first. To control a vehicle, both a transmitter and receiver are required and these control the direction and speed of movement. Beware models with only limited direction controls, like left movement only!

If you are keen to get involved try to get the assistance of local model shops and contact any local clubs. Finally, there is a high risk of damage, both to your equipment, and in the case of planes, to other people's property. So, make sure you have organised adequate insurance cover before embarking on maiden flights, voyages, journeys etc..

COSTUMES AND DRESSING UP

Trying on clothes and make-believe play acting are a very natural part of children's development and are especially used in nursery and primary school education. In addition to theatrical productions; parties, carnivals and street events provide ideal opportunities for wearing costumes and fancy dress. In youth clubs, discos and dances can also be organised to include a fancy dress 'theme'.

The actual range of potential costumes is limitless and your eventual creation can include elements such as face painting, masks or the eco-costumes described in the Eco-Activities section. In the meantime, we offer one costume example which is a perennial favourite for Halloween and Trick or Treating.

Witches, vampires and ghouls are ever popular dressing up characters. Their costumes are readily made using available materials. Black and white are very much the colours of the night, plus perhaps a little bit of fresh blood substitute!

For an easy to construct witch's hat:

- To construct this you, or the youngsters you work, with will need two sheets of thickish black paper.
- Use one sheet to construct a cone, by twisting the paper into a funnel shape. When the open end of the cone will fit over the intended wearer's head, tape it together from inside, flatten out the wide end and cut to make a circle.
- Use the second sheet to construct the brim of the hat. A compass or two round plates or saucepan lids can be used for measuring the inside and the outside of the brim. Draw a cross in the inner circle and then cut along each line from the centre and bend the four triangles back to the circle. These can then be glued together with the cone.
- Black and red wool cut about 18inches-two feet (45 to 60 cm) long can make great hair which can be attached with tape to the inside of the hat.

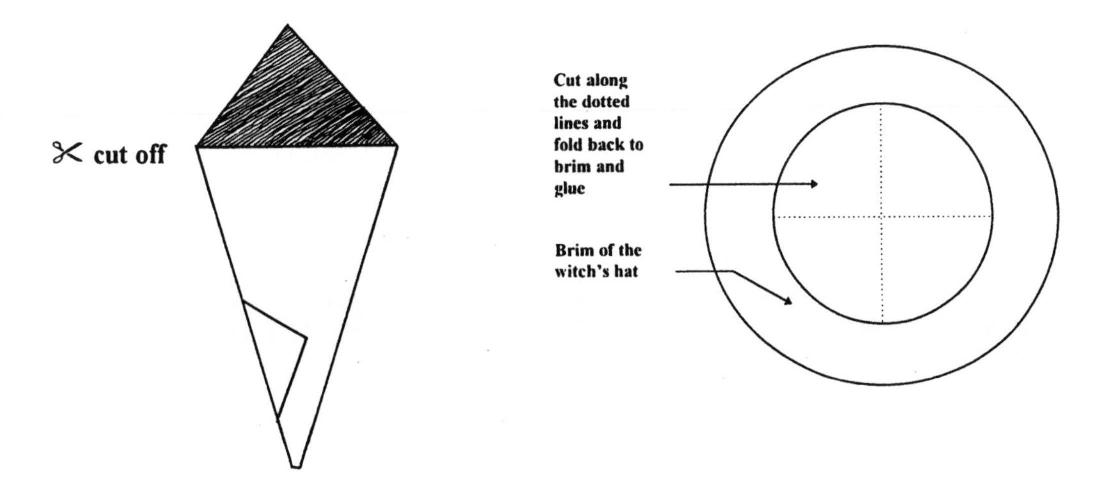

- An old bin liner, with openings for arms and head looks great as a modern punk-witch cape!
- Silver and gold stars, moons, frogs, bats or spiders can be cut out of coloured paper and stuck to the hat or cape to finish off the costume.
- Face painting or a grotesque mask will complete the ensemble.

Vampires can also be made from bin liners. Cut the bag so that the bottom of the bat cape is ragged, and as wide as the outstretched arms of the wearer. Black trousers, shoes and plenty of gaudy face paints make a fearsome creature of the night. Underneath the cape, if this area is showing, a white shirt can add a useful contrast to the black exterior.

A useful idea is to create a **clothes resource box.** This can be assembled from jumble sales, donations and charity shops. In it you will quickly accumulate items which can be cut up, modified and generally cannibalised in a creative and imaginative way. Hats, shoes and jackets are especially useful for dressing up, as are belts and scarves. An old bathing hat is ideal to form a bald head, or the basis for a fabulous wig.

For play groups and nursery groups, where pretend play is particularly important, the NES Arnold catalogue offers a range of dressing up clothes. They have specifically developed a range of clothes from Africa, Asia, China and Japan, and a second range of workers' clothes including outfits for a male nurse, police, chef and ambulance driver.

CYCLING

Most youngsters in the ten to sixteen age range own or have access to a bicycle. Many have learned, at their own or their parents' expense, a little about cycle maintenance. What we are suggesting is using a range of experiences which will harness or resuscitate some of the natural enthusiasm and interest in cycles.

In groups we have worked with, **bicycle maintenance** was first introduced because the kids' bikes were in a thoroughly deplorable state of repair. Unlike working on cars or motor cycles, only a few tools are required to do basic work. Complex work on gears is another story, and another set of tools!
The range is approximately:

> a set of five open ended spanners (Whitworth, or more usually metric depending on the make(s) of the bike(s)); a quarter and eighth of an inch tipped screwdrivers, plus a Phillips-type; an Allen (hex) key set, now used for many handlebars and seat bolts; puncture repair outfit and three tyre levers; cone spanner; pliers; hammer; and for chain and wheel jobs - link extractor and spoke spanner. Extra large size spanners become necessary when working on the steering nuts. A large adjustable spanner is an alternative. You will also need oil; SAE30 is better than the household type. Dry lubricants such as Superspray are good for chains, as are Bike Lube and Bike Eze; and grease for bearing maintenance jobs, and sometimes petrol, if you have to soak a chain etc..

We are not going to offer a how-to-do-it selection of repairs for bicycles. 'Richard's New Bicycle Book' by Richard Ballantine (Pan 1990) is a good resource for any youth group and its members. To complete our comments on maintenance – it is a good idea if you avoid becoming the youth-working, bicycle repair person for the area. The reasons, we hope, are obvious! Certainly show kids how to carry out tasks, but don't do all the work for them. Finally, we know of a couple of youth centres which have successfully operated bicycle repair services to raise money. This might be accomplished by first teaching a small group of youngsters how to repair their own bikes and then letting them offer the service. In the cases we know of, one centre offered the service to any members of the youth centre. The other put up notices in local shop windows, and used the community newspaper and local radio station to advertise the service. One might have a few qualms about the morality of competing with local traders, but in many cases these days, bicycle shops sell bikes and are more than happy to let someone else carry out repairs.

Repairing bikes with youngsters is a good activity to develop relationships between workers and kids. Building a 'bitsa' bike has been a regular activity run by Charley Mathers in Dundee. He says,

> "A good conclusion is the intrepid mechanic riding off into the sunset (sigh) or, on the other hand, botched up jobs hold the consequence of a long walk back, skinned knees or worse. Also make sure you have enough tools - it is unnecessarily frustrating to end up with a fight over essential tools."

Building bicycles to use and sell is another activity which has provided both skill-learning and money for some youth group members. Based on an ethos close to the Friends of the Earth cause, kids have been encouraged to put a halt to the built-in obsolescence, and philosophy of disposability of broken or faulty items. Often one bike can be made, or retrieved, from the parts of two useless bikes. This does not have to cost vast sums of money, and some centres, including Ferry Road in Dundee, have stockpiled bicycles which can later be cannibalised to build working models for use or sale. Odd-shaped bikes, fixed-

wheel bikes and bikes with unusual gear ratios have been made this way, as have tandems and bikes with trailers etc.. A close acquaintance with the police bike pound, the rubbish tip and the local scrap-dealers can come in useful if you are contemplating this aspect recycling!

From Dundee (again) we learned that using tandems can be an aid to learning to ride a bike, with the youngster as a passenger. Not falling off provides a boost to confidence and encourages the pupil to have a go solo. The disadvantages of tandems are that it is hard to obtain spares and that they are **lethal** in the hands of two inexperienced riders.

Safety

These days, with increasingly busy traffic, it is very important that young people get involved in at least basic cycle proficiency training. This involves learning the rules of the road, basic Highway Code, attentiveness, and through practise, an ability to stay out of trouble. Wearing a cycle helmet is also now a basic necessity. The national Cycling Proficiency scheme may be pleased to offer a course at your centre. In some areas of the UK there is the 'Bike Mate' scheme which matches learners with experienced riders.

Insurance should also be investigated. The bike itself should be covered and, if possible the riders and their potential to cause damage to others.

Other activities

Other activities involving bicycles which we have helped organise include:

Sponsored cycle rides

To do this you need a lot of people acting as marshals en route. You are also required to notify the police of your plans. In most cases they will be pleased to help, but be sensible about the roads you are using. A sponsored cycle is probably best suited to areas outside of towns, but it may be that a local park or sports centre could be used for an event, even in a large urban area. This would not provide such an interesting route, but it would ease the dangers on the road. Other points which we would suggest as ground rules are:

- Take the names of, and perhaps allocate numbers to all of those taking part.
- Check and fix (if possible) all the bikes going on the event. They must be roadworthy.
- Consider the insistence on use of safety helmets. These are increasingly becoming a necessity in urban areas and on main roads.
- Depending on the route, ensure that everyone is old enough and a sufficiently competent cyclist to complete the course.
- Choose a course which offers a challenge, but is not too demanding for the relatively inexperienced cyclists taking part.
- Have marshals' vans involved in the event, equipped with tools and first aid equipment. These could perhaps be situated in the middle and at the rear of those taking part. They can attend to any roadside problems and ferry bikes and cyclists back to the home base as necessary.
- When starting the cycle run, stagger the starters and tell them that it is not a race. We found it useful to let the fastest cyclists go first. Although this makes the event a bit longer, it reduces the amount of overtaking.
- Encourage riders to have their own drink bottles, but if, for instance, the event is fifteen miles long, have a stop for drinks at the half-way stage.
- Make sure that the route is clearly marked with direction arrows, and have difficult points attended by marshals. By this strategy you should lose fewer participants!
- The final home base should again offer some refreshment and each cyclist's name should be checked off the list.

Using the above tips and adding some of your own, say, having some staff cyclists out on the course to cut down on dangerous antics, the day should be an enjoyable, safe and profitable one.

Customising

This is not a good idea for Wayne's new twenty-one gear mountain bike, but it can be applied to the aged relic. Organising a paint-in is a good fun activity and can also breathe new life into elderly machinery. The use of an air-brush spray may be especially useful, also coloured tapes, transfers, metallic foil etc. can all add to the personal touch. Unlike the car though, we wouldn't suggest a fur seat cover unless your youngsters want very soggy backsides!

Treasure Hunt/Scavenger Hunt

As some readers will realise, in both the 'New Youth Games Book' and 'World Youth Games', written by us, we have tried to describe a whole range of games and events which can be used with youth groups of varying ages. What we are offering below are two simple events which are ideal to adapt to cycle events. Since they do not relate solely to the speed at which different competitors can cycle, we think that they are useful to consider when planning cycle-related activities. It is also well worth your while looking at Alan Smith's book on 'Creative Outdoor Work with Young People' which has lots of useful orienteering-type ideas.

Treasure Hunt: Here are two ways of organising a treasure hunt which is easy enough for most organisers to consider using.

1. This involves supplying each contestant with a sheet of clues. These can be descriptions of buildings in the local area, of objects like trees, seats, railings, bus shelters

etc.. The clues can be made as difficult, or easy, as the event calls for. With young groups, say up to twelve, you should avoid clues which are too cryptic. For instance, clues to the local church might be:

UNDER THE TALL TOWER, or
THE TALLEST BUILDING, or
FOR WHOM THE BELL TOLLS, etc..

At the intended site, leave a piece of card, perhaps with a 'letter' (i.e. **D**) on it. This ensures that contestants must go to all sites, rather than just naming them. If you want to add an extra element: when contestants have found all the letters they might have to make the letters into a word or phrase. Don't try this with groups whose literacy is poor and whom it might embarrass. Unfortunately, since the clues may get stolen it may be better to use an alternative method, described next.

2. Give participants a map of the local area with some of the details removed (i.e. street names, villages). On it, mark circled numbers or letters at points where the participants must name what they see at that particular point. The question sheet may ask questions such as, "When was the building built?" Or, "Who is the Director of this organisation?"

Scavenger Hunt

We have included a version of the following in the Eco-section of this book, but it can easily be adapted for cyclists. We believe this is an old scouting game. Each participant is given a list of articles to find and bring back. Thought should be given to likely sources, otherwise it may just be a matter of cycling home and back. The sort of objects to be scavenged might include a clothes peg; a pine cone; a nail; a particular flower; a photo of a pop group; a sea shell etc.. You should make use of available local resources, so in a town the objects might include a hamburger wrapper; an empty bottle etc.. Each youngster involved will need a good, safe shoulder bag, or preferably a saddle bag or panniers. And for this reason, keep the size of the objects small.

The use of bicycles makes these events more fun and in all types of hunts, the accent should be on participating. Bikes speed things up and can make the event into something of a local history or natural history course, where historical buildings and the natural environment are used as answers to the clues. But don't forget to stress 'safety first' to the kids taking part.

Trials, BMX and Mountain Bikes

Obstacle courses and/or trials courses are good fun and can be easily set up on a small piece of ground. See-saw planks, greasy planks, ducking under barriers are all feasible adaptations of the popular motor-cycle TV programme 'Kick Start'. British Moto Cross (BMX) organise trials events and the use of special sturdy bicycles. Local cycle dealers may be happy to sponsor events, perhaps relishing the thought of all the rough treatment these bikes have to go through! The mountain bike is really an adult version of the BMX, plus lots of gears. It has brought a lot of fun to cycling by opening up off-road routes through the countryside. Be warned, though, that not all footpaths and bridleways are legal for cycles. With youth groups, make sure permission to ride over private land has been obtained in advance. The large types of mountain bikes, coupled with the wide, straight handle bars makes them very stable. They are also durable and can carry reasonable loads for successful long distance touring.

After you have organised one of the above events, it is likely that the youngsters will ask for more. The trick is then to try and get them organising future competitions. They will prove far more devious than you!

Youth Hostels

We don't wish to write a essay on youth hostels, but it is worth remembering that they are especially suited for youngsters who are on cycling tours or just away on bikes for the weekend. Some leaders have organised very successful cycling holidays with small groups of youngsters. It is worth planning short orienteering/map reading exercises prior to embarking on a long trip. Another spin-off is that through cycling to hostels, youngsters are treated with favour by many smaller hostels. Learning the rules allows the youngsters to understand how all the Youth Hostels Association (YHA) hostels work and they can then plan their own tours. They have over 5,000 hostels in 64 countries. Their HQ is at Trevelyan House, 8 St Stephen's Hill, St Alban's, Herts. AL1 2DY.

Sponsored Events

Cycle events can raise money for charities and equipment. Most of the activities listed in this section can be adapted for sponsored fundraising. Safety, insurance and matching the event to different age groups and abilities are important aspects of the organiser's role.

DÉCOUPAGE

Literally translating from the French, this means, "cutting out, or carving out." This is only a part of what découpage art work is. It was a very popular pastime with Victorian ladies and in the last ten years, or so, has enjoyed a period of rediscovery. For youth or community work, it is a useful activity which allows people who are not very good at drawing to produce decorated items which can look stunning and highly professional. In many senses it is a development of collage work, described earlier in this book. It essentially involves:

- cutting out pictures, patterns and drawings, or using transfer or stick on decals (pictures of flowers, animals, birds etc.);
- arranging these in an interesting way on a base picture or object;
- gluing them in place using either ordinary glue, or if attempting to obtain a 3-D image, using silicone solution;
- spray fixing;
- varnishing.

The diverse range of available objects and materials which can be used for découpage make it an ideal activity for youth groups. It is cheap and flexible and as an art form can produce varied and pleasing results. As with a number of art activities it is useful to adopt a 'Blue Peter' style approach at the beginning, by showing examples of découpage and explaining the process to the participants,

"Here's something I produced in the lunch-hour...."

You know the type of thing!

With a youth group you need a good variety of both things to **cut out**, and items to be **stuck on.** To start off a group you'll need plenty of newspaper covered tables, and:

- a selection of facsimile Victorian decals/pictures, wrapping paper designs, coloured and black and white pictures (colour supplements, advertising materials, music and sports pictures etc.);
- scissors and sharp craft knives (handle with care!);
- paints for preparing some surfaces to take découpage images;
- adhesives, possibly including silicone, for producing flat and raised images;
- spray fixative for sealing;
- varnish(es) for completing the object.

For instance, one member of the group may want to decorate an old junk tray, another a flower vase, and a third is intent on attacking a waste bin. The process is the same for each person:

– choose a selection of appropriate pictures/images to cut out or transfer/stick on;
– carefully undertake any cutting required;
– prepare (clean/paint/sand down) the object or surface which will receive the images;
– test out the possible positions for the pictures. Blu-tak or similar can be useful for this purpose;
– glue the cut-out images into place;
– spray fix if necessary;
– apply a first coat of varnish, allow to dry, lightly sand, then apply the next coat. Most items look their best with three or four coats minimum.

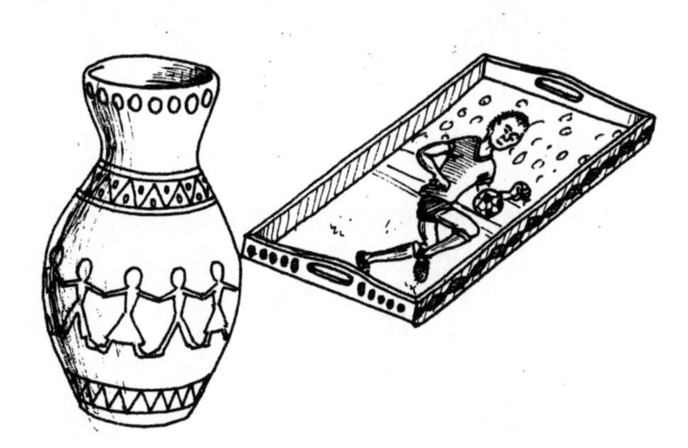

A few tips:

1. To finish off an object properly will require more than one session because of the varnishing. Explain this at the outset and plan for the follow-up.
2. An increasingly varied selection of paints, adhesives and cheap Victorian decals are becoming available. Specialist Crafts market a small range of 3-D découpage kits.
3. Don't be afraid of encouraging young people to experiment. There are no rules, and anything can be stuck to the finished object. The NES Arnold catalogue includes a glittering array of sequins, chenille, feathers, jewels, pompoms and glitter. The glitter can always be added to the layers of varnish.

4. Try using spray paint through patterned items, such as doilies, tights or stencils to produce imaginative backdrops for the cut outs.
5. With younger groups, it is best to use pre-prepared shapes and relatively blunt scissors for cutting out. Older children may be safe using craft knives – but they are very sharp and make potentially lethal weapons!
6. PVA adhesive, when slightly diluted, can be used to paint objects to give them a sheen quite similar to varnish.

DRAWING AND VARIATIONS

Many of the young people we worked with have had their creative instincts effectively removed or suppressed by experiences at home or school. Few have any regular access to materials which can encourage and develop their creative talents. If you are serious about using arts and crafts in your work with young people, then it makes sense to allow them access to materials with which they can test out ideas and fulfil some of their creative aspirations, even if this is just designing a gang logo or a football crest. The short piece on 'Spray Can Art' in the Murals section offers such street ideas.

Painting, drawing and their variations provide tremendous scope for individual experimentation and fulfilment. While painting may need some specialised materials and workspace, drawing materials can be used anywhere. So, why not try leaving out spare paper and pencils, felt pens, crayons, charcoal etc., and see what happens! Keep your fingers crossed that it is not a collection of obscenities on the walls! Having comics and magazines around can be useful to help stimulate flagging imaginations. See the Badge making section for related ideas.

What we call 'Drawing games' are also worth considering. Using what we call the **'Egg Head'** game is a good way of getting non-artists to draw. In this activity we usually photocopy a variety of heads/egg shapes:

Sometimes we start participants off with a few simple additions to aid their imagination:

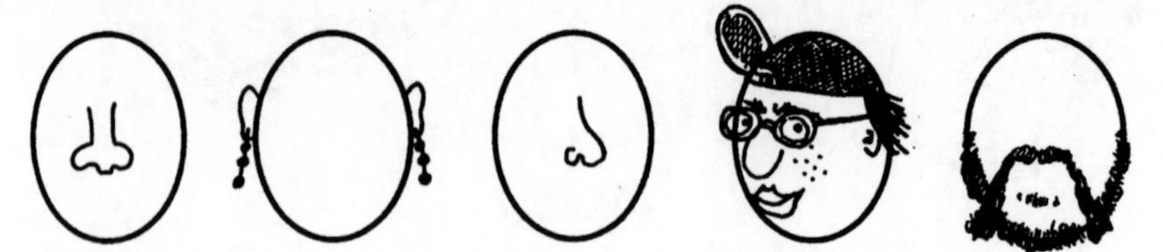

The idea is to let the young people create their own characters. Perhaps only some of them will look like you!

Another fun idea is to play a visual version of the old paper and pencil game, Consequences. We have heard the game called **'People'** and **'Figures'**. First you need to prepare a strip of paper by folding it into a concertina shape of six parts for: head; upper body; waist; thighs; knees, ankles and feet. We've found it best to prepare the linking lines which go over the fold lines. This ensures that the body all joins together.

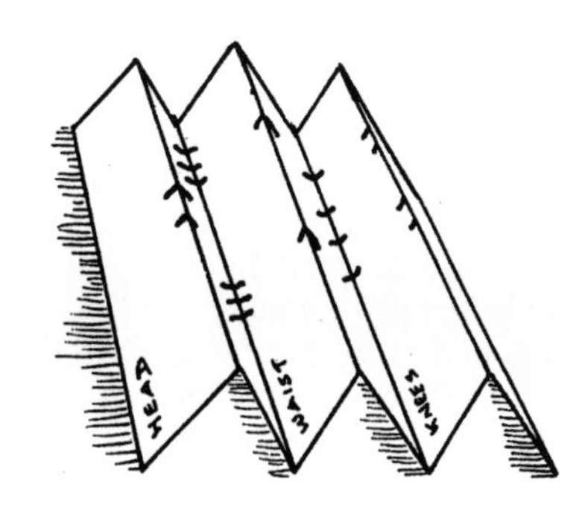

The game sequence involves each person adding a drawing of one part of the person in turn. It is much more fun if other participants do not see the drawing until the end. The first person draws a head – as weird as they like, and then folds it over so that the next person can only see the space where they can add a drawing of the upper body. This process is then repeated for each part of the body. The final creation can often be extremely strange, if at times a bit sexist.

It can also be worth experimenting with making your own **stencils** out of paper or card, to be used with paint or felt-tip pens. A number of firms also manufacture wooden or plastic stencils in the shapes such as animals, letters etc.. Specialist Crafts sell stencil card which is good for making accurate stencils which can be used to produce patterns for stencilling on walls or onto pictures. The Galt catalogue offers some nice stencils for Christmas cards and drawing. In the Lino Printing section, we have suggested a number of simple printing techniques.

Most people will have seen **pin and thread designs**, using coloured thread wound round panel pins hammered into a piece of wood or chip board which has been painted black. Abstract designs can be made by placing pins round the edge of the board with a few in the centre and experimenting with different loops and twists. Alternatively, patterns and designs for flowers, stars or ships can be achieved with a little practice.

Pens and drawing aids

Amongst our favourites are the poster paint pens in the Uni-POSCA range. These pens come with different size tips and dispense a bright solid paint colour onto just about any sort of surface you come up with. We've used them on wood, metal and paper. In fact these days the range of different drawing mediums for work with young people is enormous. Each offers a new dimension for learning and experimentation. It includes:

- pencils, coloured pencils and water colour pencils;
- wax and oil crayons;
- charcoal;

- pastels, oil pastels(the Filia range are very good) and conté crayons;
- marker pens, felt pens and pens for overhead projection transparencies;
- drawing pens such as the Edding 1800 pens and those by Rotring, Ceramicron and Mecanorma, used for accurate technical drawings and fine illustrative work, like Gubby's cartoons!
- and, see the Airbrush section at the beginning of the book.

A **pantograph** is another cheap piece of equipment which makes drawing accessible to all. The pin on the device is used to trace out the lines of a drawing, design or photograph while a pencil is drawing out the design on a larger scale. It is less automatic than its sounds and is actually quite creative. We have used the pantograph to draw a correctly proportioned outline of a 'face' or 'object', then carried on freehand. Youngsters can learn something about the scale, positioning and proportions of humans, animals and other objects. Some of the commercially available 'drawing games' are also worth considering for use with youth groups. The **Spirograph** range of drawing toys use geometric shapes for creative design and they do enable youngsters who do not see themselves as being artistic, to produce interesting and accomplished pictures.

ECO ACTIVITIES

There are a whole range of both indoor and outdoor crafts and activities which can be organised using natural environments and 'found' materials. Some of these overlap with other sections of this book such as mask making and jewellery. Others sit squarely at the intersection between activities and games playing, but since we are writing *this* book at the moment, rather than another volume on games playing, we are happy to include them here!

The leaf slide show

To organise this outdoor activity you need to have pre-prepared a set of fold-over cards, allowing one for each participant in your group.

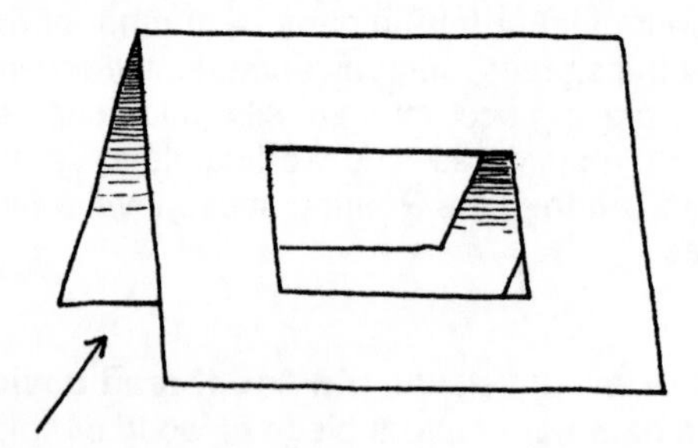

insert leaf between the flaps

The activity is a good one for using while out on a walk in the woods or on an outdoor expedition. To start with, you ask everyone to find an interesting or unusual leaf. Once they have all done so, hand out one fold-over card each, and ask each person to place their leaf in between the two sheets of card so that an interesting part of the leaf is trapped between the two holes. Then, get everyone to form up in a circle and look through their 'slide viewers' at the leaves using the sky (hopefully, sun) as a light source. Everyone is likely to be surprised at the complexity and beauty of the leaves. In turn, get the group members to pass on the slides to the next person in the circle, so that everyone has the opportunity to scrutinise each leaf. It's an enjoyable and educational way to spend a quarter of an hour in the country and works with any age or ability group.

Wide Games

These were first developed by the Scouting movement as a means of using the potential of wide open spaces for recreation. Recently, the Play movement has begun to sing the praises of these activities, especially with big groups of youngsters. Both of us attended a very enjoyable two-day Play Convention held in Perth, organised by 'Fair Play for Children in Scotland'. The Wide Games sessions were organised by Martin Rothero, who stressed that the natural resources of a woodland or beach can be effectively utilised to:

- provide good entertainment and exercise;
- get young people to make creative, positive use of the environment;
- develop their own activity and games ideas;
- work effectively in teams and develop personal initiative.

Traditional games/activities such as a **Scavenger Hunt** (see also Cycling section), are effectively a Wide Game. Participants are usually provided, individually or in pairs, with a list of objects to find. The organiser should spend some preparation time making sure that it is a 'possible' list and that obtaining the items do not involve, trespass, danger or destruction of living things. A typical Scavenger Hunt might involve participants in a half hour search for:

● something sharp ● a pine cone ● an oak leaf ●a feather ● something beautiful ● 3 pieces of human litter ● a piece of bark ● some sheep's wool ● an acorn ● a conker ● a fern leaf ● a sycamore seed.

Each participant or pair is given a bag to put their findings in, and is told exactly what geographical boundaries to work within. A recognisable call or whistle should be used to get everyone to re-group at the end of the activity, since not everyone can be relied upon to (a) have a watch, and (b) use it!

After the hunt, the organiser should praise the participants for their 'finds', make any comments on unusual discoveries, and ask about what else searchers found or saw while they were engaged in the hunt. This activity is successful with groups from about nine or ten upwards, but may not be suitable for participants with movement difficulties.

Conkers and Acorns

At the end of Martin's Wide Game session, which had involved in a good deal of running about in a couple of search and capture games, he invited the two groups of seven or eight to invent their own Wide Game. And so, 'Conkers and Acorns' was born; a simple, eco activity based on tag. To start, a playing area was defined, in this case a hockey pitch. The two goals were declared as the home bases. At the beginning of the game, each individual on one team received three conkers each, and the opposing team members were each given three acorns. These were either held in the hand or put into a convenient pocket. Each base houses a stock of more acorns or conkers, say 24 for an eight player team.

Then, the following rules apply:

– the game lasts until the organiser blows a whistle;
– only home team members can visit their own home base;
– the aim of the game is for individual players to tag opposing team players, thereby winning one acorn or conker;
– there is no re-tagging after a tag by another player;
– when a player runs out of their personal stock of three seeds, they can make one visit to their home base to replenish their stock (back up to three);
– the winning team is the one which has the most seed trophies captured from their opponents when the whistle blows.

A couple of points to consider. One: if there are lots of acorns or conkers lying about, it offers admirable opportunities for cheating! This can be averted by marking the seeds for the game with a spot of paint. Two: Try and divide up the teams in such a way as to make the ages, sizes and running abilities reasonably equal. And, if you are reasonably lucky, your reward as organiser, will be a bunch of exhausted but happy young people!

Eco costumes

Young people like dressing up and making unusual costumes and headgear. The 'found' resources of a wood or field can provide for some very interesting and imaginative creations. Say, for instance, that you set a task for a youth group of making a hat or crown, these can then be complemented by a later group making a cloak or costume to go with it.

The leaves, twigs, bark, berries etc. required for a costume can all be scavenged in the opening minutes of the session, and then, back in a workshop area, provide enough paper, card, scissors, glue, staplers, coloured papers, pens and anything else you think is appropriate to enable the construction of some unusual apparel. One result from a workshop session for training leaders can be seen in the accompanying photo. This activity can take a bit of time. We'd suggest that you allow about 1-1½ hours.

Your friend the tree!

This is an interesting sensory, eco activity which involves dividing your youth group up into pairs. It works with just about any age group, but needs to take place in a safe, reasonably flat wooded area, preferably with a variety of different tree types. The pairs take it in turns to be blindfolded, twirled around (safely), and then led up to a tree. The blindfolded person is encouraged to get-to-know their tree, giving it a hug, possibly even a kiss! After two or three minutes, the leader gently guides their partner back to a position away from the tree, gives them another twirl for disorienting, good measure, and then invites them to try and locate their own, friendly neighbourhood tree. Surprisingly, most people do find the tree they hugged, or, whatever! Then, it's the turn of the partners to swap roles and the leader becomes the led.

A pleasant, gentle way of getting young people to develop their awareness of what is growing around them.

EGG-MOBILES

These strange devices were directly a result of a BBC Television programme, in which teams designed a small, model vehicle which was capable of transporting an egg. Hence, our mate, Tony Watson's name for them – EGG-MOBILES! It's neither expensive nor difficult to organise as an activity, but you do need to plan ahead and ensure that all the materials are available. We reckon that it is best organised in quite a long session, perhaps about two hours long, with up to five groups operating concurrently, with three youngsters in each. The best age for the activity is twelve plus, and it is a good mixed ability and/or mixed age group task. Normally, the event is organised on a competitive basis, but it can be modified to be simply a co-operative, fun exercise.

The aim

Each group is given the same task to complete. You can vary the goal, but in our example the basic aim is to build an egg-mobile from the materials provided, which will propel itself over an agreed, or longest distance across a gym or similar floor. You can choose whether this also entails setting a new travelling time record, as recorded on a stop-watch.

The materials

The main requirement is that each group gets exactly the same components from which to build their egg-mobile. The following list gives an indication of the sorts of things required. These are all obtainable from Specialist Crafts, but there are also a good range of CDT accessories in the NES Arnold and Galt catalogues.

1. Standard length rubber bands (reasonably strong).
2. Model wheels, wood or plastic.
3. Balsa wood, or light weight bamboo canes.
4. Adhesive, masking tape and string.
5. Steel axles.
6. Piano wire.
7. A modelling-knife/scalpel for cutting, and possibly a small hacksaw.
8. An egg, or similar, to be conveyed.

A typical mobile may look like:

The triangular shape tends to run in a more stable way than its four-wheeled counterpart, but **don't** tell the kids **that,** or show them the above drawing!

Other competitions/activities

We don't want to duplicate the material from CDT modelling and construction projects, or our mate, Alan Smith's book, 'Creative Outdoor Work with Young People'. There are lots of examples of things to design and build, which can be turned into group work/team activity projects. Getting more ambitious, the outdoor environment does offer the chance to plan lots of 'now get out of this-style' or 'Crystal Maze' exercises, which combine brain and a bit of brawn to find a solution. Raft-building and racing, and constructing tree houses are two possibilities, along with town trails and social history projects, all of which can get young people studying their local area and its community.

FACE PAINTING AND MAKE-UP

Arm most teenage groups with a supply of face paints and within minutes you are sure to have a good selection of Draculas, Clowns, Witches, American Indians, and Animals. With a little skill and a knowledge of the available products and their application, this enthusiasm can be used as the basis for a whole range of arts activities particularly in the performance arts arena. Make-up is sexually stereotyped as a female domain, but the basics of making up a face are very similar whether it is for face painting, beauty or stage productions.

Face painting

Face painting has proved popular with many youth groups, large and small and of varying ages. It requires relatively little in the way of equipment and is an easily supervised activity.

There are quite a range of face paints to choose between for use with young people. Some people are allergic to make-up of any kind, so it is important to use paints or crayons which have been well tested. Ideally, young people with sensitive skins won't ask to be face painted, but that's not the real world! Instead, have on hand, water, soap and skin cleaning lotion. Also it is a good idea to have other, equally fun activities available just in case some members cannot participate in a face painting session.

Although it is possible for each person to paint their own face, this requires a mirror for each person, well beyond the resources of most youth clubs, unless you are running beauty classes. It is just as simple, and arguably a lot more fun, to divide the group up into pairs, with each person taking it in turn to decorate their partner's face. Adults should be on hand to offer general advice, keep an eye on the face paints and how they are being used, and (we hope) get involved in the spirit of the activity, as active participants!

Apart from when using paint crayons, each face painter will need a small piece of sponge for applying large areas of colour and a couple of paint brushes, one of which should be quite fine. With younger children, it is best if paint/colour is kept away from the eyes and hair, but with older young people, they can be encouraged to experiment more (i.e. painting arms, legs and body), and with attention to detail around the eyes and mouth. It is always best to apply the large areas of base colour first, then to add in the detail.

Face painting is a useful part of circus, carnival, street performance and drama and theatre activities. Running a face painting stall at a fete or show can provide both fun and useful funds. *Make-up sessions* run on a regular basis in a youth club, or as a workshop at an activity day or weekend, are almost always very popular with girls and young women. They may also be combined with related activities such as hairdressing and hair braiding.

Types of face paints:	***Options include:***
Face paint crayons:	quite expensive, easy to use, non-toxic, but hard to use to create strong colours or cover large areas. Some are hard to remove.
Left over make-up:	cheap, but a limited range of colours. Tends to be viewed as the province of girls and women, and therefore will not be used by boys or young men.
Stage make up:	often referred to as greasepaint, it is either oil-based or water soluble. A good range of colours are available, it is easy to apply with sponge or brushes, but it is relatively expensive. For youth group use, water-based are probably the best. Grimas, Aquacolour and Snazaroo are well known makes.
Baby lotion plus powder paint:	50:50 mix; easy to use, good range of colours, some colours are hard to remove and they may dry out the skin.

The Alan part of Howie and Alan, spent about five years of his late school and college days working part time and full time in West Sussex theatres, including the prestigious Chichester Festival Theatre. Primarily, he was involved with set design, lighting and sound, but inevitably a bit of make-up work was involved. The rest of this section is based on that work, and material from the Grimas book 'Make-up for profession or Hobby' (Grimas, 1992) and Mary Quant 'Quant on Make-up' (Century Hutchinson, 1986).

Base colour

Since the skin is a delicate canvas for painting, care should be taken that make-up will not cause harm. Ideally, anyone applying make-up or face paint should wash their face first. Acid-balanced cleansing bars or liquids are the kindest to the skin and help to preserve the skin's natural oils. When using make-up which will be worn for any length of time, it is best to apply a moisturiser. This protects the skin and helps to provide a stable surface for the foundation. The best type to use depends on the person's skin – dry, oily, normal, allergic etc..

In face painting, cake make-up (which is oil based) is used as the foundation. The colour(s) used depends on the required effect. Foundation for make-up is usually liquid or past and is best applied with a slightly damp sponge. Remember to apply to the neck as well as the face. Colours for the base and the detail can be tested on the back of the hand and later washed off.

Applying the detail

Face: Rouge for cheekbones and temples can be applied with a brush, as can water-based paints for the creating effects such as animal and clown faces. Brushes in two or three thicknesses will be needed for applying water-based colours. Blending of a number of colours together is very important in make-up. Some effects require subtlety, some boldness!

Modelling the face using rouge can achieve the effects of changing the shape of the face

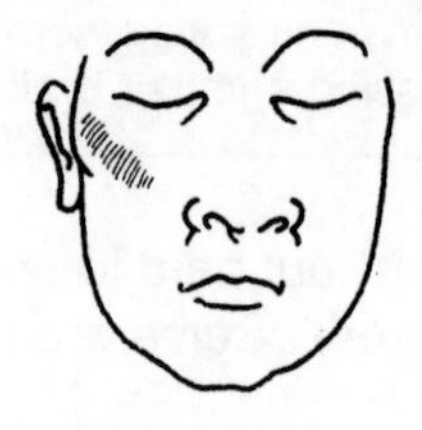

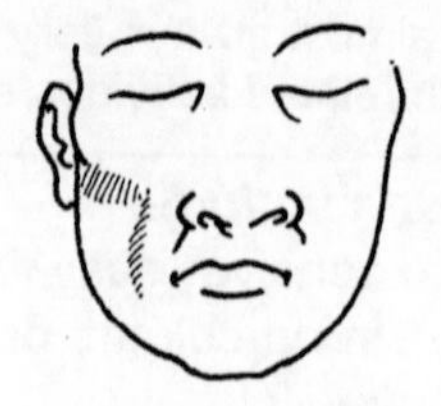

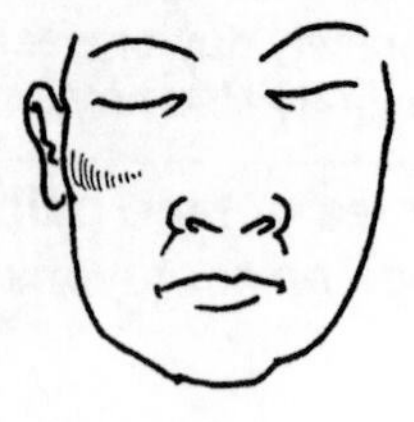

The 'rules', such as they, are for make-up and face painting are contradictory. Blending one colour into the next, using a subtle touch, is the basis for good make-up technique. In face painting, stark lines and vivid colours help to present a powerful image. Similarly, on stage, make-up is used for strengthening or changing features and this can be achieved to even greater effect when using a base of latex, but that *is* beyond the scope of this section!

Once the foundation is settled, then use a light coating of powder, including a little around the eyes. Then carefully remove the excess with a powder brush. Proper 'fixing powder' is also available, which ensures that make-up stays put.

Eyebrows

In face painting, and in ordinary make-up, building up or disguising the eyebrows is an important part of the whole design. To strengthen or re-shape the eyebrows it is possible to use small, stiff brushes, eyebrow pencils or a mascara brush. Often, more than one colour, including rouge, is used and blended for striking effects. For stage work or for elaborate face painting, eyebrow plastic may be used to block out the eyebrows. Camouflage make-up can also be used for this purpose and for masking skin discolorations.

One of the tricks of applying make-up successfully, is to use a spatula to pick up small amounts of colour, which are then applied with a brush or cotton wool buds. It is also an advantage to have a good range of brushes available for use with different colours and uses.

Eyes

False eye lashes come in natural or bright colours, even gold, rainbow and red! They require cutting to size and applying carefully with a special adhesive to the lid of the eye. If the recipient isn't used to having them applied, it can take a few attempts. The eyelash is usually applied from the inside of the eye first, moving outwards, pressing lightly into place close to the rim of the eye lid. Eye liner is used to disguise the join and if a 'natural' look is required, the false eyelash and the real lashes are blended together and shaped.

Next comes the artistic bit, colouring and shaping the eyes. The eyes are an expressive feature and putting a light colour on the eyelids with a darker colour in the fold above the lid accentuates the eye, as does the use of eye liners, which can be applied with a brush or pencil.

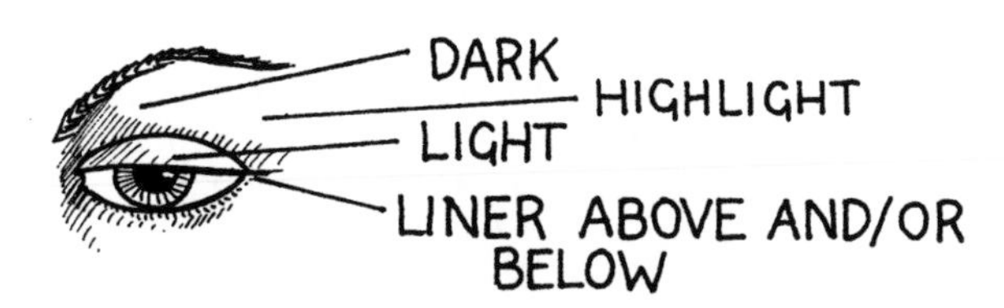

For bolder effects, eye liner can be obtained in primary colours, white and black and with a pearlised effect. A highlight can be added to great effect on the highest point of the brow bone. As with other aspects of face make-up, either blend colours for a natural effect, or emphasise the contrasts for strong, powerful effects. To prevent powder falling on to the cheeks, place a piece of tissue below the eye being worked on. Finally, apply mascara of whatever shade and colour seems appropriate.

Lips

A tiny amount of foundation applied with the finger to the lips, provides a firm base for lip colouring. Nearly all professional make-up artists use a lip pencil and then a lip brush for shaping and colouring the lips. The pencil is used to produce a clear, crisp outline and the brush to provide a uniform colour. Lip gloss is used to achieve a shiny effect and sealant. Fixing powder will prevent the lip colour quickly deteriorating.

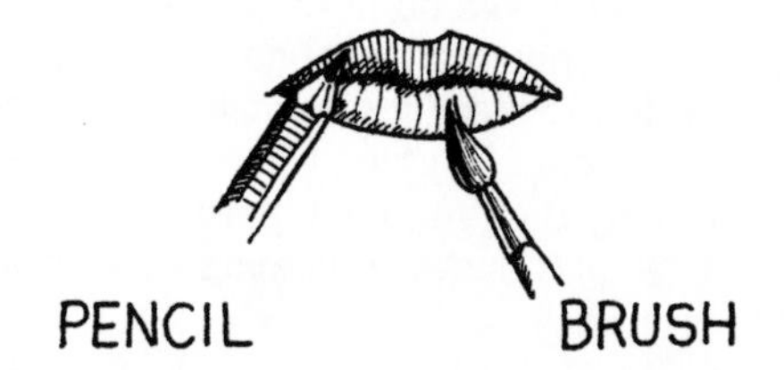

Special effects

For *colouring hair*, applying water-based colour with an old toothbrush is about the easiest method. Once colours are established, the hair can be modelled and fixed in place using a strong-hold, hair spray. *Beards, false eyebrows and moustaches* can be made from crepe wool, cut to size and fixed in place using spirit gum. Special *face glitter* creates a good party look and can be applied with fingers, brush or sponge.

Body painting uses a lot of paint but is extremely impressive in parades and carnivals. A technique which has limited uses, but which is nonetheless fun, is to paint feet using water-based paints, possibly creating mock shoes or little people on the toes.

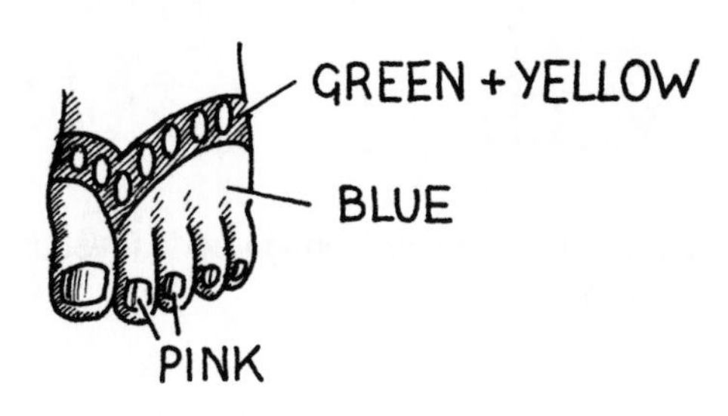

For artists, *tattoos* can be painted on or designs painted on the face. Transfers are also available. In recent years, football and rugby colours have been painted on faces; flags, animals and flowers are all popular. Finishing touches like colouring hands, arms and legs may complete the effect; likewise *nail varnish,* which now comes in an amazing range of colours.

Removing make-up

The make-up described in this section is a mixture of oil and water-based products. To carefully remove make-up, especially if you are working with a group of youngsters, you will need:

- cleansing lotion/cream;
- make-up removal oil;
- spirit gum remover;
- wool pads and cotton buds;
- eye make-up remover.

Skin cream is usually applied afterwards to offset any effects of the make-up.

Designs for face painting

Face painting and make-up sessions are the ideal opportunity for young people to display their own individual flair and imagination. We do not advocate a slavish paint-the-face-by-numbers approach. Instead, as a workshop leader, encourage both the artist and the model to experiment, to take risks and to learn for themselves how different materials work, blend, rub of, cover each other, etc.. Working with young people whose base skin colour may vary from very pale to very dark requires, particularly for make-up rather than face painting sessions, a good range of foundation colours which correspond as nearly as possible to the natural skin colour.

Possible ideas for face painting include:

CLOWN

WITCH

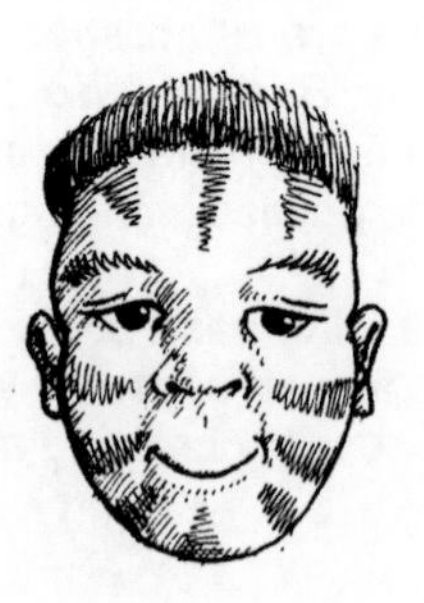

WEREWOLF

PUNK.

Obviously, for a number of occasions, face painting needs finishing off with wigs, hats and suitably bright or appropriate costumes.

FLOWERCRAFT

We guess that almost everyone has groaned either inwardly, or outwardly, at the very thought of pressing leaves and flowers. We have been among them! However, having been introduced to the craft activity of pressing flowers, it does have a number of things to commend it:

- it's cheap – flowers and leaves are plentiful;
- it's easy to achieve interesting and pleasing results;
- if you don't have , or can't afford a proper press, an old phone directory will do the job, since the paper is absorbent and the book is heavy enough to flatten out the flowers.

To collect, press and display dried, pressed flowers will require two or three sessions, so it works best with young people who do not demand instant results.

Collecting specimens

This is best done when it is relatively dry, otherwise dampness will ruin the items during the drying process, when they will go mouldy. Direct your young people to collect specimens which do not belong to someone else (in other words, are growing wild, or cultivated by you or your organisation); offer an interesting range of colours and textures, and importantly, do not destroy the only examples of rare flowers and foliage.

To preserve freshness, collect the specimens in airtight plastic bags or use a simple type of travelling press.

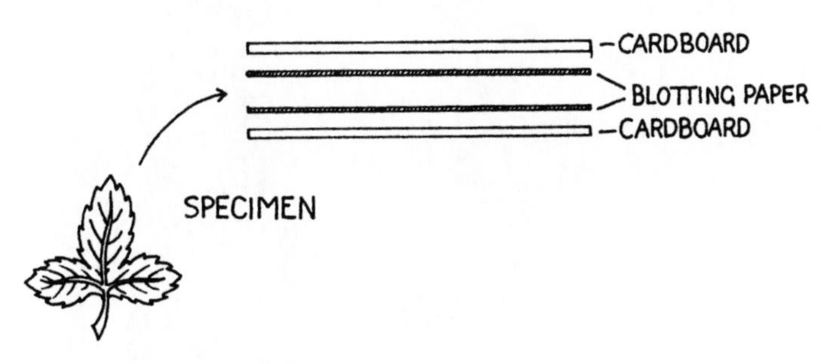

Bind these sandwiches together with a couple of elastic bands. The quicker the specimens are dried, the more effective the final pressed version is likely to be. Use small nail scissors for snipping off the flower heads, leaves, buds, stems and grasses. With some flowers, the multitude of petals make them hard to press into a two dimensional form. With these it is often best to dismantle the separate petals and dry them individually.

Try to help your group choose what they collect by considering:

- is it very fleshy and succulent? (these do not dry out well);
- is it relatively dry already? (best for pressing);
- is it a suitable size, shape and colour for the intended picture?

It may help if your group has a small guide book to wild and cultivated flowers. (The Observer's series are good, as are those from Collins and the Treasure Press).
The following are recommended for pressing:
☐ snowdrop ☐ daffodil ☐ heather ☐ anemone ☐ primula ☐ alyssum ☐ buttercup
☐ wild pansy ☐ dog rose ☐ elderflower ☐ daisy ☐ coltsfoot ☐ primrose
☐ celandine ☐ cow parsley ☐ hydrangea ☐ montbretia ☐ rose ☐ larkspur
☐ lobelia ☐ gypsophila ☐ forget me not ☐ rock rose

Ferns, leaves, seed pods and even seaweeds (if well washed) all make interesting materials for pressing.

Pressing

A small pair of nail scissors and tweezers are necessities. Many flowers and leaves are best divided up before pressing. Later they can be re-assembled in an abundant variety of ways. As we've already said, an old telephone directory can be used for pressing or you can make or buy a version of the travelling press which includes plywood panels and wing nuts to exert the best even pressure on the drying samples. A nine-inch square press is about the optimum size. The telephone book or blotting paper can be re-used almost endlessly.

Most plants take up to six weeks to become fully dry and ready for mounting on card or any other surface.

Presentation

Sticking flowers to a surface is a collage-type activity. The aim is to present a new picture which offers a unique blend of textures, shapes and colours. It can be worth discussing with young people, how symmetry and patterns can be made from the different parts of the flowers. Choosing appropriate types of surface to mount the flower parts on will also influence the effectiveness of the overall design. Contrasting colours or subtle blending of tones can both produce good results.

To attach the individual pieces of leaf and flower to the mount, it is often adequate to use a slightly damp finger to transport them about. Then use a little latex (or similar) glue to affix each piece in place. We've also used cow gum, dispensed from the end of a cocktail stick! The design aspect is always harder to teach. As with many other craft activities, it is best to encourage imagination and individuality, rather than copying any particular style. Pressed flowers are very suitable for book marks, simple greetings cards and calendars. Paper plates can make an attractive mount for a dried flower picture.

For a more 'polished' finish, some young people like to turn their creation into a proper framed picture. Oval frames are often particularly suitable. It is worth suggesting to the young people that they should spend some time considering the options for mounting material. A piece of silk stretched over a wooden backing may make the most appropriate background for a lot of flower creations. Alternatively, gluing leaves and flowers onto wood or even a stone can be finished off with two or three coats of clear polyurethane varnish, which will bind the picture into place.

Specialist Crafts and many other firms supply a good range of different sizes and qualities of flower presses.

HANDMADE PAPER

This definitely falls into the category of environmentally friendly youth activities, as you can easily recycle newsprint or office paper. For finer quality results you can now buy newspaper pulp from your arts and craft supplier, who will also sell you a starter kit if you don't want to make up your own paper making frame.

This can be a fairly messy activity, so you don't want to do it in the living room! Ideally you need access to a large kitchen sink, and you should have plenty of old newspaper handy to put on the floor and to mop up spillages.

Equipment Needed

You'll need the following pieces of equipment, most of which you can make up yourself or find easily at home, school, club etc..

- *Paper making frame.* This should be relatively small – A4 (297mm X 210mm) or A5 size is ideal. You will need to make up two identically sized frames out of one-inch wood. The bottom frame should be covered with a fine synthetic mesh and stretched tight. Alternatively you can use a fine metal mesh. The upper frame is left empty and serves to contain the paper pulp solution while the water drains away.

- *Pulp:* newsprint or office paper torn into small pieces.
- *Aquapel size.* This makes the paper stronger and resistant to waterbased colour medium. Mix in the proportion of 2% Aquapel to 98% water, and use this mixture to soak the pulp or paper in.
- *Small decorative pieces* like flower petals, small seeds, threads etc. can be used in the mixture for effect.
- *Paper making dye* or food dye if you want coloured paper. Tea, coffee or scent can be used if you want smelly paper!
- *Buckets* to mix the pulp in.
- *An electric whisk* or blender.
- *A washing up basin* or sink large enough to take the size of frame you are using.
- *A number of tea towels* or similar for drying the paper between. The material and weave of the cloths you use will give your paper different texture effects.
- *A pair of strong pressing boards* to squeeze the water out of the paper (or you can buy a pressing frame for a few pounds).

Method

Remember that you will need several sets of equipment if you are working with a group.

1. Fill a bucket with pulp or paper and leave it to soak in water. Paper should be soaked for a couple of hours or overnight. Pulp need only be soaked for half an hour or so.
2. Now take a handful of the mixture and squeeze out most of the water. Put these balls of pulp in the blender and add some fresh water. Blend the mixture for four or five minutes, adding more water if needed, until it is the consistency of thin porridge.
3. Put the pulp mixture in the basin and add one and a half times this amount of warm water. Mix together with any colour, scent or decorative effects.
4. Now arrange your frame so that the gauze is in the middle with the open frame on top. Hold the frame firmly and immerse it in the pulp. Lift it slowly out, making sure you keep it level, and allow the water to drain away before putting the frame down.
5. When you lift off the top half of the frame you will be left with a sheet of (wet!) paper lying on the gauze. Tip the paper carefully onto a tea towel on a pressing board and cover it with another tea towel. Repeat the process until you have a stack of sheets, each separated by a tea towel. Place the second pressing board on top and squash it gently but firmly to squeeze out all of the water. This can be quite messy so it's a good idea to lay the pressing boards on newspapers to soak up the water.
6. Finally, peel off each sheet of paper, keeping it on a drying cloth, and lay them out on newspaper until thoroughly dried. You can speed up the drying process by using a hairdryer.

Once you have dried the sheets of paper, they can be used for many other arts and crafts purposes. Simply painting or drawing on them with charcoal, for instance, can produce an attractive finished product. Found materials like feathers, shells, fabric etc. can also be used to good effect and will blend in well with the natural appearance of the paper. Greetings cards and calendars are also worth considering. You may well find that your young people end up writing to their 'special' friends using the handmade paper!

HOT AIR BALLOONS

Making and flying hot air balloons is an exciting project for any group aged eleven upwards. The balloons you make with your group are very realistic. They will fly, and differ only in scale and sophistication from the continent-jumping record-breakers we've seen in recent years.

Your group will need a moderate amount of patience to work with the tissue paper used to construct the balloon, but the effort is well worthwhile.

To build one balloon you will need:

- 17 sheets of tissue paper in two colours 20 x 30 inches.
- Cream adhesive or Pritt stick adhesive.
- Stiff wire about 70 inches long (strong garden wire).
- Cotton wool roll.
- Methylated spirit.
- Sellotape.
- Scissors.
- Pliers and wire cutters.
- A large table and plenty of space.

Method

1. Open out the tissue paper, fold in half lengthways and build two piles, each one consisting of eight sheets of alternate colours (fig. 1)
2. Keeping the piles as neat as possible, cut away the shaded areas shown (fig. 2). Keep your offcuts in case patches are required later. Pile 1 will form the top half of your balloon and pile 2 the bottom.
3. Now open out the sheets and stick them together to form eight panels. Glue in one thin continuous line and if possible keep the pieces separate until dry (fig. 3). Half inch overlap should be sufficient and it is important to keep the edges parallel.

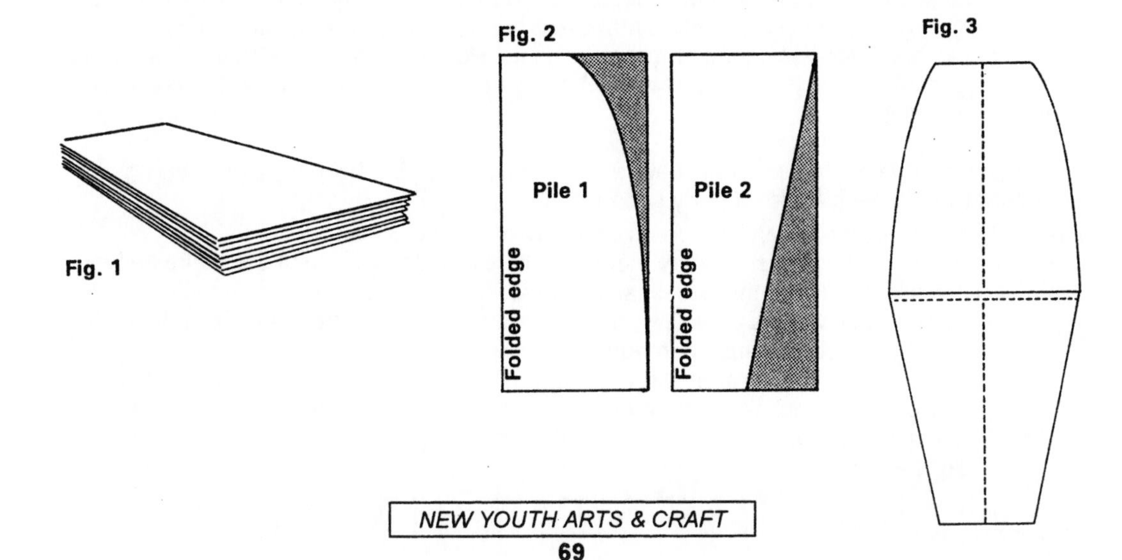

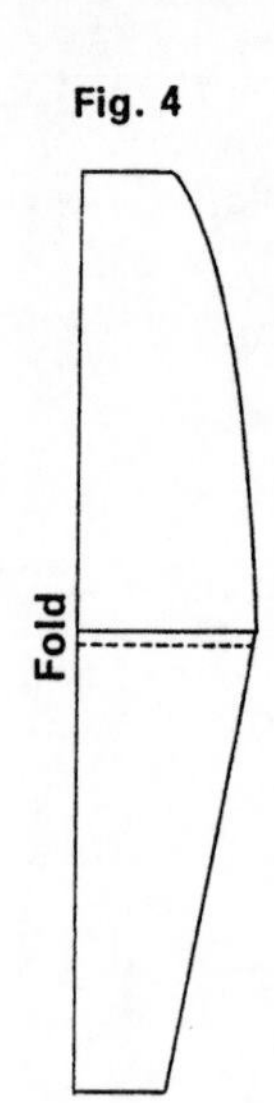

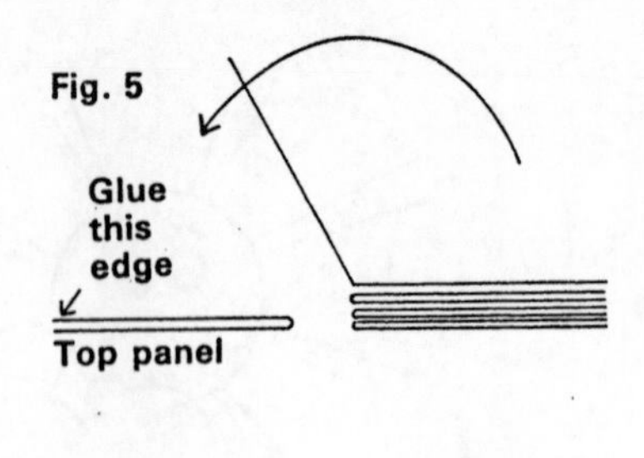

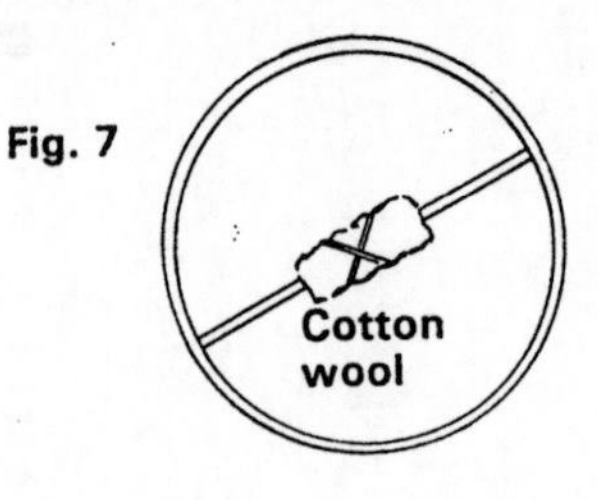

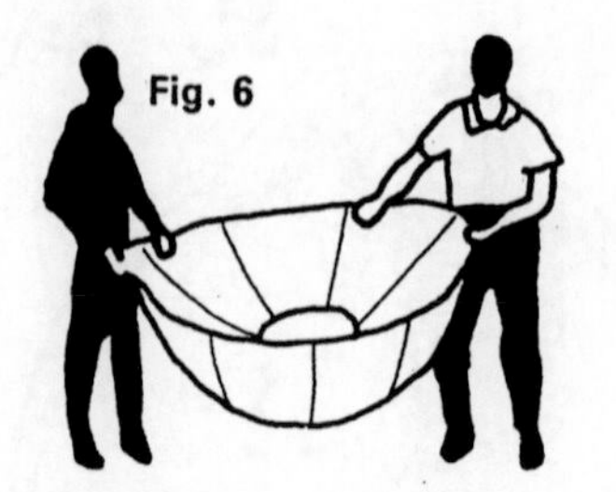

4. Fold each panel in half lengthways and build a pile remembering to alternate the colours (fig. 4)
5. The top panel is placed as shown and the top edge glued in the same way as before. Fold the upper part of panel 2 over and glue as shown. Fold the next part of panel 2 over and glue ready to take the upper part of panel 3 (fig. 5). Care must be taken to separate the two halves of each panel to prevent them from sticking. When all the panels have been stuck the first and last edges can be glued together.
6. Gently open out your balloon. Two people make this easier. Hold the balloon by the seam which runs round the centre of the balloon and shake the bottom half down into the top with the balloon upside down (fig. 6).
7. Cut the remaining sheet of tissue paper to the largest octagon possible and stick this to the inside of the top of the balloon. This is the most difficult part. Try gluing two panels at a time and work round the hole.
8. All that now remains to be done is to make a circle of wire with a cross-piece and wrap about 2 foot of cotton wool around it, tying it on tightly with light wire (fig. 7). Make sure the cotton wool is kept well away from the circle and cannot slide.
9. Fix the circle in place to the base of the balloon with many small pieces of sellotape and your balloon is ready to fly. (If there are any holes or tears they should now be patched). About a cupful of meths is plenty. Pour this onto the wick just before ignition. Alternatively, a piece of solid firelighter can be used instead of cotton wool and meths.

Read the following notes carefully before attempting to fly your balloon, and always make sure that young people are properly supervised.

- Hot air balloons can only be flown safely on windless days.
- If the countryside is very dry there may be some danger, e.g. if the entire balloon catches fire during the launch and drops to the ground.
- Choose launch sites carefully and make sure that the breeze won't take the balloon anywhere it could cause damage.
- Once the balloon is safely airborne, it won't come down until the fuel runs out. However, the wick will remain hot and could smoulder. Always have several containers of water handy to ensure that any fire hazard on take-off or landing is dealt with swiftly.

Launching

Make sure the balloon is held, fully opened out, by the middle seam with one person holding the top and with the base a couple of feet from the ground. Light the wick and wait for the balloon to fill with hot air by which time it can be safely held at the base. When the balloon starts to lift you can let go. It helps to walk with the breeze if there is any.

Good Luck!

HOT ENAMELLING

This is always a popular activity with young people, probably because professional looking results are easily obtained. We reckon that it is best used with the thirteen and over age group. Enamels are derived from powdered, coloured glass. The whole process of firing this at high temperature in a kiln to produce a glossy finish seems to have a magical quality which appeals to kids.

Starter kits are readily obtainable, and are relatively inexpensive. However, you still require a kiln. In the past we have made much use of a simple kiln (essentially a hot-plate with lid) which has a limited heat output. This makes it difficult to fire millefiori (patterned glass beads) or to achieve a scrolled effect. If you intend enamelling to be a long-term activity for your youth group it may be worthwhile investing in a more expensive kiln with higher heat output, and possibly a regulator to prevent the risk of the heating wires burning out. We liked using the simple kiln, though, and found it especially useful for soldering badge findings directly onto finished copper shapes (much quicker than glue). Unfortunately, we have had difficulty in recent years to trace suppliers for this kind of kiln. The more expensive kilns, the enamels, tools and copper blanks are all available from Specialist Crafts.

To get started you'll need the following **equipment:**

- Kiln (high output ones start at around £220).
- Enamels – available in opaque and transparent (and sometimes translucent and opalescent) powdered forms. Millefiori, enamel lumps and threads.
- Shaker jars (for enamel powder).
- Trivet (if using front-loading kiln).
- Spatula.
- Sandpaper.
- Enamelling oil and brush (helps the firing process but is not essential).
- Descaling liquid (helps prevent copper oxidising in kiln).
- Copper shapes and jewellers findings, including leather thong for pendants (jewellers findings are things like earring clips, rings, and badge pins which are glued or soldered to the completed enamel shape).
- Asbestos or other heat resistant board.

In health and safety terms, the Department for Education have pointed out that most jewellery enamels contain a certain level of toxic metals. However, it is perfectly safe to do hot enamelling work with older children, providing there is adequate supervision. When using powdered enamel it is recommended that masks are worn when sifting powder, and that young people should be advised that the powder is dangerous if it comes into contact with eyes or mouth.

Copper shapes suitable for badges, pendants, rings, etc. are easily obtainable, although you can cut your own from copper sheeting. The copper needs to be prepared for accepting the enamel powder by sanding it to a smooth finish with a fine grade sandpaper and applying a thin coat of enamelling oil if required. Descaling liquid can also be applied at this stage to the reverse side of the shape. Now the powder can be sprinkled onto the shape to provide a thin even coat. Placing the shapes on the sheets of newspaper will help when it comes to clearing up. This is the first of two coats, and should be the same colour, or lighter, than the final one. The shape can now be placed in the kiln with a spatula and fired until the surface has a shiny, wavy appearance. This only takes a minute or two, and the shape should then be removed and laid on a sheet of asbestos to cool.

Shaker Tubes and Jars for Enamel Powder

Now comes the exciting bit when you can create your own individual design. You must first prepare the shape with a second coat of enamelling powder, using a thin coat of oil again, if you like. The simplest method is to make your design or initials by removing some of the powder with a fine brush (as long as the colour underneath is a contrasting one). When fired, the design will stand out due to the contrasting colours. Second coats should be fired until the surface is smooth and glossy. If any objects to be fired are not flat, or have sloping surfaces, Tramil Gum can be used to affix the enamel to the surface ready for firing.

Once allowed to cool, findings – badge pins etc. (to transform the shape into a badge, ring, earring, etc.) can be glued or soldered on. Epoxy Resin two-part glue sets in about ten minutes and is very strong; Super Glue is quicker, but slightly less permanent. When soldering, the back of the shape must be sanded down until smooth and shiny, or the solder will not take. 'Jump rings' are very useful in making pendants. Once the little ring has been twisted through the hole at the top of the shape you'll find that it can be laced easily with leather thong and will sit nicely round the neck.

Enamel lumps and coloured threads are always popular ways of decorating shapes, and are simply laid on top of the second coat before it is put in the kiln for firing. In the kiln they will melt flat to form part of the smooth glossy surface. Young people love using the threads to spell out their initials! Millefiori can also be used to good effect but you need a good kiln if they are to melt down properly.

Simple combinations of different colours can be effective at the second coat stage and these can, when melted, be scrolled with a pointed implement to produce a swirled effect. There are several other enamelling methods (e.g. champleve, cloisonne, pique-a-jour) which demand jewellery-making skills or specially prepared materials, but can produce exciting results for those prepared to persevere.

There isn't much that can go wrong with the simpler forms of hot enamelling, and it is therefore worth trying this activity out with most older youth groups. Articles made can be used as presents, or even offered for sale at open days to swell your coffers.

Try to limit the numbers participating in enamelling sessions to about four to six young people per facilitator, and make sure you have an adequate amount of working space. Kilns get very hot indeed and can take a long time to cool down; make sure that the kids are aware of this. Asbestos gloves or a fire blanket can be used if you need to move the kiln during use or after the session.

INSTANT ANIMATION

You'll probably remember flicker books which used occasionally to be given away free by children's comics and breakfast cereal manufacturers. Well, stop being lazy, and invent your own instant version of a cinema great! A flicker book uses exactly the same technique as a cartoon animation.

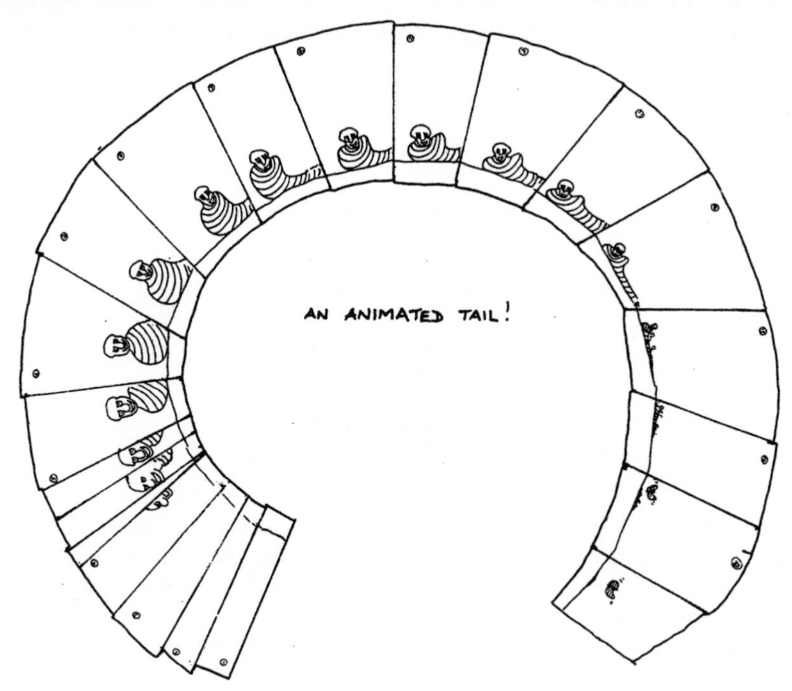

To make a piece of instant animation you'll need to obtain or cut out about 30 equally sized pieces of lightweight card (about 120gsm, for the technically minded!) Index cards are good and you can at least be sure that they are exactly equal in size.These should then be numbered in the left hand corner so you and the other artists keep them in sequence order.

Now, draw a line somewhere in the middle of each card and start drawing a simple cartoon sequence for your flicker books, using the right hand side of your book for the drawings. Keep the line drawings simple. With a group of youngsters it's a good idea to have lots of source cartoon materials available and pencils and tracing paper. Try though, to encourage some original drawings to come out of a session. Since it doesn't require too high a skill level, just patience repeating the drawings, you don't need to be a great artist to achieve a pleasing bit of dynamic action. You can get different effects by making the cartoon animation move in very small or larger gradations of movement.

Once the set of drawings is complete, tape the bundle together holding them tightly in the middle and binding them round the left hand edge.

JEWELLERY

This craft can utilise the products of several techniques outlined in other sections of this book. For example, polished pebbles can be used to make earrings, pendants and rings. Similarly, you can use brightly painted papier maché beads and shapes as raw material for these items, and necklaces as well.

In most cases you will want to use jewellers' 'findings' to help you make finished articles quickly and easily. These are the mountings used to make rings, brooches, earrings, cufflinks and even bracelets. Findings are typically made of base metal but can also be obtained with various qualities of silver and gold finishes. A vast range can be obtained from a number of specialist suppliers. You will need an epoxy resin adhesive to fix your chosen materials to the mounts.

If your budget will stretch to it, Manchester Minerals provide a vast array of jewellers' findings including ones made of solid silver and gold. Their design range is extensive and includes complex and popular designs such as butterflies, flowers, teddy bears and dolphins. Excellent results can be obtained almost instantly using these findings, and of course they are perfect when working with younger children or those with a very limited concentration span.

We suggest that you start off by getting hold of some findings to give you ideas about the kinds of material you might want to use with them. For example, you may want to glue some millefiori enamel straight on to earring mounts; silk threads and small feathers or down are also suitable to decorate earrings. With the current gender bending trends of the 1990s, including cross dressing, jewellery making (and wearing!) is no longer a predominantly female pastime. Acid, new age and rave cultures have contributed to create demand for all kinds of weird and wonderful brooches, pins and other adornments. There is often much cachet and street credibility to be gained if these artefacts are home made, particularly from found materials.

Encourage the young people you are working with to explore the possibilities of particular materials and to experiment with non-traditional designs. The following sections outline a few key techniques, and we begin with one of the newer materials now available which can be manipulated easily into striking designs.

Fimo Modelling Material

This is a versatile clay type of material which is fired in an ordinary kitchen oven to harden it. It is available in three dozen different colours, and they can be mixed together to create any specific colour you want. Fimo is renowned for its brilliant colour intensity, and of course this means that there is no need to paint the material once you have made your piece of jewellery.

Its uses include:

- beads for necklaces;
- modelled birds, animals, cartoon or human figures;
- brooches, pendants, badges and earrings;
- 3-D badges and pictures;
- braiding or marbling to produce spectacular effects, including millefiori.

Fimo produce a very helpful leaflet which demonstrates how you can make various designs very easily indeed. All in all this is an amazingly versatile material which is very easy to use.

As full instructions and ideas are included in every pack, we will not go in to detail here. However, there are one or two safety rules which need to be borne in mind:

- As with many craft activities you should not eat, drink or smoke in the activity area.
- Fimo is not suitable for use with children under eight.

- Hands should be washed after using the material.
- Fimo needs to be hardened in the oven at an exact temperature. As harmful gases can be produced if this temperature is exceeded, we recommend using an oven thermometer.

Pebble Pendants

You can use pebbles you have polished yourself (see section in this book) or bought from a supplier such as Fred Aldous or Manchester Minerals. There is a specific jewellery mount called a 'bell cap' which you will need to obtain, and you need to select your pebble carefully so that the bell cap will fit.

Before you glue the cap to the pebble using epoxy resin, fit the cap to the pebble by pressing it on to the stone. A pair of jewellers' pliers are handy for this job – these are long nosed pliers which are obtainable with one round and one flat end, or with both ends round or flat. If you are working with a range of different materials, you will probably want one of each – otherwise go for the one flat/one round version.

BELL CAP
ADHESIVE
STONE

Once you have glued the cap to the pebble you will need to leave it to set. Of course with pebble pendants, and with rings, you can't simply put them down on a table, because the finding is likely to fall off. What you need is a pot of sand or salt – then simply push your item into it to hold it in an upright position.

Pebble pendants can be completed using a jump ring and metal chain or leather thong.

Pebble Rings and Bracelets

Most rings and bracelets use a flat 'pad' type of mount. Unfortunately this means you will probably not be able to use pebbles you have polished yourself, because one side of the pebble needs to be perfectly flat to make good contact with the pad. However, these 'cabochon cut' stones can be bought fairly inexpensively from your supplier. It is then simply a matter of choosing (for bracelets) stones of similar, or complementary colour, and gluing them on.

You can obtain linked bracelets onto which you can hang a number of bell capped pebbles – and of course you will be able to use your own pebbles with these. Take care when sticking the caps to the pebbles that the ring on the cap faces the same way as the display face of the stone. Now when you put the jump ring on the cap and fix it to the necklace, all the pebbles will hang facing the right way.

Do remember that jewellery comes in for exceptionally hard use, so when you are gluing items together follow the manufacturer's instructions and allow the glue to set for the recommended time before wearing the jewellery.

Silver and Copper Wire

Simple pendants and rings can be made very easily with copper or silver wire. Generally, any metal you will be working with needs to be annealed (softened) before you start to make your piece. Do this by holding the metal with tongs and heating it with a blowlamp until it is a dull red colour; then plunge it into cold water. Rub the metal with wet and dry sandpaper to brighten it up again. The metal soon hardens up again, so you may need to anneal it a few times as you work. 16-18 gauge wire is best for this kind of work.

If you need to straighten out the wire, place one end in a vice and grip the other end with flat nosed pliers – if the pliers have teeth, cover them with cloth tape or sticking plaster so that they don't mark the metal. To provide a good grip for the pliers, make a small right angled bend at the end of the wire – now give a few steady pulls on the wire to straighten it out.

To make a simple pendant, take a length of wire about six to eight inches long, and make a small loop in one end using round nosed pliers. To do this, grip the end of the wire towards the end of the jaws of the pliers and bend it around to form a small circle. Next, change the grip on the pliers (see diagram) and bend the circle back to centre it. Now move to the other end of the wire and make another small loop (but don't centre it this time).

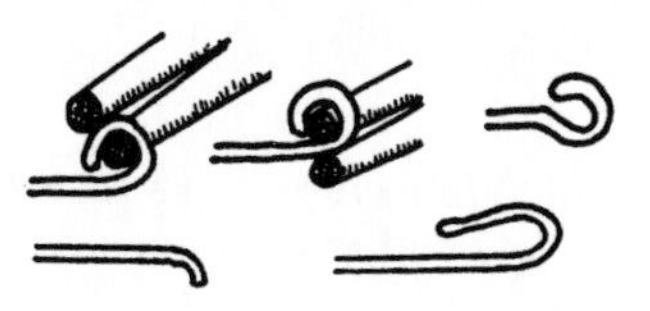

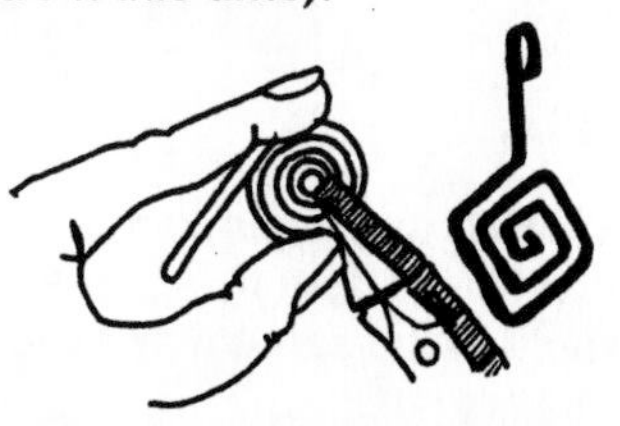

This little loop forms the beginning of the winding, circular shape you are going to make. Start coiling the wire by using your fingers to push it round the loop, and as the coil gets larger hold it firmly with flat nosed pliers. Finally, twist the original loop by 90° so that the pendant will lie properly when you thread a chain or thong through the loop.

A square shaped pendant can be made by using flat nosed pliers to make 90° turns in the wire. An interesting effect can be obtained with either pendant by flattening the wire. Young people love doing this, as it involves bashing the wire with a flat headed hammer against a metal block or anvil!

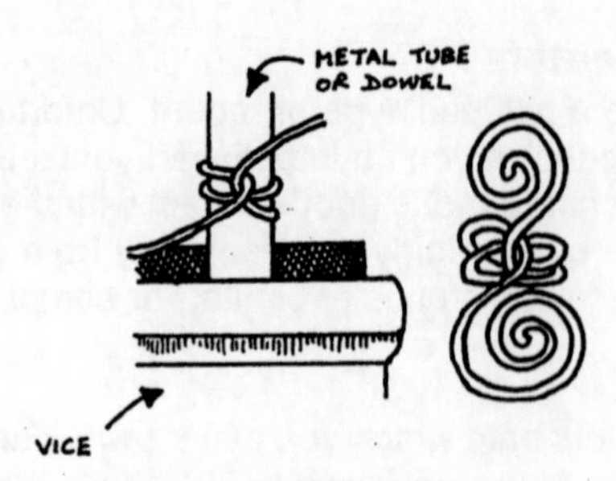

A coiled ring can be made in similar fashion by using an 8 inch length of wire and winding it twice around a suitably sized metal tube or dowel (which will need to be held upright in a vice). Now cross the ends of the wire to secure the ring. File the ends of the wire smooth (cut to adjust the length of the wire at this stage if required). Next, the two ends of the wire can be shaped into circles or squares . Again, the wire can be flattened with a hammer for effect.

Drop Earrings

These earrings can be made using headpins or eyepins and your own selection of beads. A pendant bead, or other item, can be hung from the loop of the eyepin if desired.

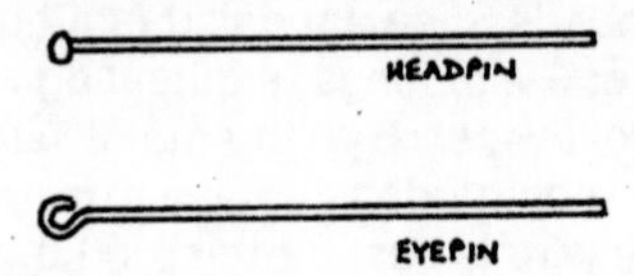

First you should thread your selection of beads onto the headpin, taking care that the hole in the bottom bead is sufficiently small for it not to fall off. Now, if you need to, cut the pin to adjust the length, leaving around 8mm at the top to form into a loop (see 'Copper Wire' above). Make sure that the loop is centred over the beads. The dropper is finished by opening the loop on an earfitting (several kinds are available for pierced and non-pierced ears) and attaching it to the dropper loop.

To start off an eyepin, open the loop by gently twisting it sideways with pliers. Hang a pendant bead from the loop and close it up with pliers. Now add your selection of beads and finish off in the same way as for a headpin.

Simpler drop earrings can be made by attaching a pendant bead directly to an earfitting without using a pin.

Shell Jewellery

Seaside shells can be used to make attractive earrings, pendants and badges. Many shells have a natural 'drop' shape and are perfect for earrings and pendants – you need do little more than fix a bell cap to them before attaching to the earring findings or to a jump ring and chain or leather thong.

Another technique is to use a flat badge finding and glue a selection of matching small shells to this to give a very attractive effect. Flower shapes can be built up easily using tiny shells. Often, you'll be able to glue a small shell, or pearl, in the centre of a larger shell to form a 'jewel.' Finally, don't discard broken shells, as they can often be used as a pendant – simply sand away any rough edges, and if there is not a natural hole to thread your chain or thong through, use a bell cap mount.

KITES

Kites have a long and respectable history, reputedly originating in China more than a few years B.C.! The Chinese, in fact, successfully developed man-lifting kites which they used as military lookouts, and Koreans and Japanese developed fighting kites – the line near the kites was coated with glue and powdered glass, the aim being to cut your opponent's line.

Kite flying has undergone a considerable revival in recent years, while hang-gliding (a derivative of the Chinese man-lifting kite) has achieved cult status. Simple kites are quite easy to make out of basic materials and can fly remarkably well. Instructions are given at the end of the section. Kites are probably best used with your youth group on residential trips or outings to the country, as turbulence created in towns by buildings and traffic makes them difficult to fly and extricate from roofs, chimneys, and the like! Similarly, kites will not fly well in forested areas. Ideal places include flat fields, the windward side of a hill, or near the sea or lake. You should not (for obvious reasons) fly one in a thunderstorm (remember good old Benjamin Franklin's experiment!). Overhead power cables are absolutely lethal and you must *always* check for them carefully before launching kites – especially in country areas where there may only be a single cable visible.

Preparing and Launching

Most kites have a bridle which attaches the kite to the line; this hold the kite at a specific 'angle of attack' – a high angle for normal wind conditions, and a lower angle for strong winds (see diagram). Make sure that this angle is correct before flying, by doing a couple of trial launches and then making the necessary adjustments to the bridle. You should find (with the notable exception of the sled kite, which you can fly at a very high angle) that the best angle of attack is between 30 and 35 degrees from the horizontal. **Always,** before launching, check the balance of the kite by throwing it gently up in the wind – if the kite keels over to one side, you will have to add weight to balance it.

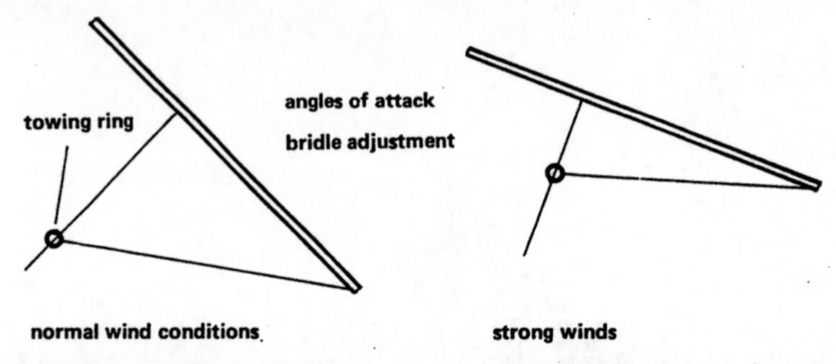

If the wind isn't too strong and you are using a kite reel (advisable for good control) you can gain height by 'winching' the kite. What you do is to launch the kite by throwing it up in the air; now allow the line to run slack until the kite almost drops to the ground, and then reel in quickly so that the kite soars up. Repeat this process (see diagram) until the kite is as high as you want, or it reaches a height where there is more wind.

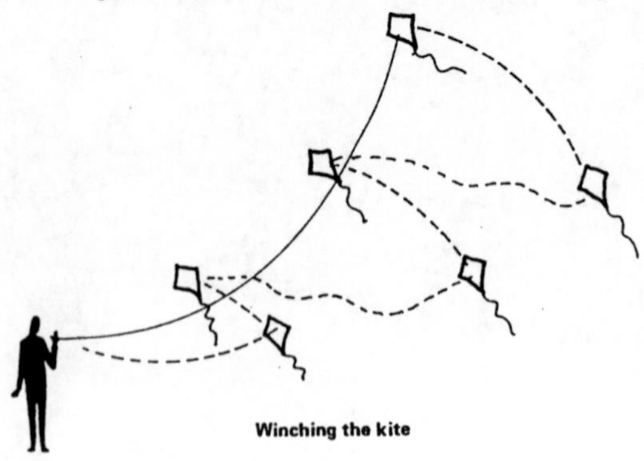

Winching the kite

You can also launch the kite with a helper by unrolling about 20 yards of line and getting her to hold the kite high about her head. As the helper launches the kite you should move backwards until it begins to rise and then slowly let out more line. Once the kite has reached a good height you can use the winching technique to make it drop and soar.

Landing the Kite

In moderate wind conditions it isn't too difficult to land the kite; reel it in slowly and steadily until it is just a few yards away, then let the line go slack to bring the kite slowly to the ground. If there is a lot of tension on the line, you can ease it by walking towards the kite while reeling it in. In high winds, extra care is needed as the kite can suddenly plunge to the ground. Ideally, ask someone to help you by walking out along the line towards the kite, pulling the line down at the same time. Once they are about 30 yards away and holding the line to take tension off your end of it, walk towards them while reeling in; repeat the process until the kite is safely down.

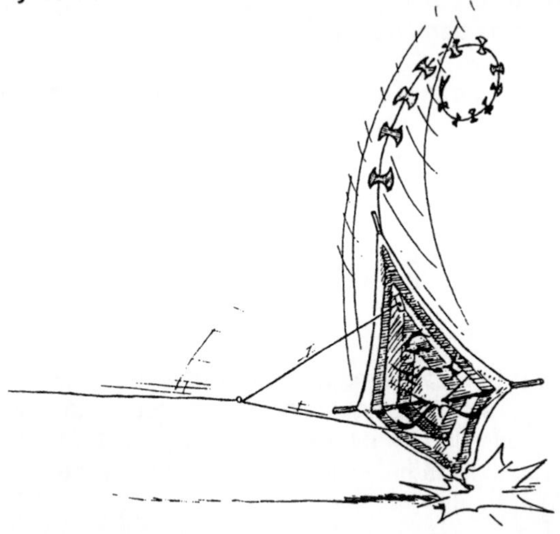

Materials and Construction

We have found that choice of materials and accuracy of construction are immensely important in creating a machine that will actually fly! We therefore include only two kite designs in this section which we found to be simple to make and virtually guaranteed to fly.

COVER MATERIAL	EASE OF USE	SUITABLE FRAME	ADHESIVE METHOD	WEIGHT	FLYING LINE
Light paper	Good	Thin stick Rice straw	White glue Sticky tape	Very light	Sewing thread
Heavy paper	Good	Cane Bamboo Rattan	Wood glue Strong glue Sticky tape	Light	Sewing thread
Silk or Cotton	Moderate	Thin stick Rattan	Fabric glue Reinforcing tape	Light	Linen
Synthetic fabric	Moderate	Bamboo Deal Light alloy Polypropelene	Sewing Sticky tape	Light to heavy	Fishing line
Nylon or Plastic film	Poor	Stick Synthetic tubing	Plastic adhesive tape	Light to heavy	Nylon
Polyethylene film	Very good	Stick Light alloy Synthetic tubing Fibre-glass	Sticky tape Cloth tape Heat application	Light to heavy	Nylon

By all means attempt to build other kinds of kite, but remember that the designs may be complex, calling for great accuracy, relatively sophisticated construction techniques, and an awful lot of patience. Most youth groups will probably relish the experience of flying kites rather than making them, so try to keep it simple. Remember that kites can be decorated and personalised – this is an enjoyable activity and helps the kites look attractive in the sky.

For those who **do** want to experiment, this Materials and Construction Chart will be useful.

Generally, a light and flexible kite will perform will in a light wind; attempt to launch it in a strong wind and it is likely to be damaged and torn.

A heavy kite, made from strong materials and able to support strong wind pressure without twisting its shape, will fly well in bad weather. In a light wind it will not even get off the ground! As a rule of thumb, flat kites should fly well in light winds, while 'bowed' kites perform well in moderate winds, and cellular kites in strong winds.

On a kite flying expedition it makes sense to take a selection of different kinds of kite, so that you have at least one or two which will fly irrespective of the wind conditions you meet.

Tails

The main purpose of a tail is to create drag and thus provide directional stability. A tail also helps reduce the side to side 'snaking' motion that often occurs. The tail should add as little extra weight to the kite as possible – remember it's the drag factor that is important. In flight, the tail should fly gracefully in the wind, counterbalancing the movement of the kite, without adding any backlash.

The length of the tail should be adjusted to suit wind speed (larger tail for high winds) but will usually be between five and seven times the length of the kite. **Do** have a few trial attempts with tails of different lengths.

Tails are always needed on flat kits.

Winding Bobbin

While not as useful as a kite reel, a winding bobbin is a reasonable substitute, and very easy to make (see diagram).

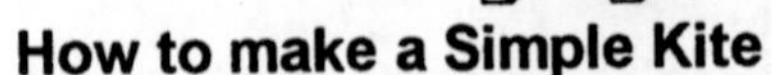

How to make a Simple Kite

This kite flies well in moderate to high winds.

You will need:

- Two spars of square section soft or hard wood
  - one of 36 inches x .25 inch
  - one of 32 inches x .25 inch.
- Lightweight cloth or crepe or tissue paper 36 inches x 36 inches.
- Line (25 kg breaking strain minimum – stronger for high winds).
- Glue and towing ring (curtain ring, washer or similar).

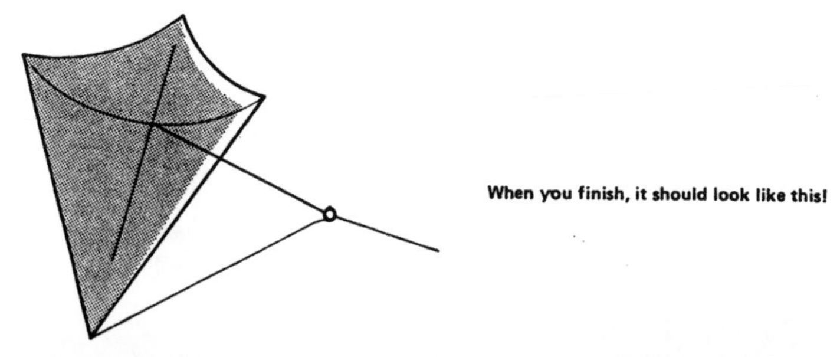
When you finish, it should look like this!

Using the long spar as the spine of the kite, tie the short spar to the spine six inches from the top to form a cross. Now notch the ends of the spars and tie line round the frame (Diagram 1).

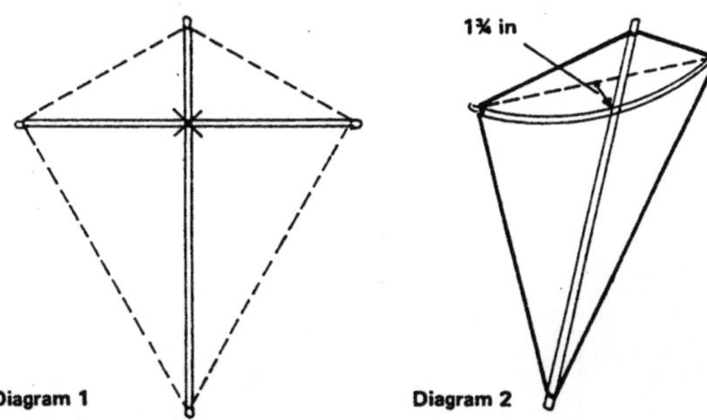

Diagram 1

Diagram 2

Cut out the cover, allowing enough of a hem to turn it over frame, and glue it down. Next, tie a line tightly along the cross-spar to bow the kite. There should be roughly 1.75 inches clearance between the line and the spine (Diagram 2).

Now strengthen two bridle points on the cover, approximately 6 inches from the top and 2 inches from the bottom of the kite. This can be done with paper reinforcing circles (paper kites), or with cloth tape or material on other kites. Pierce a hole in the strengthened part of the kite and tie the bridle ring around the spar behind. The string should be a total length of approximately 84 inches, and should be looped once through the towing ring. If you adjust the bridle so that the top part of it is roughly 36 inches long and the bottom part 48 inches, then the kite will be set at the correct angle of attack for normal wind conditions (Diagram 3). Finally, attach the line to the towing ring. The ring will remain in position as you tighten the line and bridle. Prepare to launch! A tail can be added to this kite to increase its stability. It should be made of a very light material, roughly five times the length of the kite itself.

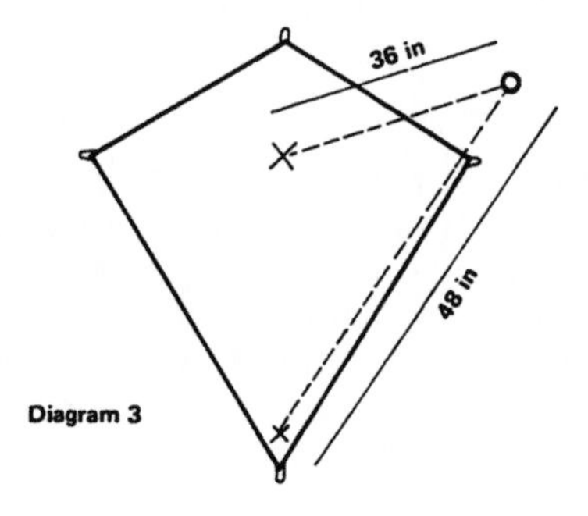

Diagram 3

Sled Kites

This kite is a recent design and came from experiments for improving parachutes. You can see the similarity to parachutes used by sky-divers. It flies well in all winds, although you may have to add twin tails for stability in strong winds.

You will need:

- Two spars of square section soft or hard wood 36 inches x .25 inch.
- 200 gauge polythene or PVC 40 inches x 40 inches.
- Fishing line.
- Strong adhesive tape.
- Metal eyelets.
- Towing ring.

Carefully cut the cover and air vents; then reinforce the bridle points with adhesive tape and metal eyelets.

Now lay the spars on the cover and fix them firmly with adhesive tape. Fix a piece of line to the bridle points as shown, laying it out round the kite to achieve the correct length.

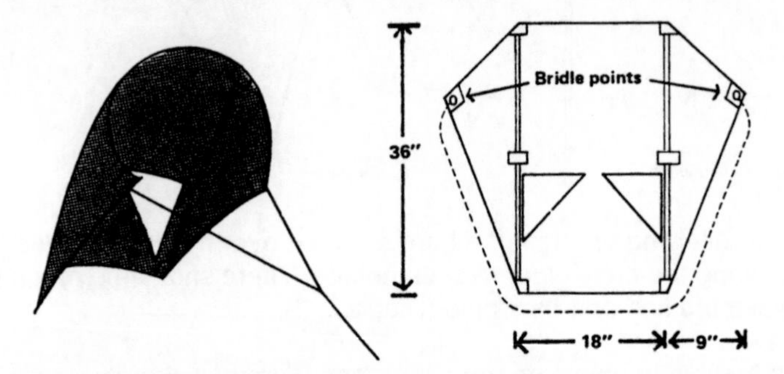

Finally, fix a towing ring at the centre of the bridle. The kite is now complete and can be attached to the flying line. Note that sled kites can fly well at an angle of attack of 50-60 degrees to the horizontal. As with any kite, if you are not happy with its balance or angle of attack in flight, make some adjustments till you get it right. It will be worth the effort!

Note that the proportions of these kites can be scaled up or down as required to make kites of different sizes – make sure to alter the bridle in line with the new dimensions.

Finally, avoid flying kites within two miles of an airport (it's actually against the law) or at high altitudes. Kites made with certain materials can show up on radar screens causing all sorts of difficulties for air traffic controllers, not to mention very real risks to the flying public.

LEATHERWORK AND PYROGRAPHY

Leather is a flexible resource for making lots of items which kids like and use, whether it is a studded dog collar for the boy or girl-friend, or bags, belts, pouches, wristbands, pendants, hairslides, pet collars and clothes, to name but a few items. Scrap leather is inexpensive and can be used to make mosaics in the form of a wallhanging, or to embellish a garment. Some leathers can be tooled or stamped with a design. You can also dye it, paint it, or stud it. Articles are usually made by cutting out shapes and joining them by gluing, stitching, thonging or riveting.

A number of leather suppliers will supply clearance, cut lengths of leather and specify their suitability for different uses. For instance, at the time of writing this at the beginning of 1996, it was possible to obtain ten belt lengths, ¾ inch wide, 3mm thick and between 432 inches and 53 inches long cost £110 per unit. It's not an activity for people who feel strongly about working with and wearing animal skins. But, virtually no suppliers in the leather trade use skins from animals killed for their skins – it is a by product of the meat industry. Some synthetic alternatives to leather and suede are available – you will need to enquire locally. Financially, leatherwork lends itself as a fundraising activity, whereby the group can help their organisation raise funds, or at very least cover most of the costs.

A fair number of fiddly bits of equipment are necessary to do some jobs properly, especially when dealing with rivets. It is possible to improvise in some cases, but you will end up with a fairly high level of wastage of eyelets, rivets, press studs etc.. Hand, hammered tools are inevitably more fiddly to use than more solid machines with special dies for applying rivets, eyelets and press studs. In the old phrase, *"You pays your money and takes your chance."*

If you want to test out the demand for leatherwork among young people you are working with, you should consider buying kits. These are useful, as you are provided with a basic pattern that can be used many times over. Because most of the leather cutting and preparation has been done for you, you can do without many of the tools until such time as the demand merits buying them. Remember, though, that kits will not keep people occupied for long as they can be completed very quickly. Since there are a number of knives involved in many leatherwork processes, it is important to match the leather projects to the age, ability and potential for aggressive behaviour levels of your young people. A reasonably comprehensive list of materials and equipment is as follows:

Vegetable tanned leather: firm, easily tooled or stamped with a design.
Chrome tanned leather: soft and supple - ideal for pouches, bags and mosaic work.
Leather thonging and needles
Stanley knife
Leather scissors with a serrated bottom for cutting
Steel rule - for making straight cuts
Awl - to score lines for cutting
Revolving punch for holes
Oblong punch for belts
Thonging punch

Stitching punch
Stitch groover
Stitch marker
Press stud tool set, plus press studs
Riveting tool set, plus rivets
Eyelet tool set, plus eyelets
Sail-Eyelet/Grommet setter
Modelling tool
Swivel knife for leather carving
Wooden or (if you can afford it) a Rawhide mallet
An Edge Shave for rounding edges, and if your group get very keen a
Safety beveller for bevelling and skiving edges (tapering thinner to join together)
Strap cutter - for cutting belt widths
Non-adjustable Groover – for decorating or deeply scoring leather (e.g. to fold)
Embossing tool and die stamps (highly recommended).

For supplies, and advice on leatherwork projects, both of the following operate nationally. Stuart Hails from Le Prevo Leathers is especially helpful.
S. Glassner, 476 Kingston Rd, Raynes Park, London SW20 8DX.
Le Prevo Leathers, Blackfriars, Stowell St, Newcastle upon Tyne NE1 4XN.

Specialist Crafts also offer a limited range of leatherwork tools and leather.

Decorating Leather

The grain side of vegetable tanned leather is suitable for decorative work once it has been moistened with a damp sponge. Very effective designs can be produced using the various embossing tools available. These merely stamp the leather with a little design (e.g. a small star). Repeated use of one or more embossing tools can quickly build up a pleasing pattern. To finish, the leather can be stained if required, and polished. Particularly popular with young people is the embossing of letters and names on to key rings, fobs, belts, and the like. You need a whole set of alphabet embossing tools.

Intricate hand embossing takes a little more skill. As before, the leather should be moistened, and then a design is drawn or traced onto it. This design should be carefully gone over with an awl or modelling tool to produce an indentation, and then scored with a swivel knife (a neat little tool that allows you to safely make intricate cuts or scores). The design is now put into relief by stamping the areas between the lines with a smooth stamp and mallet. Again, the leather can be dyed and polished to finish.

Leather is best dyed by brushing the dye onto the leather using a tightly rolled cloth. This helps to avoid streaking. The dyes used are very powerful, and rubber gloves (and an apron to protect clothes) should be worn for protection.

Pendants

Use thick scraps of vegetable tanned leather for this. Draw a pendant shape directly on the leather and then trace it out with an awl. The shape can now be cut out using a leather knife or shears.

Make a design on the shape (you can, if you like, do this before you cut it out) by:

burning	–	use an electric pen/electric embossing tool
embossing	–	use embossing punches
tooling	–	use a modelling tool and swivel knife

The pendant is finished off by bevelling the edges, punching a hole in the top and threading with leather thong.

Wrist Bands

Fearsome looking specimens are easily made by cutting out and decorating with rivets, studs and eyelets. The edges can be holed with a thonging punch, and then thonged to effect. The easiest way of fixing them to the wrist is by using a press-stud arrangement or providing holes so that the wristband can be laced with leather thong: we would stress that it is possible to make more subtly designed wristbands by embossing or tooling the leather! Le Prevo Leathers recommend finishing off the wrist band with Resolene or Carnauba Creme.

Hint – watch your stocks of rivets and studs as an inevitable spin-off of this activity is the exciting 'decorate your denim or leather jacket syndrome'. Alternatively, you can just order more studs.

Belts

Heavy leather belts suitable for tooling and dyeing can be made from thick, vegetable tanned leather. Start off by selecting a suitable buckle, and cut a strip of leather to fit the inner width of the buckle. (Use a scrapcutter or knife and steel rule). The leather strip should be a foot longer than the waist measurement. A stitch groover can be used to cut decorative grooves along the edges of the belt, and one end should be cut to a curved shape. Make sure that the other (buckle) end is cut square and then trim off the corners. A slot for the buckle prong should be cut, starting approximately 1¼ inches from the buckle end of the belt. An oblong punch and mallet should be used to cut out the slot, although you can cheat (and save money on an oblong punch) by punching two holes roughly 1¼ inches apart and then cutting out a slot between them. The slot should be wide enough for the prong to more about freely. With the buckle in place and the leather doubled over to hold it, mark out four rivet holes (for the two rivets that will fix the buckle) and then punch them out (with a hollow or rotary punch). five or six punch holes should be made out at 1 inch intervals, starting about 3 inches from the shaped end. With a safety beveller, bevel all the edges on both sides of the belt. The belt can now be tooled, and dyed if required, and only needs to be riveted at the buckle end to finish it off.

A belt made in this way will not only look good (especially if it is well tooled) but will be extremely hard wearing and as good as any expensive shop-bought product.

Suede can be used to make belts too, although the finished product will not be as tough and durable as a leather belt. This is compensated by the ease of working with the material, and the possibility of using appliqué techniques to decorate it. The main differences from the method shown above are as follows:

Allow twice the width of suede as the inner width of the buckle you are using, as the suede has to be doubled for strength; otherwise all measurements are identical. Working on the reverse side of the suede, make a line centrally along the length of the strip and apply a fabric adhesive to the whole of the reverse side. Now turn each side of the belt over to meet at the central line and press flat. Trim one end to a diagonal point and make sure that the other end is square. Appliqué shapes can now be made out of thin scraps of leather or suede, and can be ironed flat on the reverse side with a hottish iron. The shapes can be made a simple or complicated as you like (squares, circles, crescents, butterflies, etc.) and should be arranged to form a pleasing pattern before being lightly glued onto the belt. The professionals use double sided sellotape for this purpose, which avoids splashes of glue marking the suede.

A sewing machine equipped with a leather work needle can be used to fix the shapes properly - advisable because the stitching itself will strengthen the belt. The diagonal point should also be stitched to finish, and eyelets should be used to reinforce the belt holes.

Chamois Shoulder Bag

Originally the skin of the mountain antelope of that name, chamois now commonly refers to the softer side of a sheep or lamb skin. It is very soft and supple leather which is easily worked. You will need one chamois skin, at least 20 by 16 inches.

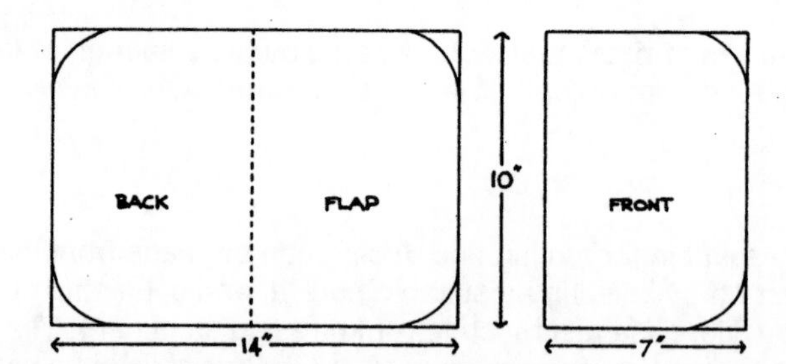

Following the diagram make a template from a paper pattern. As all the curves need to be identical, use only one template to cut out the shapes as shown - one large piece for the back and flap, and one piece for the front. Using the remaining chamois, make up a strip about 4 feet long by 1¼ inches. This forms the gusset between front and back sections and ‘runs on’ to form the strap. You will have to join pieces together by gluing and stitching to make up the 4 foot length. Now, at half inch intervals, punch holes along both edges of the strip and around the edges of the other pieces. These holes are to accommodate thonging to join the gusset to the front and back sections and to give a decorative effect to the front of the bag and the strap. Various thonging stitches can be used, but the single whipstitch is easy to do, and decorative (see diagram).

Sewing and thonging stitches.

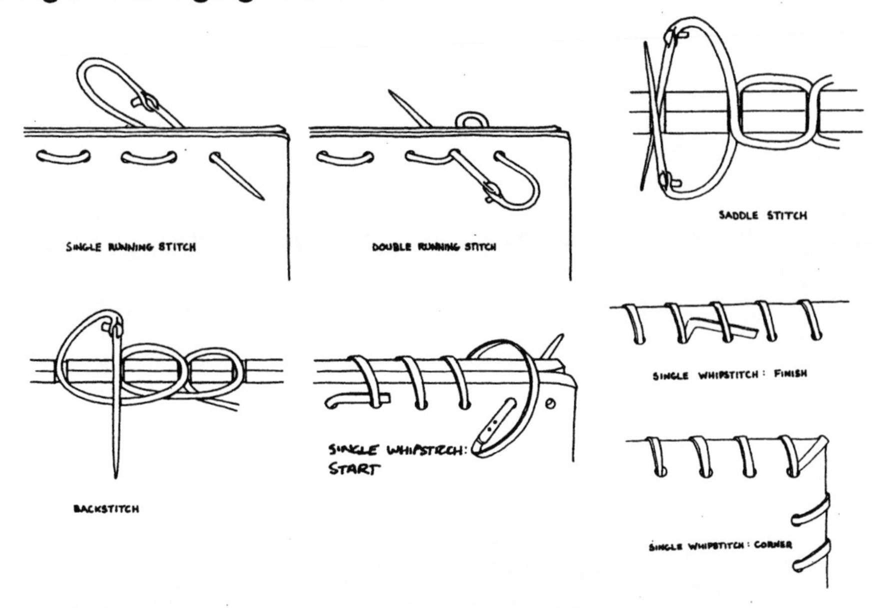

Use this stitch to join the gusset to the front and back sections, continuing the thonging along the edges of the strap and the front flap. You can use commercially available leather or suede thonging, or make up your own from chamois if you have any left. The bag is finished off by punching a couple of holes about an inch apart at the front of the bag, just below the flap - thread a few strips of chamois through the holes and knot losely for effect.

Other leather items worth tackling are belt pouches and, if you have the finances, and are happy that your youngsters have the ability, waistcoats. Pouches can be made out of leather or suede and decorated by tooling or appliqué. Pouch fastenings can be made with press-studs or Velcro. Waistcoats are best made from a soft suede leather or chamois. Simply buy a waistcoat pattern, or copy an existing one, and use offcuts to decorate the finished article.

It is worth trying to find a source of cheap leather offcuts - try any small leather goods manufacturer. Such offcuts can be used for appliqué work, and to make small items like pendants and wristbands. It is also possible to make patches from offcuts. They can then be glued and stitched onto fabric backing and used to make bags, purses, waistcoats, etc.. Big frames and handles are available from craft shops, and this provides a useful shortcut to good quality results.

Pyrography

This is the art of pokerwork, often applied to leather and wood, which burns a design permanently into place. Specialist Crafts offer quite a good range of Pyrography irons and machines for pokerwork and wood and leather offcuts, but a more specialist source for irons and wood and leather items is:
Janik Eneterprises, Brickfield Lane, Denbigh Rd, Ruthin, Clwyd LL15 2TN.

This activity is only suitable for young people who you feel are safe with the equivalent of a soldering iron, which the pyrograph tool essentially is. The best pyrograph tools incorporate a variable heat setting and can be fitted with a whole range of tips, brands and wires to achieve a variety of effects. These include decorative shapes, numbers and letters, which can be used to decorate a belt, a purse or a wooden clock or box. Janik stock a useful array of wooden pencil boxes, money boxes, egg cups, door plaques and badge shapes.

To produce a pyrography design, the artist can either draw freehand with the iron, stamp out patterns, or following a pencil design or tracing. Celtic art designs are particularly popular using this medium, but do require quite a high level of proficiency with the tool. Our own experience has shown that it is often difficult for young people to produce evenly burned imprints on the leather or wood surfaces. They can end up in tears and tantrums! This is an interesting, complementary craft to the more usual leatherwork techniques, nonetheless.

LINO AND BLOCK PRINTING

Although it is a very simple way of producing printed images, excellent results can be achieved by using this method. You can make multi-coloured prints in one go, for example, without the complication of register boards and other paraphernalia. Linoprints can be used to decorate cards and calendars or to make magazine covers, or prints suitable for framing. Because of the nature of the tools involved and the relative difficulty of manipulating them without amputating fingers, it is best to limit this activity to two or three young people working with one instructor. The cutting tools employ very sharp blades so we would not recommend it as an activity with primary school age children.

To organise a lino printing session you will need:

- Pieces of lino – available from craftshops, NES Arnold, or Specialist Crafts. It can be bought in a lino roll (4.5 mm thick) for economic cutting or in a variety of pre-cut sizes, in either 4.5 mm or 3.2 mm thickness.
- Lino cutting tools – these use sharp steel blades mounted in wooden handles, so exercise care in use.
- Consider the purchase of small G-clamps, or, bench hooks, which are like a drawing board with raised edges, used to keep the lino block in place, enabling the use of both hands for cutting.
- Ink tray or plate glass slab.
- Small rubber roller (with handle).
- Tubes of oil or water based printing ink. Alternatives are using specially formulated blockmix with powder paints, or special oil based printers' inks.
- Soft (unsized) paper or card for printing – e.g., Japanese type or Quickprint special paper, or smooth matt surfaced paper.
- White spirit for cleaning.
- Aprons.

Although the lino can be used as it is, you will find it easier to print with if you mount it on a block of wood. Water based inks are easier to clean than oil based, but many of the inks give less impressive results.

Lino and block printing involves gouging out sections of lino to leave a design in relief which can then be inked and used to print on paper or card.

Preparation

You must first draw your design onto the lino, remembering that the print you get will be a

reverse image. For this reason it is probably best to suggest to your youth group that they should avoid lettering until they gain enough skill to cut them out in reverse. Tracing can be used to make the initial design, transferring this to the lino by using carbon paper (placed carbon side down on the lino with the tracing placed **upside down** on top of it). If the design is difficult to see on the lino, cover it with a thin coat of white poster paint before the design is drawn. This makes the design easier to see when cutting out. When all the cutting and gouging has been done, the poster paint can be washed off and the lino dried before moving on to the print stage.

Remember, too, that you can achieve a positive or negative image depending on how you cut the lino. For example, if you want to print a star shape, you can simply gouge this shape out of the lino and print it. You will get a **negative** image with the star shape being formed by the ink surrounding it. If, however, you gouge away all the lino **except** the star shape, the resulting print will be **positive**, i.e. only the star shape will be inked onto the paper.

Printing

Prepare a print area for your group on a sturdy table or workbench, by spreading out some old newspapers. Then squeeze a couple of inches of ink from a tube onto a glass slab or tray and roll it out to form a thin layer. The lino block is inked by running over it several times with a roller. Now, encourage the printmakers to make a few test prints on some waste papers, applying even pressure with the hand across the inked area, or ideally, by using a second un-inked roller, or, better still by using a special printing press. Each print requires the block to be re-inked. It will take 2 or 3 test prints before the block will print evenly. Final prints (several hundred) can now be made from a lino block.

Burnishing is another method that can be used to produce lino prints. Ink the block as above and lay it face up with the printing paper carefully laid on top of it. Now, using a smooth implement like a wooden spoon, and taking care not to move the paper, rub through the paper onto the design underneath to produce a print. If you are using thin paper, you'll have to cover it with a thicker sheet as well, as the colour will otherwise come through the thin paper to be nicely smudged by the wooden spoon! Burnishing will produce very good quality prints and can also be used to tidy up imperfect prints created by the pressure method. The quality of a print can be checked by carefully turning up the corners, one at a time, and having a 'peek'. If you are not happy with the quality, replace the paper and tidy it up with local burnishing.

Multi-coloured prints

Prints of many colours are easily produced by the lino printing method. This will be most successful where the design has several discreet elements which can be inked separately. Instead of using a roller to ink the block, this method requires the use of inking 'dollies' to dab the ink on. These are simply small wads of cloth wrapped in cotton wool. Cotton buds work very well for this purpose. However, if you have a large expanse of block to ink with one colour, you should still be able to use the dollies for smaller areas. Any ink which spills over onto other print areas (or the background) can be wiped off with a rag and white spirit. Once the block has been inked up with the required colours you can proceed to make prints in the normal way. Outstanding results can be produced with this method, and it is well worth spending some time experimenting with it.

Other things to try

You can experiment with other materials to 'cut' such as vinyl tiles, hardboard, rubber blocks, different woods, etc.. In fact, almost any kind of thin, close-textured board can be cut to make printing blocks. New linoleum cuts much better than old, but you can make old lino easier to cut by warming it up before use.

It is possible to etch lino using caustic soda (this substance is corrosive, so great care should be taken when handling it. Only for use by older, responsible youth groups!). Make up a saturated solution by adding caustic soda crystals to a jar of cold water until no more crystals will dissolve. Stir it with a piece of wood using protective gloves. As heat will have to build up during this process, allow the solution to cool and then add a teaspoon of meths (this helps it spread on the lino). Now prepare the lino by cleaning it with meths. You can section off areas that you want etched by using plasticine – the caustic soda solution can then be carefully poured into the well that is created. It is also possible to paint the solution directly onto the lino. The solution should be left on for at least two hours before washing it off. The dissolved lino can be removed by brushing it off under running water to leave an interesting, granulated surface. Other interesting effects can be made by scoring the lino or indenting it with nails.

Using poster paint (the consistency of thin cream) it is possible to make prints from found objects like bits of wood, metal, leaves, etc.. Some vegetables (onion, cabbage, artichoke) sliced in half make good prints and you can also carve a design into a cut potato.

LEAF PRINT

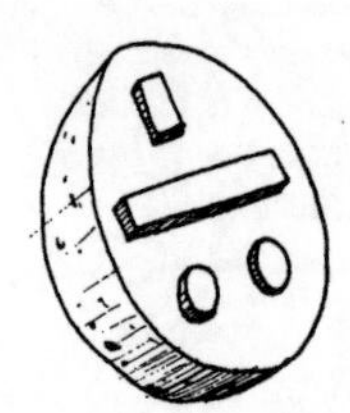

HALF POTATO

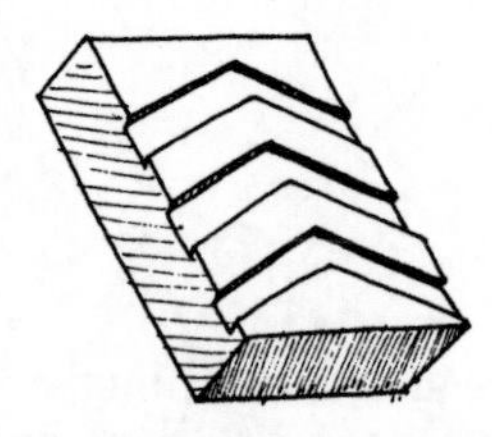

WOOD BLOCK

MAGAZINES, ZINES AND PUBLICATIONS

Many people who ultimately become full time writers, poets and musicians started off penning a few words for their humble school or youth club magazine. From there they may have progressed, or was it regressed (?), to running their own zines or fanzines; perhaps even dabbled in something more commercial. Anyway, self publishing, small scale newspapers, promo leaflets and all sorts of printed weirdness happily continue to exist. The wonderful world of publications run-off on a photocopier and stapled together is very much the domain of youth groups. Here we'll have a go at trying to tell you why its rather beneficial to the health of young people, and a bit or two about how to do it!

Encouraging youthful publications without taking them over, or acting as the Big Brother or Sister Censor, is one problem area. Another is balancing on the tightrope between encouraging young people to write what they want, and remembering that writing may also be sexist, racist or highly critical of, for instance, the people who pay for a youth project or manage it! Having said that, a youth-produced newspaper or zine can:

- help increase literacy skills;
- provide a forum for young people amongst themselves and in the wider community;
- offer an opportunity for co-operative work;
- provide a chance for young people to express themselves;
- assist young people to understand a bit about how the media works.

Before getting started

For the adults involved, it is worth sorting out what resources are, or might be made available. These may help you decide what you produce. Likewise, the age of the young people you are working with will be a factor, as should be their own personal interests and preferences. At the very lowest level, you may just produce a 'Wall Newspaper' which can be ideal for younger groups. Individual children write their own articles, produce quizzes, poems and jokes and then the whole thing is pasted up on a wall inside the building, together with any photos and drawings. This sort of thing is ideal for playschemes and the like and is much used in primary education.

With older groups, the dramatic increase in the availability of personal computers and of photocopiers, means that many of the older methods of producing short run magazines such as duplicating and even typewriting are now nearly defunct. There is also more likelihood that the local council or college, and even some large community schools may have an offset-litho printing machine. This is 'proper printing' and is used for most professionally produced books. You also need to have paper for producing the master copy of each page and paper for printing the copies for distribution. The complete list of possible resources might include:

- one or more places to work from (for writing, artwork, collation etc.)
- computer and printer
- paper
- photocopier or printing machinery
- pens
- drawing equipment for artwork, illustrations and cartoons
- polaroid camera for instant photos
- a black and white darkroom (see photography section of this book)

- a drawing table/light box for planning and designing pages
- a stapler or other way of binding.

A good way to begin

Planning *what* your group wants to produce and perhaps *why* it wants to produce something, and *who* is for it is for, is as good a way to start as any other. After this, you need to consider whether it is going to be sold or given away free, and then have a look at what funds are available. You may also want to see if there any friendly local specialists who would be willing to advise on:

- how to use the computer and related software programs
- writing and reporting
- photography
- design and layout of publications.

It is then down to thinking about who will be doing what, and what should go into each issue. As we hinted at the beginning of this section, a lot depends upon how much risk-taking you want to engage in. Youth work itself is about risk-taking within boundaries. Kids will always test the boundaries. It is the reason why some of the most innovative arts work takes place in the voluntary sector, where the workers are particularly keen to allow young people to have access to the skills, materials and means of production which allow them to produce interesting publications.

Alan, out of the Alan and Howie writing team, has been especially involved in these types of ventures. He has helped young people and adults in over a dozen youth clubs and communities in England and Scotland to start club magazines, punk fanzines, rock and counter-culture zines and 'alternative' community newspapers. His own checkered career spans involvement in the infamous *International Times* magazine at the end of the '60s, through *Sound of the Westway*, (a 1977 Punk Fanzine produced from an Acton youth centre) and described by Julie Burchill in *NME* as, " *In my day it was Fanta orange and Gary Glitter - now it is Government sponsored chaos."* More recently he helped produce *A Time to Travel? An introduction to Britain's newer Travellers* with Travellers themselves. Now, at the time of putting this book together, he is being threatened with a High Court defamation suit by a lady who identifies herself as being a gigantic dinosaur described in his local spoof newspaper, *SubLyme News!*

The contents

The answers to the questions about who it is for, and why it is being produced, shou a fairly clear set of answers regarding what type of things that should go in. If the ai publicise the programme in a youth club, it probably won't be appropriate to have a article by a fourteen year old girl on why eating meat is murder. However, in anothei of publication this might be exactly the right thing. For a lot of first time youth club-ty zines, the following is a fair list of 'possible' contents:

- interviews
- news reporting
- sports news
- favourite hobbies and recreations
- reports on what has been happening in and around the club
- future events, trips etc.
- things to do and make
- music and gig reviews
- poems
- crosswords, quizzes, word games and competitions
- cartoons and jokes
- drawings and photos
- letters
- recipes
- surveys and questionnaires
- reports from members' committee and management committee.

For more experimental and adventurous zines, young people are more than likely to make their own agenda for the contents. This may include articles on anything from Green issues to pieces about Raves, House, Grunge, Sex and Sexuality, Politics - areas such as the Criminal Justice Act, Paganism, Spiritual Things, Drugs, Festivals, Gatherings and Demos. For instance, Piglet in Swordfish catalogue #1 says:

"'If you're not outraged, you're not paying attention.' Ever noticed all the shite things going on in the world? Wars....exploitation....eco-destruction....Listen, things are worse than you can possibly imagine. We are all the victims - of the Media, of the System, of ££$$$££. Criminal Justice? ACT!"

(for lots of samples of Youthful Indignation and Creation, contact Swordfish for their catalogue of comix, zines, books, ethnic things, underground music +++ more: PO Box 26, Crawley, W.Sussex, RH11 7YS.)

The tasks

Some of the best zines and similar are run by very small groups of dedicated folk. The Levellers' mates produce the very interesting *On the Fiddle,* and the dub-reggae-house outfit, Zion Train, produce some well weird observations on life in their own highly polished *The Wobbler.* All of these and all other publications require most of the same tasks to be fulfilled:

- interviewing and reporting
- other writing
- research and note-taking
- photography
- illustrations and cartoons
- editorial tasks
- keying/typing
- graphic design/type fount design
- printing
- collating and binding
- selling/publicity/distribution.

The list clearly shows that either a few people have got to do a lot, or otherwise the tasks have got to be shared out with the aim of getting as many people involved as possible. In youth work, the latter model may be more appropriate for the official youth centre or school production, but as with supporting young musical groups, it is important to back young people in doing their own thing. The division of tasks also begs the question, who takes ultimate responsibility for what goes in and what doesn't? From this question it seems important to look at the power relationship of young people to adults in the process of production and need or otherwise for an overall editor or editorial board. A cautionary word: remember it is the writer, publisher and printer who can be held liable if you create some enemies who want to spend a lot of their money on taking you for a day or two out in the courts!

escape from reality

build your own Time Machine!

The British Government has spent millions secretly researching Time Travel. Why? We can only speculate. In the late 80's, a top security Time Research Station was set up somewhere on the south coast to house Project Victor. Now, after years of work at tax-payer's expense, government scientists have finally cracked the chronon...

We aim to expose this shocking, dangerous experiment. Classified documents from the project have been leaked to us for clandestine distribution, via "Clive", our inside PV contact...

...cret plans for Time Machine ... are now available!

The Land Comes Alive

On April 23rd, St George's Day, 300 land activists descended onto a disused airfield in Surrey. Over the course of the following week a demonstration of possibilities took place, highlighting what could be done if access and use of the countryside were not the exclusive preserve of the wealthy few. Jim Carey spoke to some insiders and reconstructs the story.

22 FRONTLINE SPIRITUALITY

The MAGIC of FINDHORN

MESSAGE from Love Lies Bleeding Deva

MESSAGE from The Devas

A few hints

Type styles: The size of type (this is called 11 point Arial) and the style of type fount **(this is called Renfrew!)** can be very important in making a publication, accessible, interesting, easy to read, and interesting or innovative. Handwriting, bits cut out of old newspapers, and graffiti art might all be considered as ways of enhancing a page of type. It is also worth looking at whether to justify type or not - this means whether to make the right hand edge of the type appear ragged (unjustified) or even (justified).
Layout: How the page is put together involves making decisions about how many columns of type are used, where to use illustrations and photos etc..
Photos: Unless you have access to a scanner (a kind of photocopier in reverse, which can scan illustrations and photos into a computer for editing) or a process camera (which turns an ordinary photo into a screened image made up of lots of little dots) you'll probably have to make do with sticking a photo on a photocopier an making the best of things. Black and white images and photos with lots of contrast work the best.
Desk top publishing programs for computers: DTP programs *can* make the job of producing an interesting page design easier, however, they can take some learning and may even inhibit more natural and creative forms of expression using a good old pen, scalpel and a can of spray mount or similar. Sometimes, it is just faster, more fun and simpler to take columns of type and headings and cut and paste them onto a page together with illustrations to make up a page of what is often referred to as CRC - camera ready copy.

At the time of writing, *Word* and *Word Perfect,* are two of the most popular word processing programs (for setting and managing type). More elaborate organisation of page designs can be handled by programs such as *Pagemaker, Quarkxpress* and *Ventura.* The learning curve can be a bit slow and fraught, but on the other hand, young people could learn skills along the way that help them in jobs in the future.

MASKS

Behind every mask is an actor trying get out! For young people this is often very true. A mask provides the security through which that person may show their 'real' selves, or it provides a facade to hide behind. Masks are best made with a purpose in mind, such as for a:

- pageant or procession
- drama activities
- dance groups
- street parties or other celebration.

Masks also present a challenge to adults when they are working with young people. Wearing a mask can unleash unusual behaviour – sometimes leaving even the mask wearer confused afterwards. Once any problems of this sort have been sorted out, it is important for the wearers to learn to move with the mask, using basic theatrical techniques.

Masks can be bought, but are often quite expensive. The rest of this section offers the cheaper (and fun) alternative of mask making. This can take minutes, hours or even days to make. Masks can be constructed out of a wide range of materials. For many youth groups cost is important, so, using what is available or easily obtainable may prove vital. In street carnivals, a mask can end up as a very complex, elaborate structure. A dragon's head might form the front of a long, cavorting chain of participants weaving down the road in a street parade.

Paper and card

Most primary age school children have made simple masks from brown paper/wrapping paper or old cereal cartons. Indeed, in the past, the cereal manufacturers have often provided pre-printed masks on the back of the packet for cutting out – anything from pirates to turtles to Power Rangers!

At its simplest, collect together some paper bags which are large enough to fit loosely over the heads of the youngsters you are working with, then mark the outside to show where the eyes, nose and mouth will be. These are then ready for the young people to take off, paint and decorate.

Using thin card, plus scissors, sellotape, a stapler, paper and paint or coloured pens, an interesting array of masks can be constructed. Imagination, a little ingenuity and a spark of talent are all that are required. By folding, bending, curling, cutting and sticking, a very impressive mask can be made. With young people it is often best to suggest a subject or theme for their mask-making. It might be an animal, monster or cartoon character.

Thicker, corrugated card may also be useful for building bigger 'Heads'. This can be accomplished by creating a cardboard cylinder. Onto this may be added (for instance):

- streamers of paper or wool for hair;
- an egg box section for a nose;
- holes for eyes and mouth;
- additional card or felt for a hat.

Once painted it can make a super mask for a carnival procession.

Plaster of Paris

Face masks can be made using wax (see Candle Making section) or with Plaster of Paris or Mod-Roc gauze, as favoured by our colleagues at Panmure House in Edinburgh. First of all you have to persuade someone to use their own face as the model for the mask. The unlucky person must cover their hair with a bathing cap, put on a smock to protect clothing and then have petroleum jelly (vaseline) applied to their face, including eyebrows, and lashes. The plaster gauze is cut into one inch wide strips, dipped in warm water, one strip at a time, and wrung out gently. The strips are then carefully applied to the face of the reclining model. The entire face, except the nostrils should be covered with three layers of gauze. Alternatively, you can leave the eyes clear. Allow the plaster to set for about ten minutes and then carefully remove from the face if set.

Once the mask has dried, the edges should be trimmed with scissors and re-inforced with strips of gauze folded over the rim. Eyeholes can now be cut and the nostril holes filled in. To model the mask further, it can be built up with modelling wax, newspaper, papier mâché, wood, wire etc., and then covered with a further two layers of plaster gauze. The completed mask is finished off with poster paint and a coat of shellac varnish. This can be a really exciting activity for kids, and most groups will have a lot of fun. However, do make sure that a hole is left in the mask for breathing and closely supervise the whole activity.

For even more life-like masks of real young people, you can take the mask made in the manner described above and use it for making a new mask. This time, the inside of the original mask is coated with vaseline, then Plaster of Paris or papier mâché strips are applied in layers to the inside of the mould. Three or four layers are applied and after they have hardened, the new mask can be eased off from its mould. This second generation mask should be really like the original face and can be gently sanded, generally tidied up and painted to produce a very sophisticated life-mask. These masks require an elastic ribbon to be attached around the back to hold them onto the wearer's head.

Papier Mâché

The section on Papier Mâché describes in a lot more detail the different techniques both to make and to use the medium. Here we offer some ideas for producing masks using this very flexible material.

Balloon mould

A very simple balloon shaped mask can be made by blowing up a balloon, coating it with baby lotion or vaseline, and then further coating it with paper strips, using the layering method described in the Papier Mâché section. Using alternate strips of newspaper and plain paper makes it easier to see how many layers have been applied. Once the mould has set, the bottom edge can be cut and trimmed to produce an open ended, egg-shaped mask.

Plasticine moulds

These offer a more sophisticated option to the balloon mould. To start, mask makers should draw on a sheet of paper the size of mask they require. This template is then placed on a piece of board, On top of this outline, a 3-D mask is made out of plasticine. This acts as a mould for making a mask using the basic papier mâché layering technique, starting with a vaseline coating and building up about four layers of paper strips.

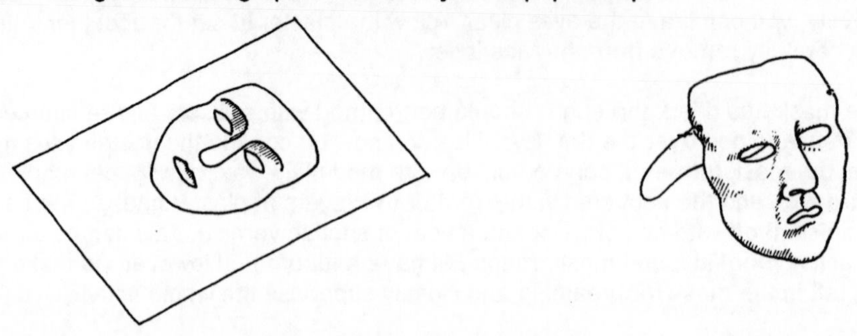

As with the other masks, it can be painted and decorated in any way the maker decides. This also requires an elastic tie around the back to keep it in place.

Wire frames

Using chicken wire, bent, shaped and secured together in the shape of the required head is a good way of making large, Big Head masks. You've probably seen some of these in street parades. Both wire netting and galvanised rust resistant wire are available from both Specialist Crafts and NES Arnold. When cutting and bending the chicken wire to form the head, make sure that there are no sharp ends left sticking inwards or outwards. For ears, nose, eyes and mouth and possibly hat/hair, add on smaller wire structures and attach them with lighter wire or string.

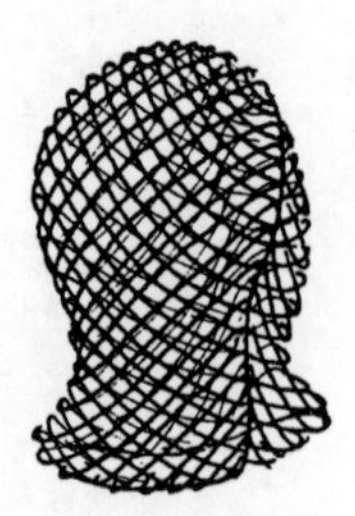

Because these heads are more complex, and take a lot longer to build, they are a more suitable project for adolescent groups who enjoy art activities. Alternatively, the wire structures can be assembled by adults and the young people can work on the layering with papier mâché strips in three or four layers. They can also decorate the heads with paint and possibly a final coat of PVA glue to give it a polished finish.

Obviously, the range of head mask types is virtually limitless; aliens, animals, monsters, gods and nursery rhyme characters are all popular subjects. In India, big headed devils are paraded around the streets for the Diwalli festival, and are eventually burned to destroy evil, in an equivalent of the UK's bonfire night celebration.

Because Big Heads are hot and unwieldy to wear, it is a good idea to:

- put in at least one extra ventilation slot into the head;
- attach shoulder pads and straps to the inside of the head to harness the head to the wearer's body, to aid both comfort and stability.

MOBILES

Mobile making is an excellent activity for youth groups, as good results can be obtained very quickly. Mobiles are hanging art forms – the dangling elements move around when air circulates, so it is best to hang them in a draught. Each mobile requires one or more wood or wire support rods from which the individual elements dangle on strong thread. The completed mobile is usually fixed to the ceiling with wire and a small hook. Wire coat hangers, bamboo or green sticks are very suitable for the rods, and sewing thread or fishing line make ideal line for suspending the materials. For affixing the items dangling from the rods, quick drying glues can prove useful, but are dangerous for young children to use.

The fascination of mobiles lies in the perfect balance between the different elements – this keeps the supporting rod(s) horizontal. There are two ways to achieve this when making your mobile. The first is to suspend your support rods from something handy – without fixing them permanently – and balance the whole thing as you add the individual elements. There are a number of ways to organise the mobiles, all of which should aim to achieve a balanced structure:

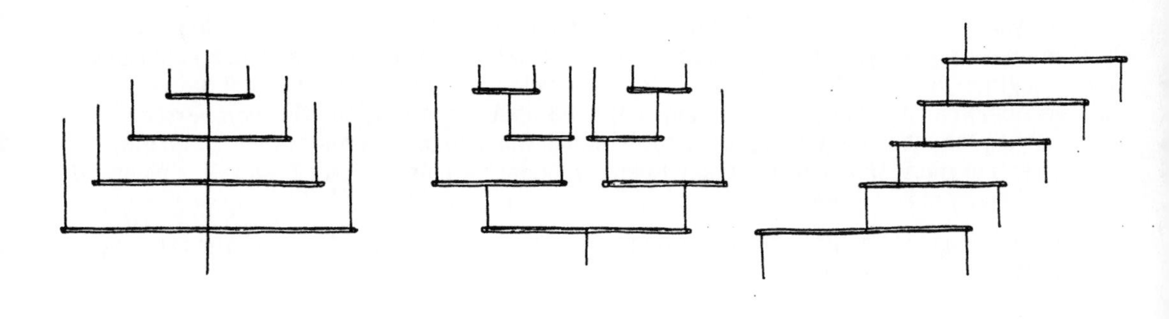

Cutting coloured, decorated card into circular patterns can look effective, as it creates a spiral:

And mobiles which spin round like propellers, using hot air are easy to make and effective.

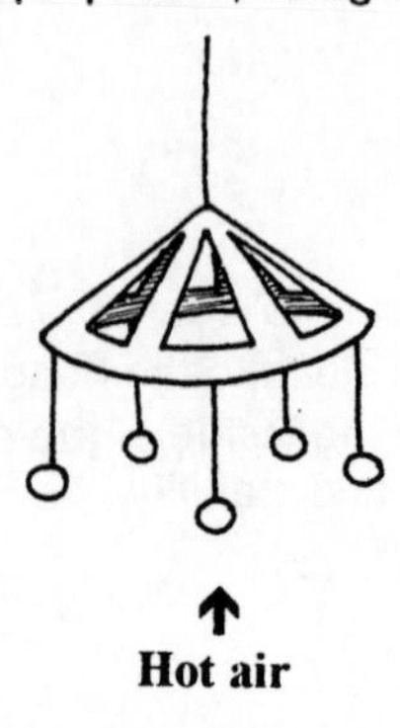

Alternatively, you can encourage young people to make the mobile just as they fancy, later adding counterweights (Blu tack, lead fishing shot, etc.) to balance the whole thing out. Elements can be of different weights and can hang at different distances from the support rod. The side with most weight on it should be placed on the shorter end of the rod.

Virtually, anything from Airfix models to glass beads, can be used to make up the individual elements of your mobile. Suggest trying materials like stiff paper, cardboard, coloured plastic, tinfoil, milk bottle tops, coins, etc.. Some mobiles, like those made of shiny bottle tops or coloured transparent plastic, are particularly striking because they reflect or alter natural light. Other mobiles are successful because they are based on a particular theme, e.g., aeroplanes, birds, geometric or abstract shapes, motor cars, etc..

A guaranteed favourite with youth groups are mobiles which spell out an individual's name, football team, or slogan. Larger letters should be cut out from card, and arranged on the mobile in an interesting way.

For youth groups or a class of youngsters, it is a good idea to turn mobile-making into a group work activity, with four or five participants, individually or in pairs, making objects to hang from the rods. The balancing of the objects may prove a bit tricky, but it pays to encourage a bit of patience and suggest that the mobiles are tested. This can be done by hanging the rods over the edge of a table, which will help to determine where to fix the objects in place. Use a 'blob' of glue to finally fix each element in place, once it is balanced.

Another idea is to make a mobile using the jigsaw principle where the individual elements fit together to form a whole.

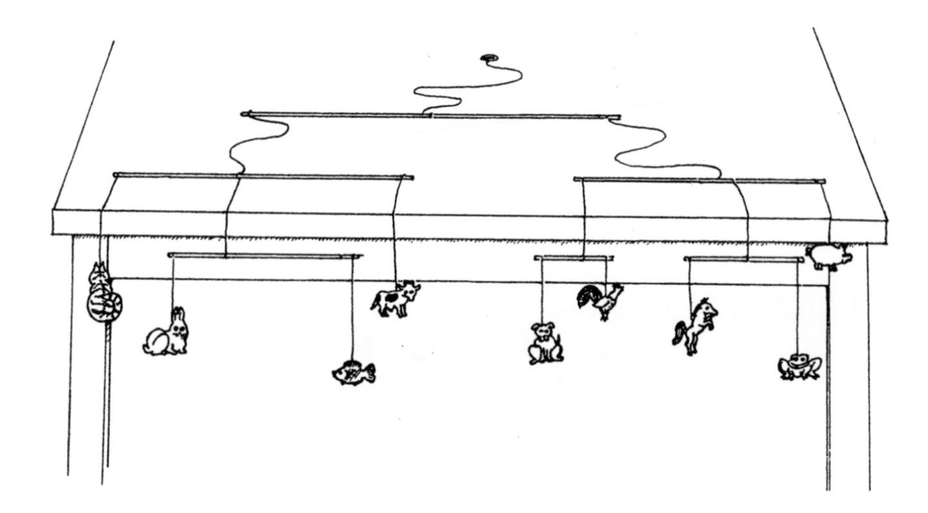

Musical mobiles are easily made out of items which make a noise when struck, e.g., tin, bamboo, shells, metal piping, etc.. The objects should be hung in such a way that they strike together when there is a draught. One way of doing this is to suspend the objects on a small circle of wire which has a heavier object hanging in the centre.

MODEL MAKING AND FANTASY FIGURES

Most parents think that children should have a go at building kits: constructing cars, aircraft, dinosaurs and the like. We suspect that adults try to force the pace too fast, and so end up doing most of the gluing and building themselves, while their offspring slouch in accustomed position on the sofa watching the box! Our experience is that model making of all kinds can be successful in youth groups, providing that the adults involved avoid inflicting the model making on the youngsters involved.

Actually, the range of potential model-building kits covers a very wide range, from:

- Airfix-type plastic models, predominantly of transport, through to the top of the range radio controlled model aircraft, boats and land vehicles.
- Plaster cast kits using clay or resin to produce chess pieces, small animals etc.. These often require some sort of baking or kiln firing. Alec Tiranti Ltd are amongst the most specialist suppliers of clay and all types of modelling materials.
- Air-drying modelling materials for producing models, playing figures etc.. Amongst a number of makes; Modair (in bright colours), Crayola Model Magic, Claykos and Modelight are all recommended for youth work purposes.
- Wooden kits for building prehistoric animals, and other animals and figures which slot together.
- Construction, Craft and Design Technology materials. For younger children, most components are made in plastic. Tomy's Popoids, Cleversticks, Jovo and Duplo are typical examples, but the range is immense. For older young people, about eleven plus, there are now large stocks of just about anything which can be used for modelling and construction purposes, including wood, plastic and metal parts, springs, propellers, gears, motors, pulleys etc.. NES Arnold and Specialist Crafts both stock extensive stocks of such materials. The Egg Mobile section in this book is one example of a simple CDT project.
- Matchstick modelling kits for building anything from galleons to houses and Romany vardos.

- Lego, Technics and other plastic construction kits which can be used to build static and moving models of all manner of types of buildings and vehicles.
- Battery and mechanically powered plastic figures such as Tomy's Zoids.
- Figures and three dimensional settings for Fantasy and Role Playing games such as 'Dungeons and Dragons'.
- Stonecraft models of castles.
- Traditional model making for train sets, doll's houses and Scalextric-type slot car racing.

One of the youth projects we worked closely with was the Pilton Youth Programme (PYP) in Edinburgh. They found that plastic model kits are, " ...unpredictably successful" with the young people they work with. Big stores often sell these model making kits at greatly reduced prices when they have become no longer fashionable, e.g. Star Wars, Batman, Power Rangers, Superman, Zoids, etc.. They made sure that kids who have no experience with models should be started off with simple kits which have only a few large parts and don't need glue (for sticking or sniffing!). Try to avoid models which are especially tricky and finicky to build. There are quite a lot which don't require any gluing, and it is surprising in more deprived areas how many youngsters have never had the opportunity to play with the ever popular Duplo and Lego sets. In Acton in West London, the youth centre advertised in the local press for Lego and Scalextric, and from what it obtained was able to create a resource which lasted three centres for a good few years.

PYP found that model making can be particularly good as a group activity which encourages co-operation and concentration. They usually have between four and eight young people and two to three adults working together around a large table. Most simple models can be assembled in one session, leaving the next session free for painting the models with enamel paint, and applying transfers. A great feeling of accomplishment can be achieved by taking a smartly painted model home to be admired.

Many of the modern models of robots and similar are capable of movement, powered either by wind-up, clockwork motors or battery motors. We especially enjoyed the Tomy Zoid models of mechanised prehistoric fighting machines. These are lots of fun for all concerned - and especially suitable for youth groups of different ages and abilities since they're made up in a whole variety of sizes and numbers of parts. Models can also be used as playing pieces for certain board games or can be used in fantasy or 'war' games. Although commercially available kits can be used to make, e.g. dragons, it is possible obtain moulds and make your own pieces; out of plaster of paris for example. Chess moulds in particular are available in many different styles. If your young people have an artistic bent, you should consider using clay to model with. Young people are often inhibited by the creative task of making something recognisable out of a shapeless lump of clay, so it does help if there is an adult around who can provide some kind of artistic inspiration and technical help. Clay models can be painted and varnished when dry to good effect.

Apart from making figures for war, fantasy, and role playing games such as 'Dungeons and Dragons', great fun can also be had in making up boards or scenarios for some games. Again, commercial models can be used, or individually modelled, clay ones. Three dimensional landscapes can be formed using papier mâché or clay to provide the perfect background for your models.

In most towns, because of adult interest one suspects, there is a 'Games Shop' of some sort. A model section will almost certainly exist and it is likely that the person running such an emporium will be an enthusiast. Likewise, many craft shops stock an interesting, but not cheap, range of craft kits. One of the tricks is to try and find a way to keep costs down. In Essex, we were able to link one youth club where we worked, together with the local, radio-controlled aircraft club. At weekends, members from the club joined the adults flying elaborate, and often very expensive aircraft for miles across the common at the north end of town. Very usefully, we have found that approaches to such committed individuals have, on occasions, provided us 'staff' for youth groups!

MURALS AND SPRAY CAN ART

At some point in time graffiti takes on a level of social acceptability and becomes a mural. The Pilton Youth Programme in Edinburgh tried to set up a measure of diversion for graffiti, by pinning up large rolls of paper on a wall of their centre. This was then used as a Graffiti Wall. They suggest providing water-based felt pens and trying to obtain large rolls of paper from printing and newspaper firms. To quote them,

> "This won't be the answer to young people expressing themselves through spontaneous decoration of your walls, but it may help."

In that particular centre, three or four large strips of paper covered the entire length of a wall. The paper was changed each week. The week's product resembled a veritable battlefield of art work. Social comments on politicians, religion, and fine drawings of sexual organs rub shoulders or wall space with debates of the greatness of opposing football teams, rock stars etc.. This sort of creativity is probably worth encouraging, and as long as not too many pens are available at the same time and an adult is nearby, say, running another activity in the same room, no further supervision is required. If there is a spate of particular interest from the youth group concerned, the activity can be quickly transformed into the type of group mural work described in the rest of this section.

For mural painters and planners we have a few tips from experience. One technique which makes high quality mural painting accessible to non-artists is to use an **epidiascope**. This strangely named object works roughly like a projector. However, it will project a full colour image of objects or flat images directly onto a wall or surface. The image can then be drawn over, thus ensuring an accurate representation. Some of the strongest images using this technique which we have seen were in Mark Hall Youth Club in Harlow, where polarised (negative black and white) images of Rock Heroes were transferred onto walls from the Melody Maker etc.. If you can't find an epidiascope, an **overhead projector** can be usefully employed to project images drawn on the clear film of OHP transparencies, up to a larger size across walls. Both are easier to use on indoor sites rather than out of doors.

Planning and drawing out a mural using **grid lines** is a useful method to ensure that a mural looks good and follows a design which has previously been planned on paper. It is also important to try and produce murals which harmonise with their permanent or semi-permanent setting. Working with young people in a large-scale arts activity like a mural involves a number of processes. Adults need to be involved in some of the decision making, but it is very important that young people are also encouraged to participate in each stage of the process.

The **stages** are likely to include:

- Deciding on a site for the mural – consultation with owners of potential spaces, the council and other members of the community are all part of this stage.
- What to paint – ideas for designs, themes and rough scale drawings, and then a decision making procedure.
- Obtaining the necessary materials, emulsion paints, brushes, cement filler, wire brush, masonry sealer etc..
- If using the grid line system, transfer the images onto an emulsioned wall or board surface using chalk or charcoal.
- Organise the painting of the mural.
- If it is to become quite a permanent mural, varnish the mural with yacht varnish.

Using grid lines

This really isn't complicated and young people quickly get used to the process. The mural organiser needs to produce a sheet or set of sheets which are a scaled down version of the actual mural site. For instance:

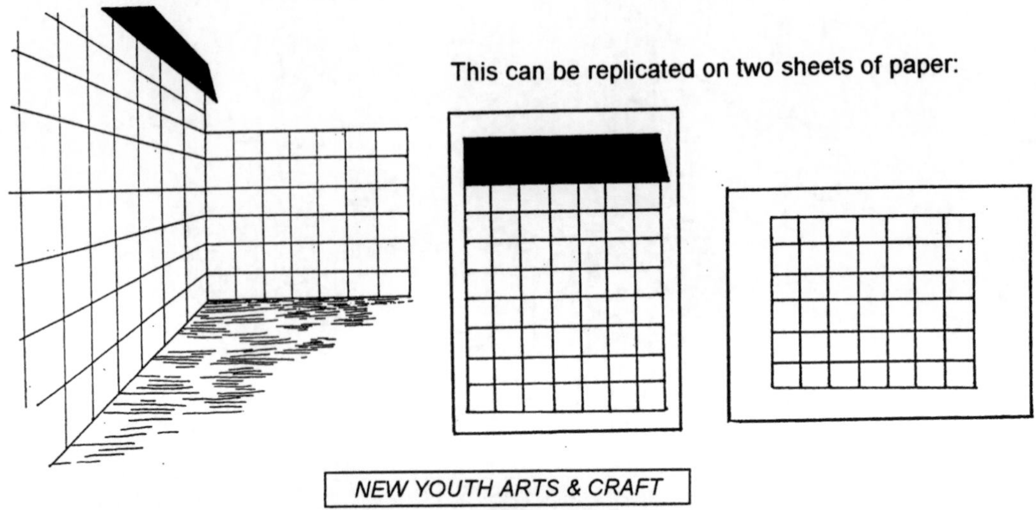

If the organiser photocopies the grid sheets for all the potential designers, they can all have a go at producing a design for the mural which will fit the designated site. The best ideas can possibly be incorporated into the final design, and the outlines can be chalked up on the wall(s).

Safety is of great importance and it is best if younger painters only work on the ground level, whilst older painters can use sturdy chairs, tables and step ladders to mark-up and paint the mural.

Ideas for designs

Both of us have attended the last couple of Glastonbury Festivals at Pilton in Somerset. There we have witnessed some of the most creative murals (and indeed performance arts) which exist anywhere in the UK. In 1995, a huge hoarding was built, undercoated and painted with the greens of Farmer Eavis's fields and the blue of the sky above. Old and young festival goers were then invited to join the bustling queue to add a small painting of themselves to the ever developing mural. To the right of the main area, a practise area was set up where the budding painters could obtain their brush, some paints and practise their own addition to the Festival Masterpiece. After five days of the festival, the end product was quite stunning. Perhaps forty thousand little figures had been added, dancing, singing, jumping, skipping and even flying across the giant wooden canvas. A truly participative mural! Alan now has a dream plan to produce a similar mural along the seafront at Lyme Regis during their Carnival week....

One useful tip: the Glastonbury mural painters used allocated painting zones, so that each painter was always working in an identifiable space (A – J or somesuch). On a smaller, more individual scale, this can provide a good model for young people to 'draw themselves into' a mural at a playscheme or youth club. One way we have organised this is to get young people to work in pairs, each drawing with chalk around the outline of their partner. Each artist then paints in the details of their own figure, individualising clothes, face, hair etc.. Other possible themes could be the town; the countryside; planets; sports; geometric patterns, or the circus.

Spray Can Art

Environmentalists have formed groups to combat the spread of this form of graffiti, but it has equally excited many modern art collectors and typographers who have found it a creative source of inspiration. Like it or loathe it, youthful artists have found spray can art a source of considerable fun. In the United States, the Metropolitan Transportation Authority's rolling stock was transformed into an enormous moving comic strip. Meanwhile, in the UK and Europe, the craze has spread and the culture of 'bombing' walls, buildings and transport has been ignorant of geographical boundaries.

Style has a lot to do with different forms of spray can work. UK street artists and wall writers have developed their own personal ways of making art statements. Often they are political and social comments; a form of challenge to local communities, the police and the authorities. Many of these artists are among the most alienated of the local youth population.

Some councils have reacted positively to the 'problem' of aerosol art. Grants have been made to groups of young artists to enable them to paint walls, underpasses, tunnels, bus shelters etc. – legally! Youth clubs in areas such as Ladbroke Grove in Brixton, Covent Garden, and Wolverhampton benefited in this way both from money and from the incentive to produce public art for their own communities. Users of this book can make their own decisions whether to experiment with the artistic streetculture of the 'Wildstyle' lettering of the spray can painters. For some youngsters you know or work with, it may be just the form of self-expression they need – to paint and tag their own wall.

MUSIC

This is not going to offer an encyclopaedic set of Guinness facts for the music world. Instead we would like to offer something of a 'brain-storming' approach to lots of music related activities which youth organisations could be offering for their youngsters. We have been involved in a number of these schemes ourselves and through that involvement, we have met a number of individuals who have been offering music as a means of developing youngsters' lives. We have always been more involved with 'popular' music and its connection with young people, so this section reflects that, rather than the tradition of formal musical tuition. In music, especially in its popular forms, there is a culture, counter-culture and sub-culture. Identification with the 'Rave' culture, or with rock personalities, the bands, and their styles of dress and behaviour, is a natural way in which many young people find a self-identity. Being a truant, an offender and unemployed are minor considerations relative to being a 'punk', 'skin', 'rasta', 'rude boy' or whatever. The choice of style may then include an aggressive rejection of society's standards, yet it is the fashion, or sub-cultural group, which gives youngsters their identity in the peer groups which they most inhabit. So, enough of this intellectualising.....how can we involve young people in contemporary music? What supports can youth facilities offer to youngsters to develop their skills and interest in that music?

We hope that the rest of this section give a few practical ideas. They are certainly not the only techniques which can be employed; however, they represent some of the initiatives which have been tried by various workers in a variety of UK settings.

Experiencing Live Music

Whether young people want to perform themselves, or not, it is almost always an exciting experience to see live music. Young people in the youth club context may be unable to afford the concert prices charged at many rock venues. Historically, this was a contributory factor in 1976 to the Punk boom, which led to many more gigs being established, even if they only lasted for a few years. It recreated the sort of pub and club rock scene which had previously existed in the rock n' roll heyday of the late-1950s and to a lesser extent the late 1960s psychedelic phase of British Rock. The point of the example is that without such small local venues, the music scene becomes a fantasised and distanced attraction which is OK as a means of diversion from reality, but has about as much real meaning as the mythical dodo. One punk, Derek Gibb, in a youth club in London wrote in an early fanzine, 'Sound of the Westway':

"When you are bored out of your mind on the dole with nothing to do, escapism has no meaning. Who wants their already depressed state of mind further stagnated by half-hour moog solos? This is where the appeal of Punk Rock lies; music to get you off your arse. Have you noticed how hippies at concerts just sit there bobbing their heads? Well, we don't. We pogo; we jump about. A dance of true expression from the heart. Who wants to wait three years for a shitty triple LP which is stale and boring and costs £12.00? Who wants to queue 12 hours for a £8/£12 ticket to see a band of raving posers that look like ants in an airplane hanger? I don't want to be made to sit down and then clap politely at the end."

Derek's indictment rings uncannily true of what came after punk as well as what went before. It was not until the rise of DJ and Rave culture in the late 1980s that the collective imagination of young people across the land was once again fired up in this way. Regrettably, the power of the Top 20 and disco managed to dissipate much of the raw energy and replace it with the harmless placebo 'escapist entertainment'. The positive side of this is where dancing, rap and bits of impromptu singing became creative and can be encouraged. At least through 'scratching' and rap the disco scene became more of a participation event. Just watch out for all those ghetto-blasters balancing on shoulders of hip-hop dancers in your local High Street. Perhaps at this point we should stop since it's getting very BOF-ish (you may not find **that** in a dictionary – ask the kids!).

Ways round the financial problem of how expensive music has become which we have used are to:

- organise gigs for young people through the youth and community service facilities;
- establish lively and relevant music tuition;
- provide practice areas;
- obtain free tickets for local music events.

Organising Gigs

It doesn't need to be as tame and tedious as it may first sound. Many fine bands have started their careers playing in youth clubs. Our own youth-working lives already span using an unknown band, 'Steampacket', which included Rod Stewart and Long John Baldry, a second-string synthesiser band which cleared a youth club dance – they were called Tubeway Army, featuring Gary Numan! Members of the Stranglers have helped out at one youth club Alan used to run; Misty in Roots members were regular artists and members at another club, and Pete Brown, who wrote most of the Cream's greatest hits donated the old Cream PA to a central London youth project.

More recently we have received help from the Levellers, Zion Train and Tofu Love Frogs. Big name bands all start on the circuit and most were, in their time, associated with youth facilities. So, don't despise two chord wonders, allow them the chance to play; organise events and perhaps establish a booking/gig system with other facilities in your area. This is a mechanism which the kids can then run themselves, with a bit of support. Often, difficulties arise through inappropriate staffing of concerts, gigs and dances. Heavy bouncers too often provide heavy scenes. It is best to run gigs with closed, or semi-closed access, building on known relationships between staff and users, rather than putting up centres as targets for inter-area gang fights. Having offered that advice, there are a number of examples of community arts facilities which offer cheap, varied, alternative media events for all who want to attend. It is also sometimes possible to make deals with commercial facilities to provide cut-price entry to clubs and venues for youth organisation members, or even to use their facilities to promote young performers, whether as mixers or muscians.

The organisation of local music festivals through the youth and community service is also a real possibility. For instance, Essex Community Education Service have been instrumental in organising events for their home grown talent and also full blown music festivals. Some of the early Rock Against Racism, Anti-Nazi League and Anti-Apartheid Movement gigs were partnership events with local youth service personnel. These proved ideal vehicles for many workers concerned with breaking down black/white prejudices, but the political base of the undertaking has been seen by some local authorities as impossible to support. Another area where change has occurred is in the yearly Arts Events run by many local authority services. With the rise in local festivals and carnivals, some of these events have been moved in the direction of reflecting young people's musical interests. A number of newer arts events are now featuring rock, folk, reggae, hip-hop, and all the off-shoots. In Scotland, estates like Craigmillar and Westerhailes have their own full time staff promoting festival events, and these have provided exciting venues in which young local bands can rub shoulders with established performers. As we comment later in this section, Rock Workshops and the like are allowing young people access to professional musicians and equipment.

Many of these workshops have promoted events which are often of a fundraising nature. The re-birth of the CND movement has also provided the impetus for a number of concerts raising money for local groups. There have also been attempts from sections of the young Labour Movement to become involved in promoting rock events. The Socialist Action for Youth group, based in London, have tried this type of show, on occasions combining it with other events such as conference and theatre programmes. Extending the use of music in drama productions is also a venture possible for many youth groups. Modern musicals such as 'The Rocky Horror Show', 'Jesus Christ Superstar' and 'Elvis' have quite wide appeal and can be adapted for youth club productions. In other cases, young bands have written their own music scores for stage shows. The Christmas Panto is still a medium for fun and variety and one which can include modern music **and** unite the local community, especially where a suitable theme is taken on board. In West Sussex, the eccentric star-gazer, Patrick Moore joins in the local Christmas show each year.

There are also literally thousands of traditional music groups and bands around the UK. Brass bands, marching bands, folk groups, youth orchestras, madrigals, choirs, jazz bands – all may find a home base, rehearsal space or performance area in the youth or community centre. They are very often the starting point where young people learn some appreciation of music and the basics of formal music knowledge.

Going to Music Shows

As mentioned before, it may be the cost of admission which prevents many youngsters from going to see live music. Where this is the case, contact with the local and national radio and television network may produce free tickets. The BBC Radio Ticket Unit is at Broadcasting House, London, W1A 1AA. This is especially useful for groups based in the major towns. Contacting the ever growing number of local radio stations can often result in an invite to the studio or, where radio stations are recording shows they have to obtain a sympathetic, appreciative audience, so they may actually welcome your enquiry. They will **not** love you if you arrive at their recording of Ossian for Clyde Folk, with a mini-bus full of Exploited fans!

As a caring, sympathetic, youth or social worker (you may remember the type!) it is sometimes possible to appeal to an impresario's finer instincts and get some cheap or free tickets for shows they are producing. Being the way of the world, you normally have to give something in return. The best and most possible return favour can be some publicity for either their show, generosity, or both.

The other major possibility for workers to assist youngsters in getting to see music, rests on the kids having some money, but no transport. Many older adolescents hitch right round the country, but for many, the provision of a mini-bus to a music festival or event is a godsend. If properly organised (by you!), this event can be a part of your youth work or group work programme, giving as it does an enjoyable shared activity. Because it is away from premises, workers must check out their legal responsibilities for accidents, etc., but it can be a good possibility.

DJ Culture

This section has been contributed by George Symington from Glasgow, who was actively involved in the DJ and Club scene for some years.

1988 saw the genesis of a new style of electronic dance music which evolved via the welding of black disco, funk and electro to white synth and industrial styles, e.g. Kraftwerk. Initially produced in Detroit and Chicago, it was mostly ignored in the US and reached Britain via DJ's holidaying in Ibiza, who upon getting the message, converted the clientele of clubs like London's Shoom and Manchester's Hacienda.

Starting off as a deeply cliquey and underground phenomenon it rapidly mushroomed (!) and has by now largely crushed the dominance of traditional rock music in the hearts, minds and feet of youth today. Dance music, splintering into a myriad of evolving factions – house, techno, garage, trance, acid, trip/hip hop and jungle – *is* the soundtrack to the 1990s and the coming of the next millennium.

Created and programmed primarily by computers, samplers and synthesisers, and characterised, according to the CJA (Criminal Justice Act) by, "a succession of repetitive beats", it is mostly heard via DJs but is also played live. The archetypal 'gig' has been superseded by massive, often illegal 'raves' – now mostly killed off by the CJA and its criminalisation of youth culture – and mainly now by thousands of clubs, some of which are a massive commercial/corporate phenomena, e.g. Liverpool's Cream. A typical teenager's weekend night out now consists of going clubbing/raving/drugging and dancing all night in an ecstatic, trance inducing tribal ritual. Hard to encourage in youth organisations, but ignored as a cultural pheomenon by the Youth Service, at its peril!

This is the first musical/cultural phenomenon to ignite the mass imagination of youth and as such its importance cannot be overemphasised. Quite simply, like the name of the club, it's 'AWOL' – a way of life. Club/dance culture is now an industry, with its own music, language, art and fashion; a subculture, that while initially demonised, has by now inevitably been sanitised, commercialised – some might even say sterilised – by regulation and assimilation, both economically and politically. So much so that there is a growing feeling of cynicism amongst the 'old school' against the hype and conformity of the mainstream clubs. A 'DIY' ethic is picking up momentum again – some of our best nights ever were held in a local youth club, believe it or not! So keeping the original vibe alive and underground has to be the way forward – getting back to our roots. Get on it!

The average teenager now dreams of being a DJ rather than a guitar hero – the DJ is the heart of the matter – the link between the studios and the club dancefloor, playing music which is often made in small bedroom studios with a minimal amount of equipment – this DIY ethic again mirrors the punk ethos – anyone could make music. The price of the equipment needed has fallen to levels whereby it is realistic to produce electronic music at home – and this democratisation of the creative process is responsible for the spread of the 'virus'! Hundreds of independent 12"s are released each week. The availability of such equipment is crucially important to young people, and any youth club which has a set-up will act as a magnet to kids desperate to get involved. A basic set-up for a youth club would consist of the following items (at 1996 prices):

2 X Stanton or similar cartridges, e.g. 500 ALs, £50.
2 X turntables with speed controls, £300.
1 X mixer (to mix the sounds from the decks), £200.
1 X amplifier, £200.
1 X double cassette deck/4 track cassette, £100.
2 X speakers (*heavy* duty!), £200.
1 X CD player, £100.
1 X drum machine, £100 – £1,000.
Slipmats, headphones, microphone, leads, £50.

All of the above can be bought for around £1,000 – £1,200.

Turntables

The only *serious* contender for turntable techniques is Technics' mighty SL1200. This is the industry standard and it performs perfectly for the DJ. These now cost almost £400 each. However Richer Sounds Ltd. have a good compromise in the Ariston 1600 at £150 each, which is quite serviceable. Other cheap copies of Technics decks are rubbish and are to be avoided at all costs. Cartridges will add an extra £50 per pair – Stanton's 500AL is standard for heavy duty mixing use.

Mixers

Mixers cost from £100 – £500 upwards depending on facilities offered, i.e. equaliser, samplers (very useful), number of channels available, etc.. Buy the best you can afford – Vesrax, Numark, Gemini and KAM are good quality.

Amplifiers

Ideally you'll need a heavy duty Mosfet power amp, the bigger the better, but 100 watts RMS will do for starters. An ordinary hi-fi amp will do if funds cannot stretch. Maplins do kit amps at low cost if you are an electronics wizard.

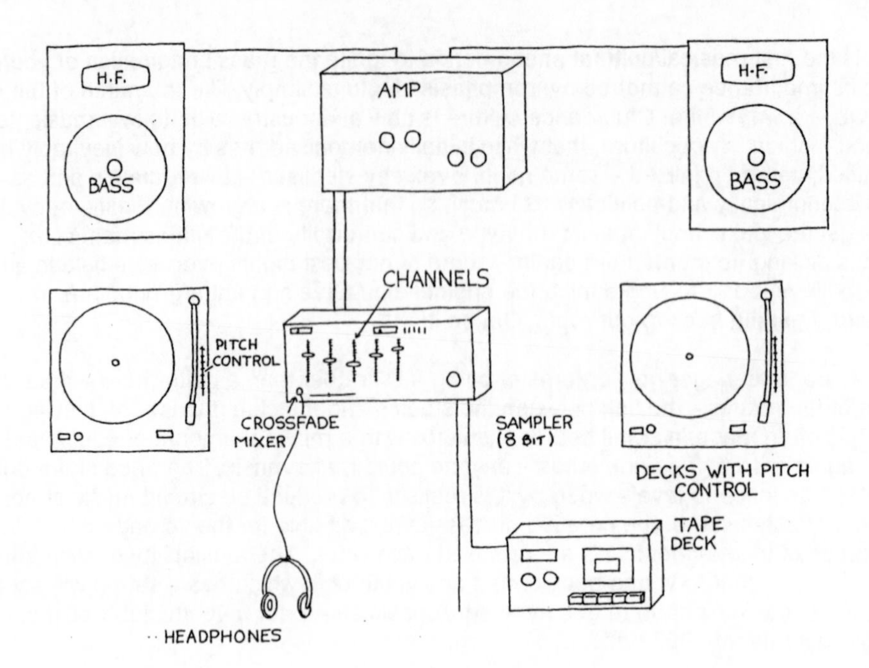

DJ SET UP

Speakers

These must match the power rating of the amplifier. Quality doesn't come cheap but will *save* on blown tweeter and bass cones. Again these can be assembled from kit form at a great discount. Firms such as Maplin and Wilmslow Audio can supply them. A good speaker for dance music is the Cerwin Vega but there are loads to choose from. Look in DJ magazines each month for models and stockists of equipment.

Tape

A four track recorder enables overdubbing and more elaborate and creative mixing techniques. Otherwise a double cassette is useful for copying tapes. Or buy two single cassette decks and link them up.

Studio Equipment

For more serious creative composing, further equipment is essential. A basic set-up should include:
Amiga/Atari computer with Cubase or similar *sequencing* software. The Amiga 300/600 range of computers can also be used to good effect with programmes such as Octamed v5. PCs and Macs with large hard drives are of course preferable, but expensive. This will be the workhorse of the 'MIDI' studio (see below).

Other equipment includes:
Sampler, e.g. Akai S1000, £1,000.
Drum Machine e.g. Roland 909/808.
Workstation – a keyboard *combining* sampler, drum machine, synthesiser and sequencer in one package – a sort of electronic one man band. Models by Korg, Yamaha and Roland are

excellent and start at around £1,000 – very good value for money – whole tracks can be put together using just one keyboard. An excellent buy.
Synthesisers – Roland, Korg, Yamaha etc., not forgetting the vital Roland TB303 bassline (*the* acid machine). The Novations 'Basstation' – a Roland 303 clone is excellent and the Roland S1X101 keyboard is like gold dust. A lot of equipment can be purchased secondhand – look in magazines like 'Future Music'.

These items are linked by *MIDI – Musical Instrument Digital Interface* – a system by which instruments can be linked and 'slaved' together to communicate intelligently, controlled by the computer and its sequencing software. Music composed can be saved on hard disks (large, one gigabyte drives are needed ideally, as sampling is memory intensive). Or you can record onto DAT (digital audio tape) or cassette, 4 track or reel to reel. In order to link these instruments a 6/12 channel mixing desk is needed – these cost around £300 – £500. It is possible to save a lot of money by using special CDs/CD ROMS which are simply a collection of *samples* of keyboards, drum machines and all other instruments. These sounds can them be sampled and used without buying the instruments! They are advertised in 'Future Music' – a good publication for general information on electronic music, midi and computing.

Studios

A studio can be set up for well under £5,000 if you look around. Buy second hand and *your* kids could be pressing up their own 12 inch singles. You could start up a label, hundreds already have, anything's possible! There is bound to be a wealth of knowledge and experience to tap into, use it, ask the kids, they are the experts! Nothing is more guaranteed to ignite the kids' interest and imagination than the possibility of making their own music. You'll have a waiting list to join in the party. Well, it beats table tennis!

Club Nights, Discos and Raves

1990s youth are into club/dance culture – it's a way of life/dedicated lifestyle. The young people of today are increasingly sophisticated. The traditional youth club 'disco' with a crappy old console and a couple of light boxes just *won't* hack it anymore. You'll need a decent PA, size dependent on hall size, anything from 500 to 5,000 watts will be required. Then all you need are two decks, a mixer, some DJs and the party is pumping! You'll need a good vantage point for the DJs and a solid platform/table for the decks and mixer. Add some smoke, strobes, moonflowers, Optokinetiks projectors (oilwheels etc.), slide projectors, ultra-violet light and fluorescent banners and you have *all* the ingredients (well, almost!) for a party. All this stuff can be hired at a cost of £200 upwards. The more spent on production, the better the show, although imagination and technique are priceless. Get the artists involved in painting banners, designing flyers and tickets, and general decoration of the hall. Keep it loud, dark and smoky and you won't go far wrong!

Lighting is crucial to create mood and reflect the energies of the evening. We used to project onto white nylon sheets using slide projectors and Optokinetiks 250s. You can get excellent slides from computers and videos – use an exposure of less than 1/15 sec for video to avoid lines/scanning on the slide.

Banners/Decor

It is easy to design and produce your own banners using old sheets, canvas etc.. Fluorescent paint can be bought in one litre bottles at about £5 each. Basic colours like orange, red, yellow, green and black will get you started. An Episcope can be used to trace designs. These banners look great under UV lights.

White gauze or nylon (fireproofed) is ideal for projecting slides onto. Use the opportunity to design a logo for your club or group, and consider organising banner painting workshops. Graffiti techniques are popular – use spray paints, UV if possible.

Club Nights

No doubt you'll have queues of aspiring DJs wanting to impress the crowd with their mixing skills. Audition them first! 'Name' DJs can command exorbitant fees – £100 is nothing for a big name. But several hundred tickets at £3 or £4 can pay for a good night – you could even *make* money – plenty do! So, running a regular club night can do wonders for your bank balance and credibility! You'll learn from the kids – they can teach you the techniques and give you the ideas and the energy and enthusiasm you'll need to make things happen.

You'll need to organise your night properly and carefully – you'll need tickets, security, a cashier, a drinks bar, cloakroom and last but ***not*** least, a *chill-out* area where people can rest and cool and calm down. It's vital to have water on tap to prevent ***heat-stroke*** – kids have died due to the combined effects of over exertion, over sweating and dehydration. *Water consumption* should be limited to a *maximum* of one pint per hour – too much water CAN KILL – be careful. You'll need stewards to supervise things and keep a watchful eye on the proceedings – softly, softly is the best approach!

Drugs

Drugs are obviously an issue and are in fact inextricably involved with the dance music scene – especially Ecstasy, which is the substance blamed for recent well publicised deaths. Fundamentally, these deaths have been caused by *heat-stroke* which is why a *chill-out room* is *vital*. Street credible information on the various drugs should be on hand. The 'Peanut Pete' leaflets and books produced by Manchester's Lifeline Project are the best around. Remember kids – *just say know!*

DJ-ing

The black art of DJ-ing is a skill requiring thousands of hours of practice and the application of a variety of techniques. Basically, these overpaid record changers (!) mix two records so that the transition from one to another is fluent and mellifluous, i.e. a seamless transition from one track to the next. This involves synchronising the speed of each record using the pitch control on the turntable so that the BPM. (beats per minute) of each track are *identical*. The DJ then manipulates the record manually using headphones so that they synchronise the bass drums (downbeats) or snares (offbeats) in such a way that when record A is mixed via the cross fader into record B, the beats merge into each other without colliding and clashing horribly.

This is a difficult skill to acquire and takes endless practice. Other techniques such as scratching, cutting, transforming etc. are beyond our scope. But a good DJ responds to the crowd, judges the atmosphere and sequences the tunes so that the crowd is taken on a musical journey par excellence. In the last two years, Alan and Howie have attended a number of club sessions at the Glastonbury Festival, in between selling their books! Orbital and Billy Nasty were particularly impressive making mixing a real 'art and music form'. DJ-ing as an art and technique started off in the gay discos and black ghettos where HipHop DJs evolved the basic techniques still used to-day. So that now, many young people might argue that the DJ, and not Eric Clapton, is God!

Thanks, once again, to George, for this valuable and interesting contribution!
(Alan and Howie)

From our experience we'd add:
- What times to operate? How does this relate to local requirements of transport and neighbours' complaints?
- Do you have any staff who have good first aid experience?
- Although it may sound 'old fashioned', it can be a good idea to provide spot prizes and competitions during a club session. We recently saw a DJ who did wonderful Rolf Harris impersonations, miming to his eccentric record. Then he got youngsters up on stage doing their versions! It was memorable! Bizarre or fancy dress can also be subject to prizes.

Helping the Budding Musician

Running music workshop activities in a club or centre is one step towards provision of a range of facilities for the young musician. Using the talents of staff who might already be working with you is one way of providing the inputs for the workshop. Another method is to contact local bands, individual musicians and perhaps any musicians' collectives which operate locally. Ask them if they would be willing to help either run a 'one-off' activity, or help staff a permanent facility linking in to your centre or youth group. There is nothing quite so exciting for budding young musicians as to meet and be coached by the professionals.

If you are thinking of running such a facility you will have to make a space available. Ideally this should include a degree of sound-proofing and be equipped with a PA. It should also be secure. The range of instruments which you provide is likely to be limited by money, but often secondhand instruments and PA can be bought to start off such a project without too great an expenditure. Again, local musicians may even be persuaded to give or lend pieces of equipment. From musician friends, we have been told that it is not the best course of action to try and teach all youngsters acoustic guitar. Although a good teaching instrument it doesn't always fire the imagination. This returns to the question of sound-proofing: it may be **drums, organ, or electric guitar** which your kids want to learn. In London at one centre we know, they lined the walls of their basement room with layers of egg boxes. (Make sure they are adequately fire proofed!). It wasn't perfect, but it provided some protection for, and from, the neighbours! So, if you can, amass a collection of instruments which young people can try. Link the lessons into seeing bands and listening to tapes and records of different styles. The music list in the Questionnaires' section of this book may be useful in those sorts of programmes. They certainly seemed popular in music groups both ourselves and colleagues have run.

Making a bit of a jump, we would now like to suggest some ways you may be able to help the individual or group of youngsters who wish to perform or record. Some of this information comes from our own experience; other ideas we have gleaned from the very helpful information packs from the BBC Grapevine Series and the old Interaction Make-it-Yourself project.

Rehearsal Space

Often youth centres and similar are quite isolated from complaining humanity. Perhaps you can follow the example of many clubs and make available rooms for youth groups to practice in. Another suggestion is to find a suitably remote school building and then pressure the local education department to make rooms available for young musicians to practice in. This will bring you, inevitably, into close contact with caretakers/janitors and their rules and regulations, but it is worth the hassle if you can enable kids to practice.

Rough recordings and live demos

A number of youth organisations have built up their own collection of recording gear. This ranges in complexity from a cassette recorder attached to a couple of mikes, through porta-studios, to eight track mixing desks with DAT recording gear and all the mikes etc., that go with such apparatus. Groups generally do not have access to anything beyond a basic cassette deck and usually really appreciate the opportunity to get even a rough recording of their sound. It helps them and it is a learning experience in itself. The sound balance of groups is normally drastically improved from a competitive, wall-of-sound, approach to a discernible 'mix' by the rigours of recording a group's range of instruments/voices/sounds. Digital technology, combined with falling equipment prices have put high quality recording within reach of many more groups. See the section on DJ Culture (above) for details of both disco and studio equipment.

It may be worth considering the purchase of such equipment on an area basis as a shared resource, or for your own centre to act as that resource, if you wish to cater for, or promote special music facilities. In our experience, it is possible to get keen engineers to build mixing facilities for the cost of components. Your local college, university, or electronics firm may well be worth a visit. It is worth briefing yourself on what you are trying to do before attacking these institutions, otherwise you may neither help yourselves or those who might come after you. We even know of a youth club studio that offers training courses:

The Basement Studio
Sefton Park Youth Centre
Ashley Down Road
Bristol BS7 9BG

The next stage of development for many groups is actually going into the studio. This can be an expensive and potentially hazardous business. Here are some of the tips offered by the Interaction Make-it-Yourself Handbook.

> "The music should be thoroughly rehearsed before going into a studio. Remember that recording demands more accuracy than performance.
> The cost per hour of a recording studio is generally related to the number of tracks the studio has. As you might expect, the more tracks, the greater the cost. The number of tracks - 4, 8, 16 or 32 is a measure of the number of elements the group's sound can be divided into .....most Make it Yourself groups, and many commercial groups, opt for the cheaper 4 track studios."

Without going through the full range of information offered by the Beeb and Interaction, the following points are worth making to groups about to part with their money.

- Know what you want to be recorded, how many hours are necessary and whether a final mix is to be achieved in one session at a studio.
- Are you willing to buy the master tape (for about £35) or will you want to rent it? Work this out with the studio in advance.
- How many cassette or CD copies of the recording are required?
- Suggestions for where to find out the cost of studios and equipment supplies may be found in a number of music reference books, which may be available in the local library. The Showcase International Music Book, 12 Felix Avenue, London N8 9TL is about the best source, listing recording studios and services.

Cutting Discs and Merchandising

The range of small circulation records and cassettes on sale has vastly multiplied in recent years. Groups with a product that they think there is local support for, may well consider paying for the production of 500 copies of a 12 inch single, cassette or CD out of their own pockets. It is not unknown for youth clubs and similar to launch into this area of small scale business themselves. It is unlikely to make anyone rich, but it's good fun and groups can use the process as a springboard to bigger things. If you, individual artist, or groups using your facilities are considering producing their own record or tape, keep the following in mind:

- It is worth demanding test copies, even if it costs extra. It is also worth checking the quality of the eventual product, whether it is to be CD, cassette or vinyl.
- Make sure you have (a) a written order (dated) and (b) a delivery note for all parts that go to make up the product: box, cover art, labels and recording. And (c) a firm delivery date. Because most small orders are competing with big orders, this may require some hassling.

The production of small run cassettes is becoming increasingly popular. On a limited scale this can be done on a domestic level linking cassette machines together and making 'same speed' or 'double-speed' copies. The time this takes make it unsatisfactory for long runs. For more than, say, fifty copies you will require the services of a fast cassette copying service. This can provide copies of your tape onto cassette on fast speed, multi-copying machines. This is quite cheap and is being much utilised by groups who, for example wish to sell 30 minutes of their music to the public cheaply. It's also very useful for groups looking for gigs who want to promote their act to promoters. Labels can be easily printed or photocopied and pasted onto card for insertion into the cassette box. Tape-to-tape duplicating facilities require payment for a master tape for their fast copier, plus a cost per tape for the fast copying. A number of firms offer this service – a substantial list is available in the Recording Services section of the Showcase International Music Book.

Labels and Sleeves

Some processing plants supply blank labels on discs free – all do it quite cheaply. A cheap label or sticker can then be added by the group themselves. Most printers can do this using the group's artwork. If the group want a commercial label, especially if it requires more than one colour, expect it to cost quite a lot of money. It hardly seems worthwhile for a small run, and it may be worth concentrating more effort on the cover sleeve. Remember to ask the pressing plant to put different coloured stickers on the A and B side of a disc or cassette, or at least one sticker on side A to help your identification for labelling.

The sleeves can be made cheaply by groups using photocopied wrap-around sheets of paper, stapled cards etc.. It requires a lot of unpaid work, however, and it is not always much cheaper than getting the whole sleeve commercially made. Get your group of youngsters to look at the range of independent sleeves for singles at the local record store. This will probably give them a number of ideas for their own article.

Distribution and Promotion

To sell music products to the trade, you may go directly to record shops. They will require a 50% mark-up. Many will ask for sale or return deals. Try to avoid this. The majority of records are likely to be sold either through distributors, who require anything up to 75% mark-up on the price you charge, or through direct selling to friends at gigs. The growth of small labels has created certain distributors' networks dealing mostly with small-run music. There's obviously quite a lot of overlap between record companies and record distributors. Many, unfortunately go bust rather quickly! Rather like the practice it takes to make a musician, there is quite a lot of research work required to find the best distribution deal. Again, the Showcase book, or the White Book, PO Box 55, Staines, Middlesex TW18 4UG contain lots of suggestions.

To promote records it is necessary to spend some money on postage and letters to accompany free copies of records to be sent to the music press and radio stations. The local press may also be worth contacting. Some groups just want to sell their recording; others use a small circulation tape/record/CD to try to obtain a recording contract, so make sure you know what the aims of the group are. John Peel and Andy Kershaw remain two of the gurus of the British Music Scene when it comes to promoting indie music and young bands. They may be worth sending a copy to, but don't be too optimistic; they literally receive thousands of tapes, CDs and records each month. The satellite TV channels now have a number of 24 hour music channels, so this is an additional route to potential airplay. Local radio is probably a better bet for many aspiring musicians.

Managers and Contracts

A word or two of warning. Getting a manager or contract for a group is not the end of all problems; it can often be the beginning of major difficulties. A record deal is useless, unless it gives musicians enough money to play. Managers who don't work throughout the British Isles are unlikely to assist a band who wants to go professional. London is still one of the centres of the musical universe. Likewise, signing a contract which ties a band to a management firm for two or three years in return for the guaranteed production of a couple of singles may not be worthwhile. Contracts of this kind usually bind all the individual members of the group, so if a member leaves, they are still under contract - not a pleasant situation. The only real answer is to see a solicitor. Community Law and Advice Centres may be able to help, but contract law connected with the record business is quite a specialist area.

Discos

Finally, one cannot complete a section on 'music' without at least reference to more traditional discos, and their world of records, equipment and style. Most Junior Youth Clubs still make use of a simple disco set up, a pile of records, CDs and tapes, a couple of coloured lights and a constant stream of would be DJs. For many youth organisations these are the only 'busy' nights. Large sums of money can be made - over £200 a night even in the youth market from promoting a successful disco. If you are hiring a disco outfit from outside of the club, even semi-professionals start at about £50 per night and for the top outfits, £200 – £400 is a more realistic sum. You are paying for the quality of the music equipment, the professionalism of the DJ, the selection of music and the time and travel costs. Running a good disco can take more planning than is usually credited.

A well run disco in the world of fast-changing fashions can satisfy one group of youngsters and start tribal warfare from another section of kids. So, either a balance is struck between the factions, or a 'theme' for an evening should be hit on. Neither will you please all your constituency of youth so, over time, various permutations will have to be tried. It is a minefield for the entrepreneur since what works once, isn't necessarily a repeat success. The question of staffing-bouncer-door control, raised earlier in this section in connection with organising gigs, is worth bearing in mind. It is likely to be crucial in respect of your being allowed by management committees to continue running discos.

It may be useful to consider building or buying a disco as an area resource. Some areas have a number of units, which are then centrally stored and serviced. Trying out as a DJ, or disco dancing could be used as an arts activity – both involve a 'performance' of a kind. Majorettes dancing groups are an offshoot of this activity.

Discos do not have a single identity and for ethnic minorities, a disco, or sound, is a means of publicising individual identity. To a lesser extent, the nature of discos should be encouraged to have a local, cultural identity, apart from purely reflecting the music which makes the Top 20.

PAPIER MÂCHÉ

When we originally tried to find out about the different ways of using papier mâché, we used our mate Nick to get his hands messy, working with a number of youth groups around Renfrewshire. On one note he wrote to us he said: "A s versitile as an egg" . We are not sure whether this is symptomatic of a brain disorder, or an acute statement on the flexible use of papier mâché! Since then we have also been shown other methods and this section is an up-to-date amalgam of our ideas on the subject. It is also worth looking at our section on 'Masks', which makes considerable use of papier mâché. Anyway, down to business.

Papier mâché was traditionally a craft technique used for making coach panels (the horse-drawn variety!) In more recent times it has proved popular in schools, youth clubs, arts and drama groups, and for carnivals and street performers. It is fun with all age groups, but young children seem to particularly love it. Two quite simple techniques are used, depending upon the type of article which is being made. Sometimes a combination of the two methods is employed giving the benefits of both techniques. The range of items which can be made is wide, encompassing puppet heads, chess pieces, masks, ornaments and candle-stick holders right through to an eight foot tall mummy! This last objet d'art graced the lawn outside a friend's house; a strange sight indeed on an open-plan, middle-class housing estate in conservative West Sussex!

Given this sort of variety, papier mâché is a useful part of your arts and crafts armoury. It is also very cheap, wonderfully messy and appeals to youngsters' baser instincts. The only drawback that we have found is the need for planning when using the 'moulding' method; the mâché takes at least 24 hours to reach the required consistency. For the purpose of this section, we offer a description of the two basic methods, plus a very limited reference to the methods of making specific articles. Once you, and the members of your youth group have mastered the two methods, the imaginations and needs of your particular group should determine what is made. So, for instance, if you are planning to produce a play, the use of papier mâché masks might well offer an added dimension to the staging. In the professional and amateur theatre this has been successfully utilised in productions as diverse as 'A Midsummer Night's Dream' and 'Equus'. Both masks and false heads can be made in this way, using chicken wire as a base for the structure and then adding layers of paper, followed by moulded mâché.

And so, on to the principal techniques, and the materials required.

Materials

We had different recommendations on what to use in the way of materials, especially the glues. Depending on who you listen to, a combination of the following are needed:

- Wallpaper paste (without fungicide); flour and water paste; Interior Polyfilla; Polycell regular; white PVA glue thinned down with a little water; latex adhesives for sticking some paper; card and fabrics; quick drying, clear adhesive for some jobs; and spray adhesive which is great for sticking paper to paper and card, but must be used in an open space or specially constructed spray booth (the vapour is unpleasant and harmful).
- A large quantity of newspapers; better quality paper makes stronger products; but is obviously more expensive. Magazines are unsuitable. Kitchen roll paper is useful for quickly building up work and tissue paper or paper handkerchiefs are good for producing a smooth, top layer.

- Art Maché is a new material which is obtainable from both Specialist Crafts and NES Arnold. We haven't tried it, but Arnold's say of it,"Instant papier mâché – but so much cleaner and easier than the conventional method."
- A variety of cardboard is good to build up basic structures.
- Two buckets; one of which should be galvanised to withstand heating. One bucket; plus a very large saucepan works well.
- Water.
- Half inch wire mesh (chicken wire) and garden wire.
- Moulds for particular objects - i.e. wooden and cardboard boxes; dishes; bowls.
- For finishing papier mâché objects you will need things like card; white emulsion paint - water based; brushes; acrylic and other coloured paints and spray paints; enamel paints; varnish; masking tape; a craft knife and a heavier weight Stanley knife or similar; scissors; etc..
- The usual drawing equipment: pens, felt tips, pencils, rulers etc..

Layering Method

With the method, the first thing to do is prepare the paste. For example, to prepare flour and water paste mix flour with cold water, stir into thin past and add one tablespoon of salt per half pound of flour. Gently heat this mixture up in a pan. As the paste begins to thicken; add more warm water. When the paste is both quite thick and translucent it is ready for use. Some people recommend using boiling water with the flour to achieve the same results.

Polyfilla and wallpaper adhesives will give instructions with them but don't be afraid to experiment with varying densities of paste.

It is worth preparing a quantity of paper strips or squares in advance. Depending on the size and shape of the article being made, vary the size of the paper squares or strips. One to two inch squares of strips are the sort of size likely to be required. You will need both a bowl/bucket of water and one of paste, ready to be put into service. You also need to make sure that the mould is coated to help prevent sticking. Again, a variety of techniques are recommended. With smooth surfaces, which are not porous; such as a balloon, or a china bowl, cooking oil or Vaseline should be rubbed over the surface to prevent it from sticking. When using boxes and other porous objects, the use of dry or wet sheets of newspaper, without the addition of adhesive, to the inside of the mould is suggested. A final note on this subject concerns the use of moulds which are airtight. The vacuum which is formed can be repaired using the layering technique described below.

Having prepared all the necessary ingredients, dip the strips of newspaper one at a time into a bucket of cold water, then coat the surface with adhesive. Layer the pieces on to the mould one overlapping the next, until an entire covering has been made. Allow to dry and then repeat the process. Approximately six layers are necessary to provide a strong surface. With items such as bowls it is a good idea to make the base of the vessel thicker than the sides. If time is limited, there are two ways in which the drying process can be speeded up.

1. Use Interior Polyfilla. Rapid setting results from use of this medium, but it is less permanent.
2. Having squeezed out any air bubbles in the strips, starting from the middle and working outwards, put the object, (bowl or whatever) into a pre-heated, medium low oven at 250 degrees and bake on a greased tray for 5 to 10 minutes. Using this technique it is not necessary to allow drying time in between the six layers.

A useful method for ensuring a smooth edge to your bowl, or similar item, is as follows:

Once the bowl has been fired in the oven attach more strips, working them over the lip from the inside outwards. Re-bake the bowl in the oven and when cooled, gently sand to a smooth finish.

The layering method can be used with cloth initially instead of paper, particularly when working with wire frames. These can be wound over the frame, followed by coatings of papier mâché. A firm frame is a necessity; otherwise all the hard work and effort will be wasted.

Moulding or Pulp Method

This is the method which most workers will remember from their own messy childhood.

Once again; a bowl of paste is made up. The suggestions for the mix are very varied. Newspapers; fabric conditioner; whiting or ground chalk; wallpaper paste; linseed oil and PVA adhesive are used together in one typical recipe. The youngsters you are working with will just love this next bit! The paper for making the mâché is torn in small shreds and put into another bowl, into which boiling water is poured. The paper at this stage should be wet, rather than soggy. Add more water later as it becomes absorbed. Once the pulp is beginning to form, squeeze out excess water with your hands. This could also be done using a pair of old tights to sieve out the water. When this has been accomplished, add paste and stir well. The stirring is really rather nasty (from an adult standpoint), if done with hands. (Not that all youth type persons would agree!) Two ways around this are: either to use rubber gloves, or to make up a primitive form of whisk. One design for this entails bending up two coathangers thus.

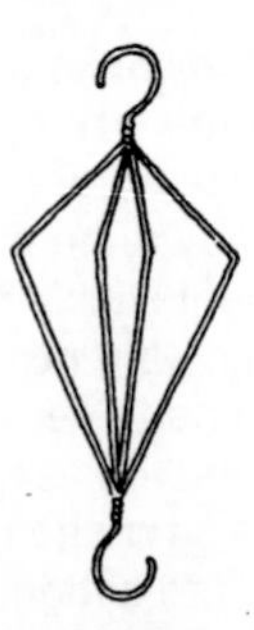

The beaten mixture of water, paper and paste will become an unpleasant looking mix with the texture of modelling clay. Some users of pulp maché suggest boiling the mix; as described above in a galvanised bucket. When it has been strained, the pulp is allowed to cool and them emptied out onto a small pile of dry newspapers. It is then ready for use. The addition of a small quantity of wintergreen makes the mixture less foul smelling. Both pulp and paste can be stored in a refrigerator and used over a short period (when making pulp it improves if left overnight before use).

What do you do with this grey, soggy mess; you are probably asking yourself? Kids being kids, the paper equivalent of mud pies will already be winging their way through your local air space! More constructively, the pulp is a wonderfully cheap alternative to clay. Therefore, if you want to make a candle holder out of a bottle first paste strips of paper onto the bottle, then add the moulded lumps of pulp.

Make sure that the papier mâché is separated by a gap from the candle wax.

Bead and Bangle making

Rather a different use of papier mâché is its use in making beads. A three foot string of beads can be made in about half an hour, though this does not take into account the lacquering. Both use the layering method, but on a miniature scale of the bowl making technique. Wetted and pasted strips are wrapped around either a tin (for bangles) or a crochet hook or knitting needle (for beads). They are squeezed to get rid of excess moisture. With the bangle, leave it dry while still around the tin; in a warm place. Once it is dry, ease off the tin, sand smooth and then layer with tissue paper to the required thickness. The beads are shaped by squeezing with the fingers, firstly while on the hook or needle, then while loose. If speed is important, they should be baked in an oven, lightly sanded, then lacquered. Lacquering is done most easily by threading the beads on a string then dipping into a cup of lacquer. Coloured nail varnishes and enamel paints are alternatives for producing lively, colourful results.

Whether it is a papier mâché model of an enormous ginger cat; or the bangles just described; smoothing, painting and varnishing will help to make an inanimate object spring to life. The important things to remember are:

1. Make sure the model is completely dry.
2. Smooth off the surfaces of the model completely with sandpaper.
3. Undercoat models with white emulsion paint.
4. The choice of top coat paint depends a bit on the cost of the paint, size of the model, etc.. With small models, enamel paint and lacquer are good mediums. Big models are more cheaply covered with poster paints and then lacquered as necessary
5. Nail varnish is good as a paint cover on small jewellery items made with papier mâché.

PEBBLE POLISHING

With a simple tumble-polisher machine (under £50) you can make good quality pebble jewellery similar to that found in many tourist shops in sunny Scotland! Pebbles are easily collected from beaches and this can provide a useful focus for an expedition or trip to the seaside. Avoid collecting sandstone, flaky shale, slate or pitted or cracked pebbles. You'll find that there are at least three grade of pebbles – soft, medium and hard. At some point these have to be separated out, as they cannot be tumbled together. It is possibly best to do the sorting back at base. Don't spend too much time trying to spot attractive pebbles on the beach – often dull, uninteresting pebbles will polish much better anyway. Try to collect a range of different shapes of between a quarter and a half an inch; this helps the grinding process as the small stones grind into the hollows of the larger ones. Remember too that beaches yield lots of other interesting items for a scrapbox – shells, for example, or small weathered pieces of wood which can be mounted to create abstract sculpture.

Apart from a tumbler and pebbles, you'll need grinding grit (silicon carbide), polishing powder (cerium oxide or tin oxide), jewellery findings, (e.g. bell caps for necklaces, ready-made brooches and rings, neck chains or leather thongs, jump rings) and a small penknife and steel file to test the hard pebble. If it can't be scratched by knife or file, it's a hard pebble. If the only the steel file scratches it – medium. If the knife does then it's soft. Manchester Minerals and Specialist Crafts supply 'Rough Rock' packs in 1 to 1½ lb quantities of either agate or quartz stones. These are pre-sorted for size and hardness, which is useful for beginners to lapidary (the posh name for this type of gemstone craft)!

Grinding and Polishing

Hard pebbles will polish up the best. Manchest Minerals stock a range of tumblers up to industrial sizes. Specialist Crafts offer a good basic machine. Follow the tumbler manufacturer's recommendations regarding the kind of grinding grit to use, but if in doubt, start off with No. 80 Silicon Carbide grit. For a small (1½ lb barrel) tumbler you'll need about 100 pebbles and a heaped tablespoon of grit. Double check the pebbles to make sure that none of them is pitted or cracked and load them into the barrel until it is almost three-quarters full. Shake the barrel to settle the pebbles and sprinkle the grit over them. Now add water until it just covers the pebbles and put the lid on, making sure that it makes a good seal. (For example, no grit trapped under the lid). Wipe the barrel to check for leaks. Place it on the tumbler and switch on the motor.

The tumbler will create some noise in use so it should be sited where it will cause minimum disturbance. Every 24 hours the motor should be switched off, the barrel removed and the pebbles checked. This is necessary to release any gases that may have formed and to see how the pebbles are progressing. Wash a few of them and examine – they should feel noticeably smoother. Now replace them and switch on again. It will take between three and six days for hard pebbles to be ground reasonably smooth. Once this stage has been reached the pebbles can be removed and washed in a colander. The waste in the barrel should be thrown away into a dustbin as it blocks sinks easily, and the barrel itself should be washed out.

Before the next stage begins, any pebble that is blemished, pitted or cracked, should be set aside (reasonable specimens can be added to the next batch of pebbles to be coarse ground). Repeat the operation as for coarse grinding, but this time using a fine grit. After five or six days the pebbles should be ready for polishing and should look smooth, lacking only the final shine. After washing, you can test for readiness by rubbing one for a few minutes with polish and a smooth felt cloth. If you can spot any pinpricks or cracks, you will have to continue with the fine grind.

The pebbles should be handled very carefully at this stage and returned to the clean barrel. After sprinkling on the correct amount of polishing powder, the pebbles should be just covered with water, and the tumbler switched on. If it sounds like the pebbles are tumbling unevenly, a small amount of wallpaper paste can be added to promote smoother running. Again, inspect the barrel daily – the polishing stage is complete when there is no improvement on the previous day's progress and the pebbles look just as shiny dry as they do wet.

It will be abundantly clear from the above, to the critical reader, (i.e. harassed youth worker) that tumble polishing is a very time consuming process. However, the time spent working with the equipment is minimal, a daily check usually being all that is necessary. The craft has obvious possibilities for groups that only meet once a week – the tumbler can be left to do most of the work between sessions and with any luck each stage will be completed within a week.

When the polished pebbles are ready they can be easily made into attractive pieces of jewellery using Araldite, Epoxy Resin or Superglue adhesive and jewellers' findings. Exercising the imagination can produce other ideas, for example, they can be used to decorate various boxes or to embellish a key ring or fob. Making a bead curtain might just be feasible and we have seen polished pebbles used to make a 'gem tree' (using silver coloured wire and small metal leaves available from craft shops).

PHOTOGRAPHY

This is an activity which, over a period of time, **all** youth groups will have engaged in to some extent. Whether it is a quick snap, or a studied portrait, there is something magical about the photographic process. A myth, however, seems to have grown up around photography; a myth which implies that photography is a complicated operation. We **are** confident that it is a myth because we have both made extensive use of photography in our work with youth groups. It is a flexible activity since it can be used:

- to record youth group activities;
- as a 'one-off' session;
- as a preparation for a week(end) away or residential experience;
- as a planned course in photography.

In this section we would like to offer examples for photography sessions suitable for any of the above contexts. Before that, we would like to offer a few comments on the basic equipment you may require, given different types of groups, ages, etc..

The equipment

In 'one-off' sessions, we have worked with both cameras and black and white darkroom equipment. The same applies to a planned course, of say, six two-hour sessions. With the holiday outing or trip to a particular event, the camera alone will probably suffice as the 'equipment', unless you are considering its use as an introduction to photography. In this case, it is likely that you will avail yourself of the cheap colour printing service which (at the latest price, 1996) will cost anything between about £3.00 and £8.00 for developing and printing 36 colour prints. With the cost of the film, this can give a print cost of less than 20 pence. We have found the Radio Times Film Service pretty reliable, PO Box 5, Eastleigh,

Hants SO53 3XW. At the time of writing in March 1996, their 27 exposure Agfa colour print film costs £2.75 including 5 x 3½ inch prints.

With most youth groups who have not been let loose on cameras previously, it is best to get them to use a simple but versatile viewfinder camera such as the Olympus range, which usually have automatic metering. (This bit of technical phraseology means that it corrects the amount of light entering the lens to suit the conditions). Many cheaper viewfinder cameras have too great a capacity for producing blurred images. The reason for this is twofold. The lenses used will not focus on subjects much closer than six feet and the shutter speed is fixed – but at a speed too slow to prevent user shakes. Finally, the lens is made of cheap plastic instead of optical glass, and even the pressure on the shutter release button may cause blurring! So, beware the cheap pocket camera unless you have tested it and found it satisfactory! One we have tried, and that is not bad for the money is the Halina Panoramic. It wouldn't win any photographic awards, but its format, producing super wide angle prints, is both fun and especially useful for sweeping land and seascapes.

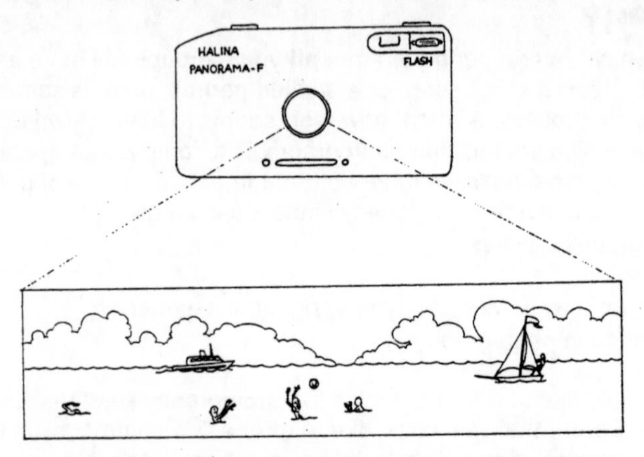

For universality, make sure that the camera you are using is a 35 mm. This is the size of the film. It is the easiest size for processing and is now the standard for much amateur and professional work. The 110 size is awkward and disc film impossible if you are working with domestic darkroom equipment. 120 roll film can produce superb results, but it is more expensive, and it is harder to work with when developing.

For youngsters who are gong to be shown basic camera techniques, you will need a camera with interchangeable lenses. It is best to stick to 35 mm format. Your local camera shop may be willing to do 'deals'. This might include the provision of good second-hand equipment. Cameras have come down in price in the past 25 years. In 'real' terms this means that a good quality single lens reflex (SLR) camera (one where you view the subject directly through the lens) will now cost less than a tenth, in real terms, of a similar camera in 1970. Many reputable makes of SLR exist. Nikon, Pentax, Minolta, Mamiya, Canon and Olympus are all worth looking at, and these firms provide cameras with both manual and automatic functioning for under £150. For teaching purposes, it is ideal if you have available a wide angle and a telephoto, or equivalent zoom lens to fit the SLR camera body. The need for extra lenses comes as a matter of teaching necessity.

In the darkroom you will need printing paper (basic, is grade 2 Ilfospeed glossy or equivalent), different developer for prints and negatives, and fixer (Hypam or equivalent).

Jessops of Leicester are very competitive and their own brand materials are good quality. They also offer an efficient mail order service for nearly anything you'll need, including the equipment listed below:

1 x double spiral 35 mm developing tank
1 x measuring cylinder
1 x thermometer (photographic range)
1 x force washing rubber tube
1 x enlarger, and spare bulb
1 x safelight and spare bulb
3 x chemical trays
3 x pairs of print tongs
1 x rubber tongs.

In the darkroom, or close by, you will also need a washing line with plastic clothes pegs to hang prints and negatives from, and a sink with a plug and overflow, in which to wash prints.

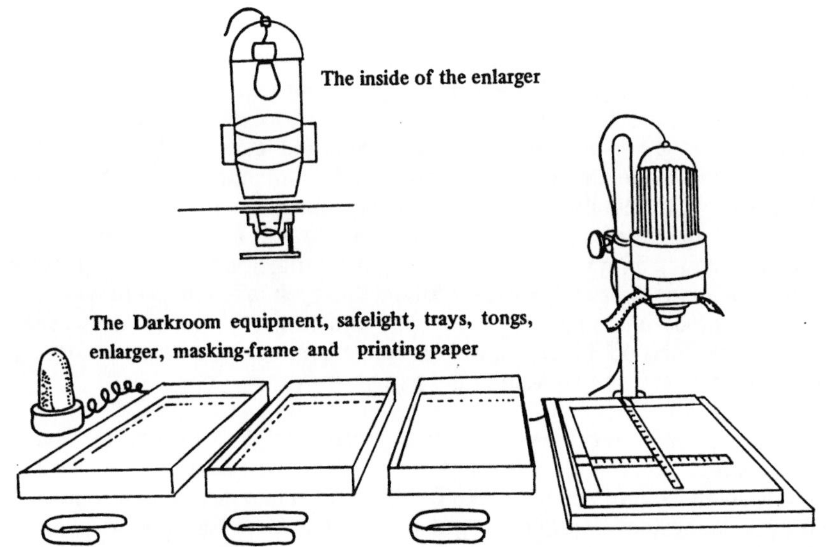
The inside of the enlarger

The Darkroom equipment, safelight, trays, tongs, enlarger, masking-frame and printing paper

A 'One-off' photographic experience

Imagine the standard issue school building, social work department or youth/community centre. Perhaps it is not a pretty 'imagining', but there are some small compensations. Among them are the availability of space for a makeshift darkroom. You need transport to get you and most of the equipment listed in the equipment section to your place of meeting. The Zenith enlarger is useful, in that it is a suitcase design, which can be moved to any site. Before offering your services, check that:

- There is a completely dark room, with enough space in which to erect one long table, or ideally two smaller, rigid surfaces.
- There is access to electric power in this room.
- The use of a sink with water supply and overflow is available, in or near the 'darkroom'.

Having ascertained that the above potentially exists, you can establish a temporary darkroom in a matter of a quarter of an hour. Do this **before** you are due to meet your

group. The only additional equipment needed for the session, are the following:
Camera(s); film – Black and White FP4 (for example); a hair-drier.

So, there you are perhaps, with an unfamiliar youth group, introduced as the 'photography expert'. All it requires is a fair degree of practice to ensure that you have the skills which give you, as the self-styled, 'flying' photography teacher, a bit of self-confidence.

Exactly how to do much of what is explained in this section is included in the section on a planned photography course. What is detailed here is a fun experience, geared to proving that photography is neither an inordinately long process or a complicated one. Try it with a group of about five. It can also be used as 'session one' with adults or youth groups who have come to do photography in eight (approximately) two-hour chunks. The exercise requires at least one-and-a-quarter hours and preferably two hours. As the group arrives, take their photos. This will probably be using flash. Introduce yourself alongside this and pass the camera around.

The 'how' a camera works should be subordinated to pre-setting the camera and getting the youngsters to feel and use the equipment. With the Olympus camera, or similar, this is a quick and painless exercise. We have also used a camera on a tripod with a cable-release attached on a 'blower' set-up. This allows for group members to take photos of themselves. Shooting a 36 exposure film in this manner will take about ten minutes to a quarter of an hour. At this point, you disappear into the darkroom and load the film into the tank, or you can use a purpose made changing bag, and load the film in a normal room. That **should** take about one to two minutes. Having previously mixed the developer/stop bath solution (if used) and fixer (all at the correct dilutions and temperature), process the film and wash it, explaining the stages of the process. This will take a maximum of fifteen minutes, if using a high concentration of fixer and a force-washer. You then take the roll of negatives from the tank, show the group and gently dry them with rubber tongs. Finally, for this stage, you hang up the film, and speed up the drying with the expedient use of a hair-drier, trying not to blow too much dust onto the soft surface of the film.

After half an hour you have a dry film. Cut it into lengths of six exposures, and explain the use of the enlarger and the three trays of chemicals in the darkroom. As is likely, the darkroom is small, so perhaps only take two or three youngsters in at a time. You can operate a shuttle system, where each youngster chooses two or three negatives which they would like a print of. They can then use the enlarger to print them. Again, it's quick and easy. If you are working well, it takes about one-and-a-half minutes, or two minutes per print, and even faster if you are stream feeding two or three prints through the chemical trays. Using Ilfospeed, resin-coated paper, only a short, three or four minute wash is required, before the paper can be hung up to dry. Drying takes approximately half an hour, but this can be reduced to three minutes or less, with a quick wave of the trusty hair-drier! In all, you can get a group of five or six youngsters each with two or three photos to take home in a very short period of time. If well handled, the group will be able to have a good shared experience, and prints which they can take away. All in the space of between an hour-and-a-half and two hours.

Using the camera – preparation for the group event or trip away

Some technical aspects of the camera need not concern youngsters. Others can be simply explained. Often, photography is treated as though the information is especially complicated. It is **not**. Even when showing twelve and thirteen year olds the basic workings of an SLR 35 mm camera, simple examples can make the process an easy one. In explaining how to take photos, it is mostly practice which determines an individual's ability to 'compose' a good photo. Getting a photo which is in focus and correctly exposed relies on simple rules which can be learned. The tips we use in explaining 'how a camera works' run roughly as follows:

SHUTTER SPEED. What are you trying to photograph? If the subject or you are moving, you require a faster shutter speed to freeze the action. An SLR or any other camera can be held at 1/60th of a second, but it is safer to use 1/125th of a second to prevent camera shake. To stop the movement of people walking, 1/125th is usually enough. For cars and people running, 1/250 - 1/1000th of a second should be used. A useful bit of information regarding camera angle: if you shoot 'head-on' with the subject coming towards you, this slows down the movement. Taking photos from the side if they are very fast-moving, for instance, in a motor-cycle race, is difficult unless your camera has a very fast shutter speed. If you want to take a shot from the side, use the 'panning' technique. This entails moving the camera in the direction the subject is travelling, keeping the subject in the viewfinder. The shutter speed should be fast enough, say 1/250th of a second, to stop blur from your movement. The panning should then stop the movement of the subject. The end product will be a shot of the subject in sharp relief with a blurred background – that's how so many sports photos convey a sense of action and movement!

APERTURE. This is the device which allows the user of a camera to restrict or increase the amount of light passing through the lens. Because of the calibration in f-numbers and the name 'aperture', many youngsters' eyes glaze over when you try to explain its use. As in the next diagram, each change in aperture allows exactly half or double the amount of light to pass through the lens as its neighbour. The 'f' numbers underneath or above the lens are the standard scale on all cameras. The largest numbers give the smallest amount of light exposure; the small numbers allow in the greatest amount of light.

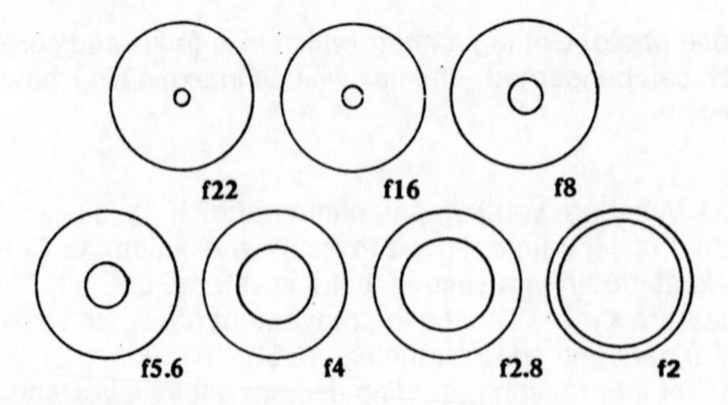

Depth of field and composition
The balance between the amount of light allowed in to hit the sensitive surface of the film by the shutter speed, and that allowed in by the aperture control, give the total **EXPOSURE,** i.e. the amount of light forming the image.

The reason you wish to alter the aperture in taking photos is to alter the **DEPTH OF FIELD** in a photo. Depth of field is basically another way of describing the amount of the photo which is going to be in focus. How this works, we have found is best explained (especially with kids) in two stages. First, remind youngsters of a simple experiment which they have probably tried on themselves as young children. It works particularly well with those who wear glasses normally. Taking off any glasses, clench a hand, making a small pinhole space through the fingers. Look through this. The world should appear a sharper place to see! This can help explain how you use aperture controls. As a rule, the smaller the hole, the sharper (more in focus) the image. With SLR cameras, the lens can be detached from the body of the camera, so that you can show youngsters the effect of opening and closing the aperture control. (If your camera has an automatic switch, make sure that it is in the manual position, otherwise the demonstration will not work).

The actual depth of field is related to the distance away from the subject and the type of lens you use. Briefly, the longer the lens - standard is about 50 mm - the less depth of field is available to the user. Therefore, a wide angle lens, say 28 mm, will offer the greatest depth of field. In the diagram below the depth of field is charted, using different apertures. When explaining this subject, remember that there is a greater depth **beyond** the subject than in front of it.

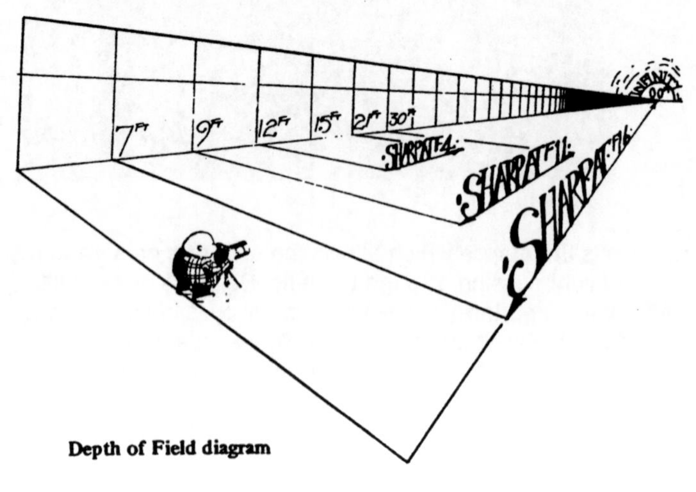

Depth of Field diagram

The use of an exposure meter, either in-built to the camera, or used separately is a great aid. You should be able to use the information on speed and aperture as a guide to settings. Basically, the film speed is set on the meter, then the meter is aimed at the subject. (Close metering – taking the meter to the subject is recommended for accurate readings). A range of options which will each give the same overall exposure are then obtained. The choice you or your group make should be based on **(1) the nature of the subject**, and **(2) the type of photography you wish to obtain**. This second variable brings one on to questions about composition. Finishing the subject – depth of field – it is useful to experiment with different apertures to achieve very different pictures. For example, using f16, the picture will generally all be in focus, useful for landscapes and large groups etc.. At f2 the background can be thrown completely out of focus, giving a photograph which centres attention on an individual or object. Two very different end products from the same vantage point!

Taking youngsters back into their murky pasts of art lessons may remind them that **COMPOSITION** has a number of important elements. Some worth considering are:

- The overall **shape** of the object. Is it interesting? Avoid rows of objects, and images where one part of the subject becomes muddled with another. Triangular shapes are one powerful option.
- **Tone and texture.** This is important, if you wish to photograph natural scenes, trees, the sea, etc..
- **Size.** Too many photographs are taken of ant-like people in the middle distance. Most cameras will focus as close as five feet. Some can be used as close as two feet from the subject. Think big, it gives interesting, vivid results.
- **Lighting.** The beginning and the end of the day produce the most interesting natural lighting and strong images. Noon, despite the intensity of light, produces generally bleached results which are flat and lacking in any dynamism.

The use of different lenses and filters can offer a range of unusual results, many of which add a very professional element to the work.

Planning a photography course

Through experience, we have found that it is best to have prepared a fairly comprehensive set of notes on using camera equipment, a darkroom and the related issues of composition, lighting etc.. Use as many illustrations as possible and try to strike a balance between 'doing' and 'explaining'. Your ability to take good photos will not be enough, unless you can actually teach in a simple way, which makes photography come alive. Try, if possible to avoid too much 'classroom teaching'.

Because of the time-consuming nature of colour darkroom work and the fumes, and type of chemicals used, we have based the considerable darkroom emphasis of courses on black and white photography. When talking about the taking of photos, both out of doors and indoors, some of the requirements of using colour can be introduced. The use of cheap processing for colour prints has now made it much cheaper to have colour prints commercially processed than home producing black and white pictures. It's all to do with the economics of large scale production.

The rest of this section is intended to fill the gaps about photography which we would wish to see plugged. Our emphasis in planning a sequence with kids is to give them a range of photographic experiences. The sort of balance we might be suggesting would be:

- Introductory, 'Instant Photography Session' as described.
- Two Outdoor Sessions, for instance on a beach and at a motorcycle meeting.

- One Indoor Session using flash and photoflood lighting.
- Two or three Darkroom Sessions.

Photo tips

Before launching into an explanation of how to use a darkroom imaginatively, here are a few tips from our experience.

BULK FILM. If you buy a canister of 30 metres of black and white film, it saves a lot of money over purchasing individual films. To load films into empty 35 mm cartridges, you can either use a bulk loader, or it can be cut into length in a **totally** dark room and then taped onto the inner spool of the cartridge. It's especially useful if you want to use a short length of film and do not want to waste the remainder.

CAMERA METERS. Using the meters on many cameras today offers aperture or speed priority. These terms indicate that you select either speed or aperture and the camera then automatically adjust the other variable to the correct light setting. Many cameras have a needle which reacts to both variables being adjusted, and the user makes the best compromise to suit the subject being photographed.

LOADING THE DEVELOPING TANK. If youngsters are going to develop their own film, practice sessions feeding a piece of useless, exposed film into the tank spiral in total darkness are necessary. When finishing a film in a camera, try to rewind it back into the cassette, leaving the end tab of the film showing. Then, prior to loading, take the tab, pull it and cut off the narrow section. The first one and a half inches or thereabouts of film are already exposed, so you can safely thread this section onto the spiral before finishing the threading process in total darkness.

DIFFERENT LENSES. If money or available resources permit, the use of different lenses gives greater flexibility. The next diagrams help to explain the different sort of results you can expect from using different size lenses:

50mm

35mm

200mm

500mm

20mm

FILM SPEED. For most purposes the film speed required will be in the 100-200 ASA range. A slow speed of film indicates that the silver oxide coating of the film is very slow to react to light, therefore it is unsuitable for use in poor light conditions. It does give very high quality prints. A slow speed is about 50 ASA. Medium speed film, which we recommend using (100-200 ASA) is good for most situations and will produce good results up to about 10 x 8 inch size. Fast film, in the region of 400 ASA, is essential for use in poor light conditions, or where high grain effect is required. It is useful for shooting fast moving subjects. The quality of film coatings have progressively improved and some fast film is now almost as good as slow or medium speed film was ten years ago.

PAPERS. Printing paper is available in a variety of grades, depending upon the manufacturer's scale. The lowest numbers offer the least contrast. Higher contrast is obtained by using the harder paper. This sort of paper is particularly useful when negatives are very grey coloured overall. A short exposure coupled with hard paper will normally give a balanced print. With resin-coated papers, the surface to which the print eventually dries can be chosen in advance. Glossy is the best high-quality surface; matt and semi-matt are popular for exhibition work where reflections can ruin the impact of a strong image. Grade 3 Ilfospeed glossy or Jessop's grade 2, are good all-round papers for use in the darkroom. The size of paper you choose depends on the use to which it is to be put and the cost. You may need a couple of boxes of different size (and grade, perhaps) paper.

FILTERS. Below is a chart of filter effects on different colours using black and white film. Filters are especially useful to heighten the effects of clouds, seascapes, etc.. In contre-jour shots (into the sun) filters can accentuate the silhouette. The use of filters restricts the amount of light entering the lens and this must be compensated for by allowing a greater exposure.

	RED	BLUE	GREEN
FILTER			
RED	LIGHT	DARK	LIGHT
GREEN	DARK	DARK	LIGHT
BLUE	DARK	LIGHT	DARK
YELLOW	LIGHT	DARK	SAME

A contre-jour design!

USE OF LIGHTING. In the course of a series of lessons, you may, if you have the equipment, wish to consider using both flash and photo-floodlighting with the group. Photoflood bulbs are expensive and do not last very long. However, they give the opportunity for planning the effect of lighting on subjects, i.e., lighting from one source at the side, underneath, behind, above. This sort of lighting is useful with the extension-release system. A flash guide to aperture settings is usually situated on the side of most flashguns. This will give an indication as to the aperture setting to be used at various distances. If there is powerful available lighting, decrease the aperture; if it is dark, or the room in which the photo is to be taken is large, increase the amount of light by opening the iris of the aperture. (smaller f-number).

IN THE DARKROOM. Producing prints is a perfect example of being able to give kids' groups almost immediate gratification. It takes a few sessions before kids are confident enough in their use of the enlarger and the chemicals to be left alone. Therefore, make sure that you are supervising, otherwise you will be confronted by large wastage of printing paper. Ideally, you will have a timer to estimate exposure times. If you don't, like us, count: "one hundred - one hundred and one - one hundred and two- etc.," to give an indication of the number of seconds an exposure lasts.

In the enlarger, there is a negative carriage. The negative strip, usually of six frames, should be placed in the carrier with the image upside down, glossy side up. Most enlargers have a red filter which allows for positioning printing paper under the image while the light is on. You can use a frame which keeps the paper flat and gives a white border to prints. However, this is not really necessary as modern printing papers lays pretty flat on the base board of the enlarger. Getting the exposure time right is a matter of practice, which can be aided by the use of a test strip.

Use of the strip allows for experimentation, without undue paper wastage. You slide a sheet of paper over the strip of paper progressively every two seconds, so you end up with a sample of exposures of different lengths. Because of the way the lens aperture works, giving greater depth of field with a closing of the iris, it is obvious that there is more chance of obtaining a distinct image with the use of a closed down aperture. For normal use, close down about two stops from the fully open position.

The instruction for mixing chemicals both for developing and printing films are given on individual bottles. The temperature is more critical on developing films and the times should be adhered to as closely as possible. For printing, the first tray contains developer, the second tray in the sequence contains stop solution. If it is not available, ordinary water can be used, but it will only wash the developer off, it will not halt the development process. As mentioned earlier in this section, we advocate a strong solution of fixer, to speed up the process to approximately 30 seconds duration. The diluted fixer can be stored in an air-tight bottle. The use of a different pair of tongs/forceps is recommended for each tray.

OTHER TECHNIQUES. Given that producing quick photos of self and friends is fun, there will not be too much boredom in the darkroom. Having said that, there are a couple of other quick techniques which we have successfully employed with youth groups.

THE PHOTOGRAM. This is a form of simple black and white image, which can be assembled in the darkroom. Instead of projecting light through a negative, the paper is placed on a flat surface and objects are placed on top of the printing paper. This is done under a red safe light. When solid objects are on the paper they will leave a negative image on the paper. This means that white images (shapes) appear on the paper, surrounded in black after development. More varied prints can be obtained by using objects such as combs and leaves, which are translucent. Items such as feathers will leave an image which displays texture. A combination of negatives, coins, petals, leaves, screws, keys, combs, etc., can produce a very unusual photogram.

SCREENS. Enlargements can be made through some sort of screen, if a special, textured print quality is desired. Rather like using different grades of paper, i.e., grade 0, to achieve special soft and subtle effects and Grade 6 to lose halftones (the greys), the use of screens can add or detract from the contrast of a subject. Mostly, they will add texture. Screens can be bought in negative form. These are used in conjunction with the negative. Extra printing time is required, but the texture can be worth the wait. Ranging from 'stucco'; 'old master' to 'dot' screens and 'concentric circles', the right screen has to be chosen to suit the characteristics of particular photos. With old tights, tacked to a frame or muslin, etc., and the frame placed in contact with the print paper, screens can be used without the expense of using the commercial items.

Into the future

In the professional photography arena, there is now a generation of digital cameras which do away with the need for film altogether. Pictures can be viewed on computer or TV screens and prints obtained from high quality laser printers. Whether this will become the 'norm' for photography in the next few years is still open to speculation. A competitor, the film based APS-Advanced Photo System, is aimed at the amateur field. The cartridge fits only specially made cameras, and loads automatically, with the film retracting back into the cartridge after use. There are no negatives to handle – reprints are ordered from an index print of the miniature negatives retained inside the film cartridge. The main advantage of the system is that it offers three different print formats: a standard print similar to 35 mm; a panoramic view 10 x 3½ inches, and an in between size of 6½ x 3½ inches. The small size of negative makes the print quality poorer than with 35 mm film, but the format will also be compatible with the digital transfer system of the future. However, it does mean that for youth groups it could make the darkroom redundant, perhaps to be replaced by the computer on screen edit programme!

PUPPETS

Where drama and acting can be intimidating to many children, puppetry is much more like 'play' and 'fantasy'. The characters and the plots are only limited by imagination, but, and it is a big BUT, there is a lot of preparation behind any sort of puppet show. Making puppets, inventing characters and then learning to manipulate them is all part of the fun. Individual youngsters will make their own decisions as to whether they are natural puppet makers or performers; still others may enjoy preparing scenery and props for the show. The adult(s) involved should encourage young people to participate and try on the different roles, and generally act as facilitator to ensure that planning and preparation will turn a puppet performance into a success.

As far as this section is concerned, we are assuming that making puppets will be a major part of the activity. However, you may also wish to buy ready-made puppets. Large toy shops such as Hamleys in London's Regent Street have a good range to choose from. NES Arnold offer an imaginative range of finger and glove puppets, including a selection of 'family' puppets covering different racial and occupational groups and a variety of animals. Galt offer a nice range in their 'Imaginative play' section, including some nice 'creepy crawlie' hand puppets and purpose built puppet theatre. Specialist Crafts sell basic marionette figures. We particularly liked the Igel hand puppet range from Germany which are available from the Big Top in Glasgow. (see Suppliers' Section).

Glove puppets

So called because they are made to slip over the hand like a glove, enabling the fingers to operate the puppet. They are much easier to make and manipulate than the marionette type (which is operated by an arrangement of strings from a control bar). An almost infinite variety of glove puppets are simply made using materials that you can probably purloin from your Dressing Up and Scrap Boxes. Even if you have to buy materials, you won't be much out of pocket.

The message with glove puppets, is simply to think of a character and then make it, no matter how improbable! Frankenstein, Miss Piggy, Batman, Power Rangers, favourite School Teachers – all are possible, and just as easy to make as the social worker puppet we saw being so lovingly (!) fashioned in one Intermediate Treatment Centre. Needless to say, this particular artefact was put to great therapeutic use in ventilating repressed feelings about the social work/client system, particularly as it affects the teenager in the deprived urban context (and if you believe that you'll believe anything!).

Simple Puppets

Very simple glove puppets can be made quickly and easily, and are especially suited to younger groups. The basic material could be a sock, ping-pong ball or old glove which is decorated with wool, buttons, sequins, etc., to make a face.

Alternatively, simple rod puppets can be made by drawing and painting characters on pieces of card, which are then pinned on to doweling or garden canes. A sleeve puppet can easily be made, adding simple materials to a shirt or pullover sleeve. It is easy to adapt this method to arrange for a moving mouth. The sleeve puppet can be used as it is in a 'Punch and Judy' type show with the body (supposedly) out of the audience's line of sight. If you wish though, you can add a stuffed body and legs to the sleeve.

Heads

Puppet heads can be made in many different ways, one of the simplest being to use an old (but clean) sock or stocking. This is stuffed to give it shape with an old tennis ball, foam rubber chips, or fabric. Cut off the sock at the heel and tie securely before gluing it to a conical tube (made out of cardboard, for example). This serves as the neck, and also provides a hole for the operator's fingers.

The basic head shape can also be made out of foam rubber by gluing it around a cardboard tube, and adding on shaped pieces of foam to provide features. This basic shape can be covered with material (or an old sock or stocking) before being decorated.

Large head shapes (e.g. for animals) can be formed by making a cardboard 'skeleton'. Do this by cutting out a cardboard profile of the head and then gluing or slotting on ribs. More cardboard glued between the ribs will strengthen the skeleton which can now be encased with layers of thin card. If you're clever you can form the neck (and space for the operator's fingers) at this stage, but it can just as easily be glued on at the end. Finish off by covering with cloth, fur or a thin coating of plastic wood.

Fabric covered heads can be made to vaguely resemble inhabitants of the humanoid or animal species by decorating them with buttons or sequins for eyes, wool for hair, material or cardboard for hats, etc..

Large human-type heads can be modelled from polystyrene or softwood. Use a coping saw or rasp to cut the basic shape out of polystyrene and carve fine details with a craft knife. The head should now be covered by gluing on small pieces of paper or newsprint. This adds strength, provides a final opportunity for modelling and renders the head suitable for painting. It should be covered with a final coat of glue (use woodwork adhesive, as most others will dissolve polystyrene) and sanded down. The neck can be hollowed out and strengthened in a similar way, adding a cardboard extension if necessary. Egg boxes can also be adapted to make good heads, with the hinge acting as the back of the head. By punching holes in the hinge area, the operator can open and close the mouth.

Bodies

A simple glove puppet body can be made up by sewing or gluing two shaped pieces of material together. What you are making, in effect, is an elbow length glove; this should be loose fitting, especially if it is to be used by more than one person. Depending on the kind of puppet you are making, you can include arms and hands in the cut out shapes, making sure that there is enough space for the operator's thumb and finger. This gives you a basic glove which can be glued to the head and neck. The puppet is almost complete now, needing only to be dressed and have legs added. You can use slim cardboard tubes for the legs but more permanent ones can be made by firmly stuffing tubes made of fabric with foam chips and sewing or gluing them to the glove. The puppet can be dressed by gluing appropriate bits of fabric to the glove or by making up loose fitting clothes to suit.

Animal bodies can be made by decorating the glove to suit (with fur fabric for example) or by making a stuffed animal body that is sewn to the glove so that it rests on the wrist and forearm. The cardboard method of making an animal head, mentioned above, can be adapted to make complete large bodied animals like alligators, whales, hippos, etc.. If you are using this method remember to fashion a hole in the underside for the operator's hand. A small spar of wood should be fitted into the hole for the hand to grasp, as this makes it much easier to manipulate.

Using the puppets

Glove puppets are ideal for a Punch and Judy type show, although the puppets that your kids have created may well be more suited to titles like 'Sid Snot's Ravers' or 'The Merry Mutants' Dance'. Although dialogue can be improvised, it is best to at least get the main story lines of the show committed to paper. Use of the story board technique can help a lot here (see Video Section), and you may even want to make a film of your show. The young people you work with may have strong ideas about the characters of the puppets they have made. This can help in working out a storyline. So, for instance, a robot and a dog might be marooned on an alien planet after their spaceship crashes.

The physical requirements necessary to put on the show are easy to arrange. A cloth draped over the front of a table will, at the same time, give you a playing surface for the puppets and hide the operator's legs. A good backdrop simplifies the whole undertaking as it means that the operators can sit in relative comfort while manipulating the puppets. The backdrop should ideally be supported on stand, a washing-line type arrangement, or hung from the ceiling or wall. During the show, you may want to change the scenery a number of times, as in a theatrical production. Once again, planning and preparation count a lot towards accomplishing a professional puppet show.

You can have as many puppets (and operators) as you can fit into your play area, remembering that it is possible for one operator to manipulate two puppets. All that remains now is to do some quick coaching to perfect puppet-type voices. Depending on whether or not your show would be rated a U, PG, 15 or 18, certificate, you may want to try taking it on tour to local old folk's homes, nursery schools etc..

QUESTIONNAIRES

The name conjures up rather unfortunate images of hours of laborious form filling, but in practice a well designed questionnaire can be the basis for a fun activity. Really! In addition, the nature of questionnaires is close enough to the range of available puzzle books to make the task of filling one in an enjoyable, rather than daunting, experience. To start with, any adult working with a group of youngsters should have an identified aim for using a questionnaire. Is it:

- to obtain information about an individual (or group) and their attitudes?
- to introduce a particular theme, issue or activity to a group?

In the first instance, the questionnaire format can be introduced by using a non-challenging version (see below). Since children generally like talking about themselves, this can be a tool which is easy to use. Why not try a questionnaire in the form of the old, star pen profiles, much loved by the teen pop papers of the 1950s right through to the 1990s. These run along the lines of:

Name	*Town*
Colour of eyes	*Colour of Hair*
Favourite Colour	*Favourite Popstar*
Favourite Food & Drink	*Dislikes*
What work you would like to do when you're older	*Favourite animal*
	Sport you are best at.

The variations are limitless and it is a relaxed sort of enterprise, without the overtones of prying too deeply. For a starter, you (as the adult) could duplicate/photocopy a sample sheet. If the group get into the exercise, they should be able to design their own forms. A little gentle control may be necessary to prevent people designing forms and questions which are too threatening or awkward for their friends to fill in. For instance, some youngsters may find the question, 'which of your friends do you like most' too intimidating. With adolescent groups, this sort of questionnaire can include questions about boy/girl friends, stars you would most like to go out with, etc.. It's not very far removed from an old commercial game called 'Tell Me', which had a spinner which gave the participant a letter and they then had to say the name of a famous actor, tree, animal, etc..

Questionnaires can be used to either assess what activities young people may wish to involve themselves in, or to introduce a specific subject to a group. As with the previous activity, it is imperative that an adult, or two, get involved in the activity, rather than using it as some sort of package which can be given to a group to keep them quiet. Really engaging with young people in this kind of process can be a revelation in gaining insight to their lifestyles, attitudes and aspirations. Youth workers, through a youth council perhaps, can use questionnaires in a variety of ways. It might be a list of alternatives for a night out in the mini-bus; it could be related to the provision of facilities in the community. The 'Rights Questionnaire' shown below has been revised by Bob Stead of Lothian Region's Welfare Rights team. It is based on a questionnaire used by the Pilton Youth Programme in the 1980s.

Rights Questionnaire

1. A policeman asks you to empty your pockets. Do you say:

a) Bugger off.
b) Do you have a warrant?
c) Why?

d) You've no right.
e) Say nothing and obey.

2. If searched would you allow:

a) Examination of your clothes.
b) Taking of a blood sample.
c) Taking of your fingerprints.

3. A policeman knocks on your door and arrests you. Would you:

a) Allow a search of the house without warrant.
b) Insist on a warrant.
c) Step out and close the door.

4. Police can question:

a) Suspicious persons only.
b) Witnesses only.
c) Both A and B.
d) Anybody.

5. When questioned you:

a) Must answer.
b) Must stay and listen.
c) May walk out without listening.

6. If arrested you:

a) Must answer questions.
b) Must stay in the police station.
c) Must make a statement.
d) Must agree to a search, etc..

7. While in custody you have the right:

a) To see a solicitor.
b) To visits (parents).
c) To be cautioned or charged.
d) To telephone a solicitor.
e) To bail.

8. Police have right of search for:

a) Prohibited drugs.
b) Firearms.
c) Eggs of protected birds.
d) Papers relating to terrorism.
e) Evo-stick.

9. Police could class as an offensive weapon, a:

a) Knife.
b) Penny.
c) Broken bottle.
d) Cosh.
e) Spanner.
f) Contraceptive.

Rights Questionnaire (Answers)

Question 1
The police have the power to search you if they believe you are carrying an offensive weapon or any of the following: drugs, firearms, stolen goods, birds' eggs, or anything connected with terrorism. They therefore have the right to search you for many reasons, but you can still ask why. You should only be searched by someone of your own sex. Just remember that the police have a lot more power than you have, and that you won't do yourself any favours by being rude or cheeky.

Question 2
If the police want to do more than just search you, they'll probably want you to 'go to the station' with them. In this case you can either be arrested, detained (for up to six hours), or you could go of your own free will. If you go of your own free will, the police may ask you to sign a voluntary certificate as evidence that you were not forced to go. If you are not being arrested or detained you should be free to go whenever you wish, but it may mean that you are kept much longer, as the police might detain you for six hours as soon as you ask to leave. *Ask the police whether they are arresting or detaining you.*

Unless you have been charged you would only need to allow the police to examine your clothes and take your fingerprints. You should not be subjected to any physical examination unless the police have a warrant. If you are proved innocent things like photos and fingerprints should be destroyed.

Question 3
The police do not always need a warrant to arrest you, so you cannot insist they have a warrant, but if you are arrested in your home the police may search for evidence of your guilt with or without a warrant. Ask them why they're searching though, and what they're looking for. The police have the power to enter and search any time of day or night and any day in the week if they have a warrant to search.

Question 4: 'd'

Question 5: 'b'
All that the police can ***demand*** to know is your name and address. If you are under 16, tell the police your age as well, as you have different rights.

Question 6: 'b/d'
You don't have to say or sign anything, but don't be rude or awkward as you'll only make trouble for yourself.

Question 7: 'c/d'
If you have been arrested or detained you should be cautioned (warned that anything you say can be taken down in evidence...) as soon as possible. You have the right to have a message sent to a solicitor and to one other named person. If you are under 16 the police must inform your parents straight away, and you shouldn't be interviewed until they or another adult of the same sex gets there. Once you have been charged, the police can either keep you in custody (in which case they must bring you to court within 24 hours or 48 at weekends), or they can release you on bail. If you are released you will have to sign a pink bail form or agree to appear in court on a certain date. If you don't turn up you could be fined or imprisoned.

Question 8 : All except 'e' as stated in question 1.

Question 9 : All except 'f'

Working with questionnaires

In many cases, young people can be encouraged to design, distribute and analyse the results of questionnaires. These can be particularly useful in the context of social skills and social education work, or to complement another activity. For example, a group investigating the history of their own local area could design a number of questionnaires to suit, e.g. on lifestyles, industry, ghosts, landmark events etc..

Utilising questionnaires in this kind of investigative way is usually a fairly challenging activity, particularly when it involves the need to approach the general public 'cold' in the street. A high degree of planning, confidence and social skill is required to persuade a 'punter' to stop and complete a street questionnaire. In using questionnaires to introduce a subject area to a group, we are pleased to offer examples of forms designed by Simon Jacquet, now of Youth Clubs Scotland, plus lots of bits from Alan and Howie! They were used as part of a loose course on **music**. The sessions involved learning to play instruments, listening to records and going to see live performances.

The purpose of the questionnaires was to broaden out the areas of music which youngsters were prepared to listen to. Records from the 1950s, 1960s and 1970s were played, and Simon himself taught riffs in a variety of music styles. Often, the members of the group, which met at Canongate Youth Project in Edinburgh in the 1980s, could relate the 1950s and 1960s lists to music their parents played at home. As this new version of the Youth Arts and Crafts Book is being published in the 1990s, we have complemented Simon's lists with ones from the 1980s and 1990s.

Perhaps, in all, a marginally devious way of introducing new music to a new generation of young people, but certainly a successful and entertaining way of doing it!

HIT RECORDS OF THE 1950s

Name ....

Here are some of the greatest rock 'n' roll songs of the fifties. Put a (✓) beside your 10 favourite records. If one of your top 10 is not there, add it to the end of the list.

Rock around the Clock, Bill Haley and the Comets	Smoke gets in your eyes, The Platters
See you later Alligator, Bill Haley and the Comets	Dream Lover, Bobby Darin
Shake, Rattle and Roll, Bill Haley and the Comets	Here Comes Summer, Jerry Keller
Putting on the Style, Lonnie Donegan	Good Golly Miss Molly, Little Richard
Rock Island Line, Lonnie Donegan	Tutti Frutti, Little Richard
Singing the Blues, Guy Mitchell	Johnny B. Goode, Chuck Berry
Sixteen Tons, Tennessee Ernie Ford	Blueberry Hill, Fats Domino
Just Walkin' in the Rain, Johnny Ray	Oh Carol! Neil Sedaka
Diana, Paul Anka	Bo Diddley, Bo Diddley
Great Balls of Fire, Jerry Lee Lewis	Not fade away, Buddy Holly
Whole Lotta Shakin', Jerry Lee Lewis	Be Bop A Lula, Gene Vincent
Chantilly Lace, The Big Bopper	Hound Dog, Elvis Presley
Dream, Everly Brothers	
Bye Bye Love, Everly Brothers	
Cathy's Clown, Everly Brothers	

HIT RECORDS OF THE 1960s

Name ....

Here are some of the greatest rock 'n' pop songs of the sixties. Put a (✓) beside your 10 favourite records. If one of your top 10 is not there, add it to the end of the list.

Lay, Lady Lay, Bob Dylan	Honky Tonk Woman, Rolling Stones
I'm Free, The Cream	As Tears go by, Marianne Faithful
All Along the Watchtower, Jimi Hendrix	Whiter Shade of Pale, Procul Harum
She Loves You, The Beatles	Tired of Waiting for You, Kinks
Hey Jude, The Beatles	House of the Rising Sun, Animals
Strawberry Fields, The Beatles	My Generation, The Who
Get Back, The Beatles	I'm a Boy, The Who
Watcha gonna do about it, Small Faces	Walking Back to Happiness, Helen Shapiro
Light my Fire, The Doors	Sound of Silence, Simon and Garfunkel
Ferry Across the Mersey, Gerry and the Pacemakers	She's not There, Zombies
Fire!, Crazy World of Arthur Brown	The Mother people, Frank Zappa
24 hours to Tulsa, Gene Pitney	A World Without Love, Peter and Gordon
Sunshine Superman, Donovan	Sunny Afternoon, The Kinks
White Rabbit, Jefferson Airplane	I'm a Believer, The Monkees
Anyone who had a Heart, Cilla Black	
Satisfaction (I can't get it), Rolling Stones	

HIT RECORDS OF THE 1970s

Name ....

Here are some of the greatest rock songs of the seventies. Put a (✓) beside your 10 favourite records. If one of your top 10 is not there, add it to the end of the list.

Stairway to Heaven, Led Zeppelin
Sailing, Rod Stewart
Brown Sugar, The Rolling Stones
Watching the Detectives, Elvis Costello
Mull of Kintyre, Wings
Dancing Queen, Abba
London Calling, The Clash
Jean Genie, David Bowie
Rhiannon, Fleetwood Mac
My Sweet Lord, George Harrison
Hot Love, T Rex
Down Down, Status Quo
Casey Jones, Grateful Dead
I'm not in Love, 10 c.c.
When I Need You, Leo Sayer

Anarchy in the UK, The Sex Pistols
Roxanne, The Police
Message in a Bottle, The Police
Heart of Glass, Blondie
Your Song, Elton John
Stayin' Alive, Bee Gees
Baker Street, Gerry Rafferty
All Right Now, Free
Imagine, John Lennon
Message to Rudi, The Specials
No More Heroes, The Stranglers
Bye Bye Baby, The Bay City Rollers
Virginia Plain, Roxy Music

HIT RECORDS OF THE 1980s

Name ....

Here are some of the greatest rock 'n' pop records of the eighties. Put a tick (✓) beside your favourite 10 records. If one of your top 10 is not listed, add it to the end.

Brass in the Pocket, The Pretenders
Atomic, Blondie
Geno, Dexy's Midnight Runners
Don't Stand so Close to me, The Police
This ole House, Shakin' Stevens
Stand and Deliver, Adam and the Ants
Tainted Love , Soft Cell
Under Pressure, Queen and David Bowie
Don't you Want me?, Human League
Land of Make Believe, Buck's Fizz
House of Fun, Madness
Fame, Irene Cara
Come on Eileen, Dexy's Midnight Runners
Eye of the Tiger, Survivor
Pass the Dutchie, Musical Youth

You can't Hurry Love, Phil Collins
Billie Jean, Michael Jackson
Let's Dance, David Bowie
Uptown Girl, Billy Joel
99 Red Balloons, Nena
Wake me up before you Go-Go, Wham!
19, Paul Hardcastle
Into the Groove, Madonna
Dancing in the Street, David Bowie and Mick Jagger
Rock me Amadeus, Falco
Don't Leave me this Way, Communards
Nothing's gonna Stop us Now, Starship
La Bamba, Los Lobos
Pump up the Volume, M/A/R/R/S

HIT RECORDS OF THE 1990s

Name..

Here are some of the most popular records of the nineties. Put a (✓) beside your 10 favo records. If one of your top 10 is not there, add it at the end of the list.

Feel like Making Love, Pauline Henry
Echo Beach, Martha and the Muffins
Shimmer, Trans Global Underground
Justified and Ancient, KLF
What time is Love? KLF
About a girl, Nirvana
All that She Wants, Ace of Base
Phorever People, Shamen
Hope Street, The Levellers
No Limit, 2 Unlimited
Little Fluffy Clouds, The Orb
What's the Frequency, Kenneth?, REM
She Bangs the Drums, Stone Roses

The Universal, Blur
Movin' on Up, Primal Scream
Wonderwall, Oasis
It's oh so Quiet, Björk
Love Rendezvous, M People
Mile End, Pulp
Changingman, Paul Weller
Cigarettes and Alcohol, Oasis
Protection, Massive Attack
Stay Together, Suede
Life is Sweet, Chemical Brothers

And for our next question............

RUBBINGS

Well, if you thought the only thing that could be rubbed was church brasses, you can think again! Virtually anything can be rubbed, from coins to manhole covers, signs to machine parts, bones and stones.

The basic technique will be familiar to most of us, who will at some time or another have done coin rubbings using paper and soft pencil, viz:

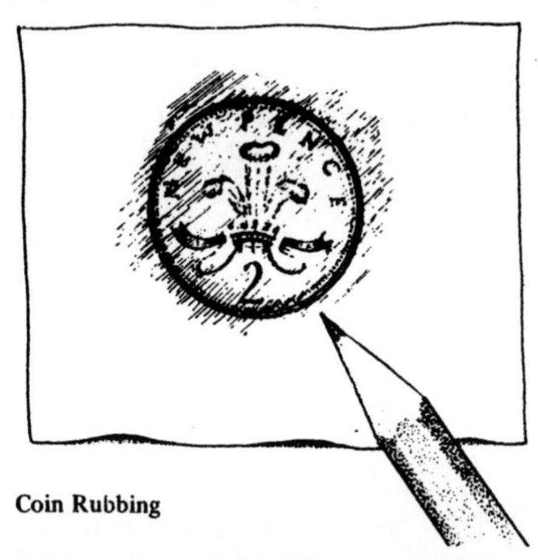

Coin Rubbing

It only takes a little 'brainstorming' and an imaginative attitude to materials to come up with interesting rubbings of a wide range of subjects. Try walls, pavements, metal plaques, decorative door handles and plates, wood, shells, fish, fencing, bark, tools, leaves, flowers, seed pots, etc..

Various kinds of paper and rubbing materials can be used. The general rule of thumb about paper is to use thin paper when a faint image is to be rubbed. Consider using different coloured papers, or newsprint and don't forget about Dayglow for mind-boggling effects! Rubbing materials like crayon, graphite stick, charcoal, tailor's chalk, Dayglow crayon and heel-ball, and Cirencester sticks (available from Specialist Crafts), especially made for brass rubbing, can be used to good effect. Half the fun is in experimenting to find the best combination of materials, e.g. white tailor's chalk on black paper.Special black and white brass rubbling paper is also manufactured to ensure the highest definition for rubbings that are important.

Project work can combine rubbings with other visual materials to form a collage. Or, young people can combine different elements together to form a 'picture' to be rubbed. The following list of materials and the rubbing method are for brass rubbings, but can easily be adapted for other purposes.

Materials

- Paper (white) – decorators lining paper is cheap and useful for practice purposes. It tears easily though, and yellows with age. Architect's detail paper is best for most purposes, bought by the roll. This is a 'rag' type paper. You'll need scissors for cutting the paper in lengths.
- Heel-ball/Cirencester sticks – these are the special wax sticks used for rubbing, made from bees-wax, tallow and lamp black.
- Brushes – two kinds. A fairly soft bristle or nylon brush for cleaning

the surface. A toothbrush to remove grit from the incised lines of the brass. Brushing the brass in this way, and freeing it of particles of grit, greatly reduces the chances of the paper tearing.

- Dusters – to remove final traces of grit after brushing.
- White cloths – one to be used before rubbing to press the paper into the incised lines of the brass – helps to get a sharper contrast between the black and white areas and gives you the **outline** of the figure – don't rub beyond that. The other cloth is used to wipe over the finished rubbing to give it a good polish.
- Masking tape – to secure the paper to the stone, wall or mounting. If the stone is in poor condition, the tape may not stick – weights can be used instead.

Method

1. Clean the brass and surrounding area thoroughly with brushes and duster to remove all traces of grit.
2. Unroll enough paper to cover the brass – cut the required length from the roll and fix it to the surrounding stone with masking tape.
3. With a clean cloth, press round the outline of the brass, and into the incised lines – this helps give a good impression and prevents you rubbing over the edge of the outline.
4. Begin your rubbing, using a blunt piece of heel-ball. It doesn't really matter where you start rubbing – it is usual to do it from the bottom up. Use firm strokes of even pressure to obtain even contrast. If your heel-ball and paper are good quality, you shouldn't have to rub too hard. When the rubbing is finished, rub it over with the second cloth to give it a good polish.

Storage

Rubbings can be sprayed with a clear plastic fixative to prevent damage. Large rubbings must be rolled (unless mounted) to store. All rubbings are affected by moisture – crayon and heel-ball can be damaged by high temperatures. If desired, rubbings can be mounted onto board for display purposes.

Although brass rubbing is rather specialised, ordinary everyday objects can be rubbed without using highly specialised materials. The technique provides a good introduction to understanding the basic print process and can be used in combination with drawing and painting to produce unusual collages.

SCRAPERBOARD

High contrast drawings and illustrations can be produced quite simply using cutting tools on scraperboard. The techniques can take a little bit of practice to learn, so it is usually best introduced to young people who can already draw reasonably successfully with a pen/pencil, AND can be trusted to work safely with the relatively sharp cutting tools!

Usually scraperboard comes in sheets of white card onto which two surfaces have been added. Underneath is a white chalk base, over which is added a thinner film of dense black ink. There are also white, silver and copper versions available, which, when cut into expose the different colours underneath. Some youngsters can also enjoy experimenting with coloured inks or coloured permanent markers. Used on top of white areas, the colours can enhance the starkness of the black and white image, but remember that this will prevent the image being photocopied, if that is the intention.

To create a scraperboard picture, cutting tools are used to lightly scrape/cut the surface thereby removing lines and small portions of the black surface. The contrasting images exposed are very striking. The cutting instruments are like old fashioned pen nibs and holders. Most manufacturers make four different nib types, which offer different thicknesses and styles of cut. Even simple results can be very powerful, providing a range of images and textures, and it is a useful medium for posters, greetings cards and book illustrations.

Scraperboard images can be designed freehand, as with Alan's little cartoon of Howie, or a tracing can be used. Chalk is spread on the reverse of a sheet of tracing paper and when a pencil is used on the top surface, the chalk lines are transferred to the scraperboard, ready for cutting.

The subjects you suggest for youthful artists will make the scraperboard work easier or harder. Copying simple designs and decorations, drawing flowers, animals, simple scenes, Christmas images – all are possible to achieve without too much practice. Usually it is quite difficult to correct mistakes once they've been made, but as long as it isn't necessary to re-cut any area, a fine line, black felt marker can be used to cover up unwanted white lines.

This is not a technique for young groups, but scraperboard is a useful medium with adolescent groups. The tools are cheap to buy; the scraperboard is a bit expensive, but relatively small pieces can be cut out for each artist.

Two final tips:

1. Attach pieces of scraperboard to a firm surface using masking tape. This ensures that it doesn't move while the drawing is being completed.
2. Scraperboard marks very easily and sweaty fingers leave greasy marks. So, when a piece is being worked on, place a sheet of paper under the hand to protect the artwork.

SCREEN PRINTING

This technique has more to do with inks and inspiration than with Bogart, Stone, Willis an other big screen stars! The screen referred to is a fine piece of cotton organdie (transpare muslin) which is stretched down tight over a wooden frame. By fixing a stencil to the underside of the screen, ink can be squeezed through the top of the screen to form an image on paper or fabric according to the design of the stencil.

This method of printing is a versatile one and can be used for posters, cards, T-shirts, carrier bags and signs. There is great potential, therefore, for club or group designs and motifs. In fact, groups who become proficient often find that they can earn some spare ca by printing small poster runs to order e.g. for Community Centres, local groups, discos, et It is also possible to make Christmas or New Year cards with the same equipment that yo use to make posters or T-shirts. Screen printing can be used to make very effective desig on fabric (e.g. for curtains or a wall hanging). This is done by repeatedly screening a desi (or designs) on to the fabric until you achieve the desired effect.

This section will deal with making a basic screen and stencil and the printing process. For more detail on the extremely wide range of potential materials available, we suggest that you refer to the Specialist Crafts and NES Arnold catalogues.

The Screen

You can buy screens in various sizes (or adjustable ones) relatively cheaply, but they are quite easy to make if you want to save money. Use ordinary planed softwood (2 inch x 1 inch) to make a frame 17 inches x 15 inches – this will be suitable for most purposes. The corners must be square and can simply be butt-jointed and reinforced with metal fasteners or flat angle brackets. Make sure that the frame lies perfectly flat. It must now be treated with two coats of polyurethane varnish to prevent it twisting and warping when it is being cleaned.

The next step is to fix the fabric tightly over the frame. Cotton organdie is best, but you ca also use terylene voile, polyester mono or multi filament fabric, or very high quality nylon gauze. Cut the fabric with a big enough overlap to turn it over the edges of the frame. Nov staple (with a staple gun) or pin it tightly, once, in the middle of each side. Carry on stretching and stapling the fabric working from the centre out and stapling opposite sides a the same rate (if you do one side at a time the fabric will be too slack). When you get to th corners bunch the fabric up and pull it very tightly before stapling. Now make an ink reservoir by masking the edges of the fabric on both sides of the screen to a depth of 2 inches minimum, with a waterproof cloth tape or masking tape. (If you are only doing a short run, simple gummed paper tape will suffice, but cloth tape is advisable for long runs) This is done to provide space for the ink. The unmasked area formed is your maximum print area for this size of screen (15 inches x 13 inches approximately). Congratulations! – you now have a completed screen. With most materials you will need to degrease the surface using a special paste of crystals. Pre-prepared screens are usually already degreased.

A 'squeegee' is used to draw the ink across the stencil. This is simply a long rubber blade with a wooden handle. The squeegee can be exactly the same width as the print area of th screen (in this case 13 inches approximately) or smaller, in which case you will have to make two sweeps with it to fully cover the print area. They can be purchased in a variety c sizes.

Apart from ink and a stencil, this is all you need to do simple prints on paper, card or fabri

Suitable inks are, for paper and card: Hunt Acrylic, Coates Ecoject, Specialist Colours or NES Arnold own make. For fabric: Sericol Texiscreen, Rowney's Fabric Dyes or Hunt's Textile ink. We are grateful to Specialist Crafts (DRYAD) for permission to reproduce their charts on screen meshes and inks – these are shown at the end of the section and offer options in greater detail.

Tursub can be used for thinning paper inks, Universal Screenwash for cleaning screens and squeegees, and Actisol to free clogged screens or after a break in printing. Ink Retarder can also be used to prevent clogging.

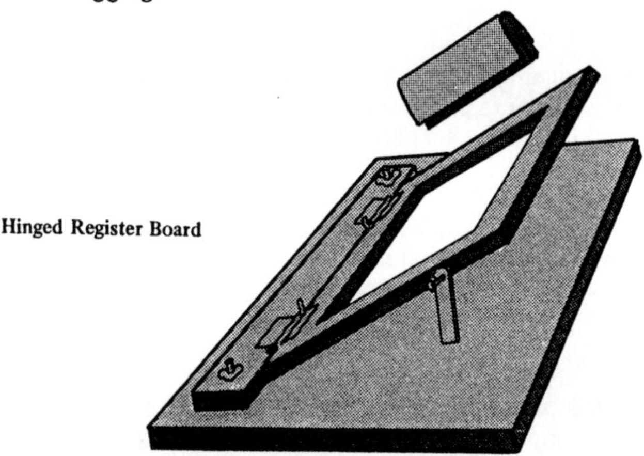
Hinged Register Board

If you intend doing two-colour prints (easy enough to do) you should prepare a hinged register board for your screen (see diagram). The hinged screen arrangement is very useful and is recommended as it keeps the screen supported in the 'up' position between prints.

The Stencil

A simple stencil can be made from paper. You can cut out letters to make a name or slogan, or cut out a design. When printed, this will give you a negative image, as the ink will pass through all areas of the screen **except** your design or slogan – this will therefore appear as white (or whatever the colour the paper is that you are printing on). A positive image can be achieved by cutting out letters or a design from a large (screen-sized) piece of paper. In this case, ink will only pass through your lettering or design, leaving the rest of the print area blank.

Paper stencils must be made from newsprint or a similar lightweight paper. They are very fragile as stencils go, and will only last for a dozen or so prints. However, they have two major advantages over all other types of stencils – they are very easy to make (and cheap!), and they do not clog up the screen (e.g. as Profilm does). This means that you can use the same screen up to about 10 times with different paper stencils, as long as the screen is carefully cleaned after each print run.

A paper stencil is fixed to the screen with ink. First lay out a couple of old newspapers as padding with a piece of paper on top. Now arrange your stencil on the piece of paper in exactly the position you want it to print. Carefully place the screen centrally on top of the stencil and paper, and have someone hold it steady. Now ladle some ink into the top reservoir (it should be the consistency of thick cream) and distribute it evenly with the squeegee. Holding the squeegee at an angle of 45-60 degrees, place it behind the ink and pull the ink down across the screen with a smooth, steady motion. If you are using a small squeegee do this twice or until the whole screen area has been covered with ink. Now repeat. Carefully lift the screen up and you will find that the stencil has stuck to it. You are now ready to make your first print.

Another method of making stencils suitable for short runs is to use French chalk or talcum powder. This should be sieved evenly onto a dark piece of paper. It can now be drawn on with fingers, needles, feathers etc. to create a pattern or lettering. Carefully lower the screen onto the chalk, ink it and squeegee (as above). Now carefully lift up the screen and you will find that the chalk has stuck to it to form a stencil. About 15 prints can be made with this method.

A longer lasting, traditional method of making a stencil is to paint out the areas through which you do not want ink to pass with Shellac varnish (you can also use stencil medium, glue or lacquer) on the underside of the screen.

If you draw your design or lettering with Shellac, a negative image will be produced when it is printed. However, you can make a positive image by painting your design or lettering onto the screen with wax or ink and then painting the whole screen with Shellac or filler. The Shellac will block all of the screen, except the image drawn in the oily ink or wax. When the Shellac or filler is dry, the ink or wax can be removed with white spirit. A positive image can now be printed.

Detailed stencils can be cut from Profilm or Stenplex. This is a layer of Shellac mounted on transparent backing paper. The design should be cut through the Shellac layer, but not the backing paper (this may take a bit of practice), and the parts to be printed removed. The stencil should now be placed, glossy side down, onto the underside of the frame and ironed through the paper at a low heat. This will fuse the stencil to the screen, and the backing paper can then be peeled off. Although it is possible to remove this kind of stencil from the screen after use with white sprit, it is a long and tedious process, likely to dispirit the keenest youngster (not to mention youth leader!) There is also the probability that the Shellac will not be completely removed, and that the next print run will suffer. On balance it is probably best to discard the screen material along with the stencil and to make up a new screen.

Photo-Stencils

High quality results can be achieved from a variety of image sources (including photographic negatives) using this method. It involves making a stencil by shining UV (ultra violet) light through the artwork onto Polycron, which is a light sensitive stencil film. The process is quite simple but you will have to get hold of a couple of UV lights and mount them in a frame above a baseboard. The positive from which the stencil is cut can be hand made by arranging anything opaque (e.g. black paper, doylies, gaskets, cut out shapes etc.) on a sheet of clear acetate. This can also be drawn on with opaque paint, ink, Letraset or Rotring pen. Super prep green film, red Sellotape can also be used to mask out large areas. Photographic effects can be obtained by using an enlarger loaded with a negative to make a positive on special photographic film; this is then used with UV light to cut the stencil onto the Polycron. You may find a print workshop locally which will provide this service.

The process is as follows:

1. Switch on UV lights to heat up.
2. Place Polycron shiny side up.

3. Lay artwork face down on top of Polycron and cover with a sheet of glass to hold the acetate firmly in contact with the stencil.
4. Expose for ten minutes.
5. Switch off lights.
6. Put Polycron shiny side down in a tray of hydrogen peroxide and water (1:4 solution) for one-and-a-half minutes.
7. Remove from tray and leave for one minute.
8. Wash with hot water.
9. Put stencil face down onto screen and leave to adhere.
10. Peel off plastic backing.
11. Tape the remainder of the screen (with paper or cloth covered tape depending on the length of the print run).

The key advantage of photo stencils is that you can produce a large number of prints from a stencil. A number of other photo stencil methods are available, which use, for instance, fluorescent or mercury lights. Your choice of a particular system will depend on the material you intend printing on, and the number of prints your require from each stencil. The cost of these systems varies and we recommend that you contact a specialist supplier such as Specialist Crafts to discuss your specific needs.

An alternative method is achieved by using the Hunt Speedball Easylight stencil emulsion, which is sensitive to an ordinary 150 or preferably 250 watt light bulb. Trial size quantities and full 'group' size bottles are available. Basically the technique involves mixing the emulsion with a sensitizer and then applying a positive stencil onto the squeegee side of the frame. The surface is exposed for between 10 and 15 minutes and this will produce a quality print screen. The sensitizer is a strong chemical and must be handled carefully. This process will produce around 50 prints from a single stencil.

Printing

The printing process itself can be quite messy, especially if oil-based inks are used, as they can only be cleaned with a spirit cleaner (water-based inks can easily be cleaned with water). So... have plenty of rags handy for cleaning. The provision of disposable rubber gloves, aprons and sleeve guards is highly recommended – not only does it make everyone look weird, but it obviates the need to spend half the session cleaning yourself up. You'll need a large table for printing on, and a big basin or sink with plenty of hot water on tap. You'll also need a line with bulldog clips (or clothes pegs) to hang prints up to dry.

It will be clear from the above that the printing process needs to be closely supervised and should be limited to two or three people at a time (unless you have more than one screen). However, others can be involved in designing and preparing stencils, or drying prints (with hair-drier or fan heater).

Place the piece of paper to be printed on the table and centre the screen and stencil on top. Now ladle some ink into the reservoir at the top of the screen (it should be the consistency of thick cream) and distribute it evenly across the top of the screen with the squeegee. With someone holding the screen to steady it, place the squeegee behind the ink and pull it firmly across the screen once or twice. With any luck you should now have an immaculate screen print. Remember to draw the spare ink back across the screen to the reservoir after each pull. The squeegee should always be pulled at an angle of 45-60 degrees and should be sharpened every now and again with fine sandpaper to achieve crisp prints.

Check the quality of the print and work out how many pulls are necessary for the best quality (most prints can be made with one or two pulls, although fabric may need more). When printing T-shirts or fabric always do a test print on a piece of paper. Insert a piece o card between the front and back of the shirt to prevent ink passing through, and pad underneath with newspaper for good contact with the screen. For fabric inks, follow the manufacturer's instructions – most have to be ironed for a few minutes with a hot iron through a thin cloth. Lettering stencils can be used to quickly produce printed slogans.

A separate stencil is needed for each colour if you intend doing multi-colour prints, and a hinged register board is essential for correct positioning. The process involves making prir in the first colour; allowing them to dry; cleaning the screen; changing the stencil and then overprinting with the second colour and so on. This is a time-consuming process, and it makes sense to attempt to get by with the minimum number of stencils. You can also use coloured paper. For example, with two stencils this could give a three-colour print. The register board is used by positioning the first piece of paper to be printed centrally on the board and marking the position with a piece of masking tape along each edge. Subsequen prints can therefore be easily positioned using the register marks.

Tiles

It is possible to print your own designs onto plain tiles using the screen printing method. Obviously a smaller screen is necessary for this, but otherwise the process is identical to that described above. 'End-runs' of tiles can often be obtained from manufacturers at little or no cost.

Screen printing is a relatively inexpensive craft, the major cost being that of the Polycron sheeting if you choose to use photostencils. For good results, a reasonable amount of care has to be taken at most stages in the process and it is therefore difficult to 'do' a screenpri quickly. The best way of tackling it if you have limited time (or young people with a limited concentration span) is to prepare stencils in one session, and spend the next session printing them. However, we have found that most youth groups can produce good quality results quite quickly. Happy printing – squeegees rule OK!

Screen Printing Meshes

Type of Mesh	**N221 Organdie 100 TPI**	**P725 Nylon Screen Mesh 100 TPI**	**P238 Multi-filament Polyester 80 TPI**	**P073 Mono-filament Polyester 122 TPI**	**P072 Mono-filament Polyester 196 TPI**
Screen Preparation	Use degreasing crystals (P075A).	Initial preparation with No. 23 degrease abrade paste (P066). Thereafter degrease crystals (P057A).	Use degrease crystals (P057A).	Initial preparation with No. 23 degrease abrade paste (P066). Thereafter degrease crystals (P057A).	Initial preparation with No. 23 degrease abrade paste (P066). Thereafter degrease crystals (P057A).
Stencil Use	Any – Profilm, direct emulsions, indirect film.	Any – Profilm, direct emulsions, indirect film.	Most – direct emulsions, indirect film. Not for use with Profilm.	Most – direct emulsions, indirect film. Not for use with Profilm.	Most – direct emulsions, indirect film. Not for use with Profilm.
Ink Usage	Reeves screen printing water colour, Coates watercolour, Hunts textile inks.	Any inks.	Any inks.	Any inks.	Any inks.
Results	Best results on fabrics. Not for fine detailed work.	Will produce basic prints on fabric. paper and card.	Will produce detailed work on fabric. Also suitable for paper & board.	Will produce fine detailed work on fabric, paper & card.	Produces extra fine detailed work. Excellent for multicolour graphs, printing on paper, card, board and fabrics.
Screen cleaning	Ink – universal screenwash (P053). Stencil – dependant on stencil used.	Ink – universal screenwash (P053). Stencil – dependant on stencil used.	Ink – universal screenwash (P053). Stencil – dependant on stencil used.	Ink – universal screenwash (P053). Stencil – dependant on stencil used.	Ink – universal screenwash (P053). Stencil – dependant on stencil used.

Screen Printing Inks

This chart contains information and suggested usage procedures for a range of inks.

Inks	Specialist Colours Screen Printing Water Colour	Printex Fabric Colour	Pearlised Screen Colour	Specialist Colours Water-Based Inks	Hunt Textile Ink	Hunt Acrylic Screen Printing Ink	Water-Based Paper & Board Ink	Coates Ecoject Spirit Based Inks
Materials used on	Paper & board Fabrics (limited fixability)	Most fabrics	Paper & board Fabrics (limited fixability)	Fabrics (cotton, polyester, poly/cotton, acrylic, felt etc.)	All fabrics	Paper, board, wood, plastic, metal (limited fabrics)	Paper & board, some grades of PVC	Paper & board
Kind of Stencil	Paper or card	Paper, card and most water resistant stencils	Paper & card	Paper, card and all water resistant films & emulsions	Water resistant films & emulsions	Water resistant films & emulsions	Use with water resistant films & emulsions P550, P987, P963	Spirit resistant film & emulsions
Mesh Type	All types	All types	All types	All types	All types	All types. Best with multi-filament & mono-filament polyester	All types and grades. For best results mono-filament polyester	All types Best with mono-filament polyester
Thin with	Water	Water	Water	Water or water based retarder P056	Retarder P962	Water or retarder P962	Water & retarder P995	Spirit thinner (P051B) & spirit retarder (P052)
Clean with	Soap & water	Soap & water	Soap & water	Soap & water or universal screen wash (P053)	Soap & water	Soap & water or universal screen wash (P053)	Spray with activator (P996) then rinse with water	Spirit thinner (P051B) and universal screen wash (P053)
Washing instructions	Not washable or dry cleanable	Washable and dry cleanable	Not washable or dry cleanable	Washable and dry cleanable	Washable and dry cleanable	Not washable or dry cleanable	Not washable or dry cleanable	Not washable or dry cleanable
Drying Instructions	Air dry within 12 hours	Air dry within 4 hours	Approximately 30 minutes	Cure dry 5 mins 140°C oven. Air dry 2 hours	Air dry within 4 hours	Air dry 20 mins. Heat dry 5 mins 275°F	Air dry 20-30 mins. Heat dry at 50°C for 15 seconds	Air dry 15 mins. 20 seconds using hot blower (hair-drier)
Indoor/ Outdoor Use	Indoor only	Both	Indoor only	Both	Both	Both	Indoor, limited outdoor	Indoor, limited outdoor
Colours in Range	10 colours	8 colours & binder	6 colours	22 colours & base (inc. fluorescents & process colours)	12 colours and base	14 colours and base	11 colours and base	12 colours and base

We gratefully acknowledge permission from Specialist Crafts (Dryad) to reproduce the two charts on screen meshes and inks.

STAINED GLASS

Traditional methods of making stained glass panels are beyond the scope of this book (though not beyond the scope of the determined youth group we suspect!) Here, we offer short-cut options for achieving the distinctive effect of stained glass using very simple materials, which are easy for young people to use.

The method, called cloisonné, involves using a pewter-coloured stained glass relief divider (which comes in handy tubes) together with stained glass paints to create the pattern of your choice on a piece of glass. There are a number of manufacturers including Cern Coleurs, Marabu and Specialist Crafts. It is also possible to add self adhesive lead strip to glass, which can be flattened using a roller. This creates very authentic looking lattice type windows and is ideal for work on terrariums.

To create stained glass type effects you will need:

- Tubes of stained glass relief divider.
- Solvent based glass paint plus stained glass varnish, or colourless medium to lighten and increase the transparency of the colours (colours may be mixed and diluted with alcohol or white spirit) OR water-based stained glass paint plus neutral cutting fluid to lighten the colours (dilute with water). Makes include Vitrail, Marabu-Decorglass and Specialist Crafts glass paints and cold enamels.
- Paint brushes.
- Tracing paper and pencils.
- Pieces of glass from your craft supplier, or other surfaces like glasses, jugs, bottles, acrylics, PVC sheets, plastic or metal foil.
- Methylated spirit to clean the glass.

Method

1. Either create, or trace a suitable pattern (e.g. from a stained glass pattern book) onto paper.
2. Clean your piece of glass with meths and place it over the pattern.
3. Trace out the pattern on the glass with the squeezed out relief divider. You should really leave it for a couple of hours before applying the paint, but if you work carefully, we haven't really found this necessary.
4. Now apply the paint by 'flowing' it with a brush inside the cloisonnés. The edges of the paint will round off by themselves. The thicker the coat, the denser the colour you'll get. For pastel shades, lighten the paint with neutral cutting fluid or varnish, as appropriate.
5. Allow to dry.
6. Some paints require a further coat of hardener.

Both small scale and large scale glass panels can be tackled using this method, and used to good decorative effect in school, youth club or home.

STONE PAINTING

We're sure that you've seen these rather quaint painted stones, which both young and old seem to enjoy turning into odd animals, birds and the like. Once painted, the finished objet d'art can be used as a paperweight, doorstop, ornament, but preferably not Lethal Weapon 5! Painted stone throwing is not to be encouraged!

With younger groups it is a good idea to use water-based paints – they are easier to remove from hair, hands and clothes. Older young people can experiment with a variety of paint mediums such as:

oil paints; gauche, acrylics, enamels, nail varnishes and Posca pens, which are instant paint pens. Permanent felt pens can also be used effectively.

In preparation for a stone painting session, you need to co-ordinate a stone-collecting session. If you have a nearby beach, this can be turned into a fun activity in itself, or the

search can be combined with a beach expedition. Before painting, it is useful to wash the stones in tap water and then thoroughly dry them. To enable drawing rough shapes onto the stones it is easier to use light coloured stones. It is easiest if only the top half is painted. The adult facilitator should encourage everyone to draw out the basic pattern on the stone before beginning painting.
For instance:

It can be useful to suggest some ideas for subjects in a stone painting session.
Invite the young people to try to turn a stone into a:

- cat
- dog
- rabbit
- clown
- butterfly
- frog
- hedgehog

The organiser should tell all the participants to keep their designs simple. As with any art project it is well worth encouraging individual expression. Stone painting has often been used successfully in art therapy sessions and because it lends itself to imaginative interpretation, it works particularly well with young groups and with people who may in other circumstances exhibit learning difficulties. Many of the most colourful and unusual painted stones are often produced by people who would normally not be viewed as 'artistic'.

When the stones are finished, it is well worth varnishing them with polyurethane yacht varnish or similar. Do not allow stone painters to stir the varnish too thoroughly, as this causes bubbles to form which may ruin the finished stone. Rather obviously, brushes will need to be cleaned well, after being use. Use white spirit for varnish or oil based paints, and running water to remove water-based paint from brushes.

If stones are to be placed on wooden tables or scratchable surfaces, it is a good idea to get some pieces of felt, which, once cut to size, can be stuck with PVA glue or similar to underside of the stone.

In all, you will or may need:

- at least one stone for each group member
- paints
- paint and varnish brushes
- pencils
- coloured paint pens
- varnish
- scissors
- glue
- felt
- paper towels/newspaper
- white spirit.

STORYTELLING

It is only a few hundred years since storytelling was the main mechanism for relaying news and current affairs information from community to community. It also acts as a transmitter of culture and tradition down the generations.

Nowadays, culture and information is likely to be recorded on newsprint, books, audio and video tape – and increasingly on CD Rom and computer disks. In many ways this can be seen as an advantage as a permanent record exists, but it can be argued that these media are essentially 'dead' or 'wooden'. For example, there is usually no comparison between a recorded musical work and a live version. Similarly, a book or poem comes to life if it is read out loud by the author or a skilled reader.

Although we are not suggesting a return to the days of oral information sharing and tradition, there is much to be said for the atmosphere and 'engagement' which is created by a skilled storyteller. We should recognise that people (and young people especially) love a good story and try to find ways in which we can re-create this lost art.

At a very basic level, groups of young people can be entertained through the reading of short stories. While this will not suit all groups there will be times, e.g. Halloween when most group will be open to a topical story. Of course, it is essential that the person reading the story has an expressive style – otherwise the story will not 'live' and individuals will rapidly become inattentive and bored.

We recommend that you look at the 'New Youth Games Book' as there are a few techniques in the relationship games sections which can be used to assist a group of young people to create their own stories. A simple technique which works well is for each person in the group to contribute a few sentences to a story as it goes round the group. Although this may sound banal in the extreme, it usually proves to be popular and quite often someone will come out with a punch line or contribution which is side-splittingly funny. It is also worth encouraging young people to work in small groups to create their own stories or 'yarns' – this provides pee support both in the creation and telling of the stories.

Children and young people *are* essentially creative, and if adults encourage this, some amazing results can be had. If an adult is prepared to make up and tell a story, then a challenge can be offered to one or two young people to create their own one for next week's session . Often, the results can be surprisingly good.

Finally, we leave you with **another technique** and a reminder of one of our games which ca be used to good effect in honing storytelling skills.

Put a number of objects in a box – at least one for each person who is participating. These objects can be anything at all – household items, holiday mementoes, bits 'n' bobs etc..

Invite each person to choose an object and then ask everyone to wander around the room thinking about something to transform their object into. For example, if you've picked up a book you might decide to transform it into a pot of gold. Encourage people to attach a little history to their transformed object – so the pot of gold could have been created by Merlin the magician just before he died in the Scottish Borders.

Now tell the group to stop and swap their object with the person nearest to them – along with its complete history. Continue in this fashion for another two or three swaps and then invite the group to sit in a circle and tell the stories attached to each of the objects they now have. This is a painless way of encouraging people to be inventive and demonstrates how stories can be built-up bit by bit. The technique also shows that no matter how strange or ludicrous, a story always has some information or entertainment value.

The **Telephone Game** can be quite a challenge but you'll find that if you have an extrovert or chatterbox in your group, they will usually jump at the chance of giving it a try. First of all you need to come up with a few punch lines. These could be something like: "I told you the guy next door was a policeman", or , "And there is absolutely no way I am going to do that", or , "I am a born extrovert".

A volunteer is needed who selects one of the punch lines (which have been written on cards) and sits in the middle of the group. The volunteer is challenged to invent a telephone conversation with an imaginary person and must finish the conversation with the selected punch line. It's important that you don't push young people into trying this technique, as it can be very difficult for some. When run on this kind of voluntary basis, you'll find that the natural actors and storytellers will come to the fore and that the results can be absolutely hilarious.

TIE-DYE AND FABRIC PAINTING

This method of producing fabric designs was thought of long before the Hippies 're-invented' it in the 1960s. As far back as the 6th century AD, tie-dyed silks and cottons were popular in India, China and Japan. The basic technique is very simple, ideal for work in youth groups, and involves knotting, folding or pleating the material before tying it tightly with thread or string and dyeing it. Obviously, as the dye cannot enter the tied-up areas, a pattern is produced. To a certain extent, the way the fabric is tied will determine the pattern, but there is always an element of uncertainty which adds to this craft's appeal.

Good results can be obtained very quickly with a minimum of effort which makes tie-dyeing suitable for work with most groups of young people. The equipment needed is neither complicated nor expensive and is easily obtained. You'll need a large metal tub or pot to use as a 'dye-bath' – plastic will do if you are using cold water dyes only. Apart from this, you'll need the dyes, something to stir with, rubber gloves (unless multi-coloured hands take your kids' fancy!) some string and the fabric to be dyed.

Tie-dye can be used to pattern any kind of material, including clothes. Think about tie-dyeing T-shirts, skirts, shirts, scarves, sheets, curtains etc.. Natural fabrics like linen and cotton should be dyed with colourfast cold water dyes, while synthetic fabrics are best treated with hot water dyes (not as colourfast as cold water types).
Dylon provide one of the largest ranges of different dyes currently available. NES Arnold sell Handcraft Craft Dyes, which are water based and fixed with a special F15/6 fixer. Specialist Crafts stock a new product, which is **tie-dye string**. Available in nine colours, these cut out the usual more complicated process. To use requires only about half a dozen of the strings to be tied to a T-shirt, or whatever, then the garment is boiled for 30 minutes. Adding salt fixes the colours permanently.

The usual tie and dye method

This involves thoroughly wetting the fabric before dyeing to produce the best contrast in the pattern. Although a good pattern can be produced with just one dye, it is possible to use several different colours to create intricate designs; remember though, that where two dye colours mix, a third colour will be produced! The fabric can be subjected to second and subsequent dyes either before or after the ties have been removed – or the original ties can be left intact and extra ones added. Retaining the ties intact means that some of the material will remain undyed in its original colour.

Fabric can be tied in several different ways to create markedly different patterns - a graded pattern can be made by tying the fabric in thick bunches as this affects the penetration of the dye. Try the suggestions given in the following diagram which can produce some interesting and attractive designs:

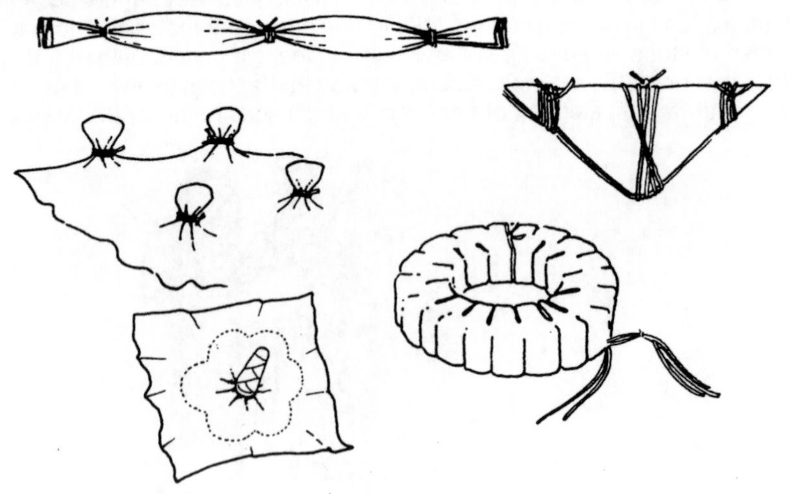

Stripes: Pleat lengthways for vertical stripes, diagonally for diagonal ones, and horizontally for horizontal stripes. The folds can be ironed to make them crisp, and should be tied at regular intervals. If more than one dye is being used, the ties can be positioned for good effect - add the new ties first before removing the old ones, so that the pleating is undisturbed.

Triangles: Pleat the fabric lengthways into four then fold it back on itself into a series of triangles, concertina-style. Bind the ends and the centre with string.

Circles: Dried beans, marbles or stones can be tied into the fabric to create a pattern of small circles. If more than one dye is to be used, the beans should be tied in different places when the process is repeated.

Sunbursts: These bigger circles can be varied depending on the number and position of the string bindings. Arrange the fabric to form a peak and bind it at various distances from the peak to produce concentric circles.

Ruching: Lay out the fabric with a length of double string across one corner. Roll the fabric diagonally around the string before forming it into a circle, ruching it tightly along the string and tying the ends.

Stitching: This can be used for initials, names and motifs. The design should first of all be pencilled onto the fabric, either freehand or with the aid of stencils. Strong thread (knotted at the end) can then be sewn over the outlines with small tacking stitches. The fabric should then be ruched tightly along the stitches and secured with a knot.

Finally, for the best results, remember to follow the dye manufacturer's instructions about fabric preparation, washing and rinsing.

Fabric Painting

A whole host of new dyes and pens for working on silk and cotton have been developed. We have experimented with Marabu-Silk, which can be applied with a brush, or washed in using the tie and tie method. Deka Silk, Elbéfix and Elbesoie are other similar product ranges. Some require fixing with a hot iron, others require steam fixing.

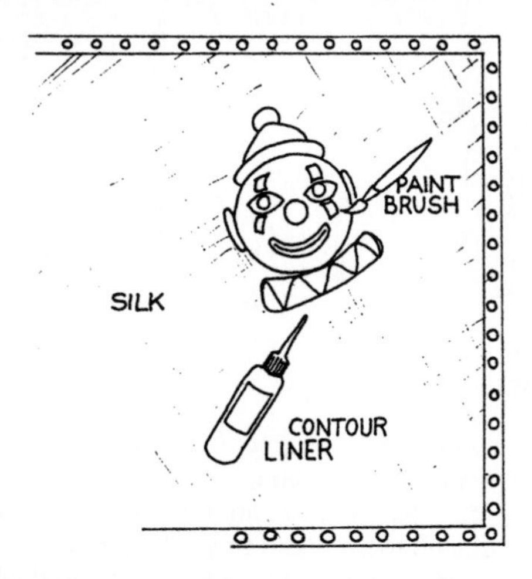

To use the Marabu-Silk method utilising a brush, the silk is stretched and tacked on to a frame. Then the contour lines for a design are painted in from a jar or squeezed from a tube with a fine nozzle. This provides frame-lines, rather like the leading on stained glass work. The contour lines can dry colourless or to a colour such as black, white, gold or silver. Then the silk dye is applied, being careful not to go over the lines. Once the dye is dry, the paintwork can be permanently fixed to the silk by applying an iron to the underside of the fabric for two minutes, with the iron on the cotton setting.

The same company manufactures some rather wonderful fabric paints called Marabu-Textil. These can be applied to virtually any smooth fabric using methods such as:
● print blocks ● stencils ● airbrush ● screen printing.
Once the paints are dry they can be made coloufast up to 40° C using an iron. They are pretty easy to use and the Marabu leaflets give precise details on paint dilutions.

Also available are a wide range of fabric paint pens and paints which can be applied with a brush. Some are specifically designed for working on silk, others will work on virtually any fabric. Galt offer fabric fun pens, metallic and glitter paints and Multicrom, which is available in a variety of colours and works on almost any surface. Javana silk paint pens and marbling inks are available from NES Arnold. Specialist Crafts can supply textile markers which are permanent and do not require ironing to fix.

VIDEO FILM MAKING

This is your chance to hit the big-time – to propel your youth group into the mysterious world of Video, Digital Cameras, the Jump Cut and the Big Close Up! Making a film can be a very rewarding activity for groups of young people, as the medium itself – film or video – has a definite glamour associated with it that creates interest and excitement and helps boost the self-image of those taking part. It is also a co-operative activity which encourages teamwork and clear communication.

Film or video can be used as a very powerful tool in work with kids. If you are trying for example, to make initial contact with young people in a particular neighbourhood, you could do worse than simply set up your equipment in an accessible location. You'll find that 'streetwise' kids will rapidly latch on to you (and to your equipment!). This kind of informal introduction to making videos can lead young people to use the equipment to explore and investigate issues that are of concern and interest to them (don't ask us what they are – ask the kids!). The medium can be particularly potent when used to represent young people's views to adults and can act as a lever in, for example, promoting the need for specific youth facilities.

The instant replay capacity of video creates the potential for a different kind of film making which has increasingly been used by youth groups. 'Social Skills' work can range from simply reflecting on how individuals and groups are perceived by the objective television eye in real life situations, to more sophisticated role play exercises which may be designed to encourage good interview skills, personal presentation, clear communication etc..

Choice of format

The choice of formats has changed dramatically since the first edition of this book when 'Super 8' was a moderately priced option for the aspiring *film* maker. Video systems have continued to reduce in price and size while becoming increasingly sophisticated. Compact cartridge formats and batteries have become the norm, making some new systems virtually pocket size. Traditional celluloid film making has become an expensive professional option – with the advent of cheap video mixing desks, video systems now reign supreme.

The newest technology to impact on 'home' movie making is the digital imaging capacity of modern computers and software. This enables images from a digital camera – still or video – to be 'downloaded' directly into a computer without the use of film or videotape. The stored image can be replayed on the computer screen or incorporated in 'multimedia' documents. Images can be cleaned up, enhanced, edited, distorted or otherwise manipulated.

Needless to say, this is immensely powerful technology which is impacting on all areas of visual communication – television companies have been using ENG (Electronic News Gathering) cameras for some years. In early 1996 a black and white digital video camera was available for little over £100. The 'QuickCam' records at 15 frames per second and gives a 160 X 120 pixel image. It produces quality black and white images and has a built in microphone.

The main drawback of digital video cameras is the small image produced on screen – it takes an awful lot of computer processing power to make moving images! Many state of the art multimedia computers can already support full screen 'real time' video images – in a couple of years, entry level computers will undoubtedly be capable of similar performance.

When buying your Camcorder the current choice is between VHS and 8mm *video*. In terms of quality there is not much to choose from, but the 8mm machines are typically more compact, as the tape size is much smaller.

With the VHS system you can buy a standard domestic sized video cartridge adapter – you simply slot your small VHS tape cartridge into this and you can then playback on any domestic VHS player. The 8mm system is different as the tape size is not compatible with domestic players.

However, the wonders of modern technology come to our rescue once more and you can in fact connect the 8mm Camcorder directly to the television or video player and playback from the 8mm machine itself. If you want a permanent domestic version of your 8mm tape you simply record from the 8 mm machine directly to a VHS tape in your domestic recorder. Thereafter you can play the VHS tape without linking up the 8mm machine.

If you have access to the funds, we recommend that you buy a video mixing desk because of the editing capability this gives you. These are available at High Street shops for between £50 and £100. The more expensive ones offer additional facilities such as titling, date recording etc..

A complete **portable video system** comprises:

- Camcorder (camera and recorder in one)
- Microphone
- Power pack and rechargeable batteries
- Tripod
- Blank video tapes/cassettes
- 'Monitor' or television
- Video light(s)

The instant replay facility of video systems makes it the ideal medium for training and social skills work.

The notes that follow are suitable for both video and film making. Although purists will cringe, we use the term *film* as a generic one encompassing the use of videotape and digital cameras.

The Type of Film to be made

It is important that the young people are involved in choosing the kind of film they want to make, and have an investment in. With luck and practice they will be creating a unique work of art! Most groups will want to make 'horror movies,' 'gangster films' or a documentary about 'our neighbourhood,' and should be encouraged to overcome some of the consequent difficulties (like learning to make someone up like Frankenstein, or getting hold of a suitable representation of a Capone-type sub-machine gun).

There are other kinds of film which you can choose to make, each requiring a different blend of production, camera, wardrobe, make-up and scripting skills. A necessary first step is to break down the chosen film type into skill areas, and to allocate roles and resources as appropriate.

The following list of film types should give you some ideas:

1. **News Film:** This is a record of events which is recorded factually using a news-programme style. It uses a 'presenter' or news reader and may incoroporate film shot on location and added into the newsroom footage. Obviously, the interest value of this type of film depends totally on what you choose to include. As long as you have interesting, exciting, or funny events to 'shoot,' then the film will be successful. This is one of the easiest

kinds of film to make – you don't need special effects, wardrobes or sophisticated camera work. Just ideas, an interviewer and a camera crew!

2. **Documentary:** The difference between documentary and news film lies in the interpretation of events; statements are being made about the events which reflect the feelings and attitude of people making the film. It requires more planning and editing to present a coherent, balanced, or polemical point of view.

3. **Concept:** The aim here is to convey some king of concept, mood or impression. For example, you choose a pop song or poem and film images to go along with it of a complementary or contrasting nature. You can easily work out how to convey a particular mood by carefully selecting subject matter, lighting and the 'pace' of the images you use.

4. **Instructional:** This kind of film either conveys information, or shows you how to make or do something. The essence of the information type of film is in selecting the most important aspects or facts that you want to get across. The 'How-to-do-it' type of film needs very careful preparation in that skills and techniques needed (e.g. how to make a go-kart) must be broken down and arranged in a logical step by step progression, ready for filming.

5. **Fiction:** This is your actual storytelling type of stuff! Essential to this kind of undertaking is the ability to devise a plot, establish a setting and develop character through the medium of film. There are several categories of fictional film, like drama, comedy, fantasy, satire and tragedy; and each of these can be set within different genres, e.g. mystery, romance, western or science fiction. Obviously, careful preparation is a key element in making a fictional film – the basic 'story board' technique outlined in a later section will be useful. As experience in film making is gained, increasing attention can be paid to the use of techniques like repetition, symbolism and the juxtaposition of shots to create special effects.

6. **Animated (Cartoon):** Some video cameras ofer a single frame facility (being able to film one frame at a time). This can be used to make cartoons. The technique, although tedious is very simple. Indeed we have found that two or three young people will often work together happily for a long time to produce their own cartoon. The production of animated films is a fascinating process which can easily tap young people's creative potential. See later section for further details.

7. **Experimental:** Young people often like to try out unusual effects and techniques. Indeed this is how film makers are created. Shooting through filters; panning through 360 degrees; filming at extreme angles or even upside down; filming very short, almost subliminal shots can all be tried, along with any other ideas your youth group has.

Film Jargon

This section will clue you in to some of the jargon beloved of film makers, e.g. 'cue the shot,' 'give me a BCU,' 'roll em,' 'scene 37, take 1335,' 'give me a nice long shot,' etc.. Seriously, though, the language of film making is important – much of it is a sort of technical shorthand which speeds up and clarifies communication between, for example, the director of the film and the camera crew and actors. Young people are inveterate users of slang and easily pick up film jargon.

Frame: A single image on a length of film or video.

Shot: A number of consecutive frames which have been filmed in one continuous running of the camera. There is no standard length of shot, although a short one will usually last for just a few seconds while a long one will run for maybe 10-15 seconds.

Sequence: A number of shots which develop one particular idea. This is the key unit to use when working with young people. If you consider your film as being made up of a number of scenes, each containing several sequences, then preparation and filming should be relatively straight forward. The concept of sequences can be easily understood by referring to comic strips, as they are invariably structured in this way. They can also be used to illustrate other terms used below (LS, MS, BCU, etc.).

Long Shot (LS): A shot which is taken with the camera a long way away from the subject **or** a shot where the camera **appears** to have been a long way away (e.g. by using the zoom lens).

Medium Shot (MS): A shot which is taken close to the subject, but which includes some of the surrounding as well, e.g. a shot being taken from the waist up.

Medium Close Up (MCU): Usually of a person, showing the upper half of the torso.

Close Up (CU): Where the camera is, or seems to be, very close to the object being filmed, e.g. a shot where a person's face completely fills the frame.

Big Close Up (BCU or XCU): The camera is, or seems to be, extremely close to the subject, with one feature (e.g. a person's nose) completely filling the frame.

Pan: The camera follows a moving subject horizontally, or moves across a stationary subject.

Zip-Pan: A fast horizontal rotation of the camera across the subject which produces a blurred effect.

Track The camera actually moves towards or away from a stationary subject, or follows a moving one.

Zoom: The camera appears to be moving towards, away from, or following the subject, but the effect is produced by using the zoom facility on the stationary camera. Zooming in towards a subject is often referred to as 'tightening the shot.'

Camera Angles: Normal (where the camera is level with the subject), high or low. Referred to as NA, HA, LA.

Common Problems (and how to solve them)

Reversal: This arises when separate, consecutive shots are taken in front of and then behind the subject. In the second shot the subject will appear to have reversed position or direction. In essence, the camera cannot be moved through more than 180 degrees when filming a stationary subject without creating a reversal problem.

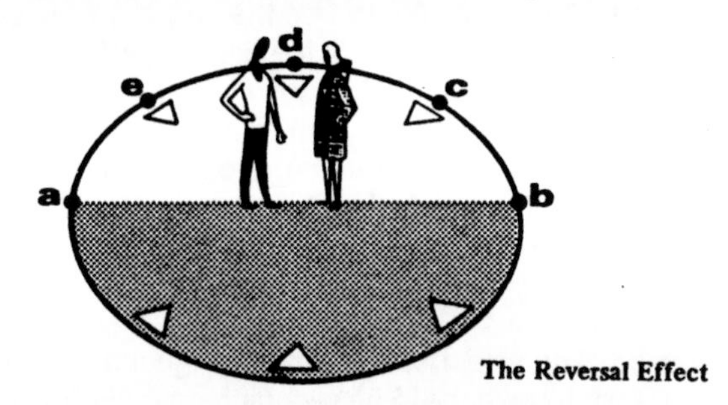

The Reversal Effect

Look at the diagram, if the camera starts off at point **a**, it can be moved as far as point **b** (or as near as dammit!) within the shaded section without reversal cropping up. If, however, the camera were to be moved as far as point **c, d** or **e**, the resulting film would show the subjects suddenly changing position. The only solution is to either avoid traversing more than 180 degrees or to show that you actually have gone behind the subject by keeping the camera running while you track around.

In some cases you may decide you actually do want a reversal effect.

The Jump cut: This is probably the most common difficulty you'll have to cope with. It arises mainly when two separate consecutive shots are taken of the same subject, and the subject (or the camera) has moved slightly between shots – the effect is that of a 'jump' or 'jerk' in the film. For all the technical prowess of our television companies, jump cuts can still be seen on the small screen now and again – watch out for them! If used sparingly, the jump can impart a shock effect to the audience if desired.

A 'Cutaway': This shot can be used to solve the jump cut problem. This involves taking a shot of the main subject, then a shot of another person or object before taking the second shot of the main subject. This is a useful technique to master as it is obvious that, say, in filming a long interview, you may want to take it in stages and therefore stop the camera several times. Cutaways can be inserted at the editing stage, in which case you need to make sure that you have a good selection of cutaway shots to use (e.g. interiors, clocks, passing traffic, etc.).

Another solution is to 'tighten the shot' (i.e. zoom in a bit) each time the camera is re-started. This will lessen the jump cut effect. Finally, you can if you wish change the camera angle or position by more than 45 degrees, as a **substantial** change will suggest to the audience that some time has elapsed, and this may solve the problem. (If changing the camera position, take care not to move it so much that you get a reversal effect).

Special Effects

Some, but by no means all video cameras offer the opportunity to experiment with special effects, such as:

Slow Motion: As normal operating speed is 18 frames per second, you will have to film at 32 f.p.s. or higher to get a good slow motion effect on playback.

Fast Motion: Film at 12 f.p.s. or slower.

Fade: Some video cameras have a special button for 'fade in' and 'fade out' effects. However, if you have a manual exposure control on the camera which can over-ride the automatic system, you will have no difficulty in achieving this effect. **To fade out:** set up your shot with the camera adjusted for manual exposure control. Use the exposure setting, if you have one, e.g. f8 which is indicated by the automatic system, and begin taking your shot. As you near the end of the shot, slowly move the exposure dial up the scale as far as it will go (i.e. towards f16 or f22). This will darken the picture. **To fade in:** set the camera to the highest exposure setting and begin shooting; gradually move the exposure control down the scale until you get to the correct setting (f8 in this case).

Appearance/Disappearance: The effect of a person or object appearing or disappearing 'on screen' is startling, but easy to arrange. The technique simply involves stopping the camera during a shot and making the appropriate change in the subject. It is crucial that the camera is firmly set on a tripod and a remote control cable should be used if possible – the camera and its settings must not be disturbed. If actors are involved in the scene, they must 'freeze' while the changes are made. Filming can now recommence, and the camera should be run for a minimum of 5 seconds after the changes have been made.

Diffusion/Distortion: These effects are obtained by filming through material which alters the image seen by the camera. Filming through a piece of glass lightly smeared with vaseline will give you a soft, diffuse effect, while fog or mist can by simulated by the use of a white or light coloured nylon stocking. Bottles, patterned glass or prisms will produce various distorted effects.

Editing the Film

Whichever way you choose to make your film, you will probably want to have a go at editing, as it greatly improves the quality of the final product. If you are using the 'film as you go' method, you may get away with using editing simply to cut out any 'duff' bits of the film. The professional method involves making up the film at the editing stage by piecing together the various scenes you have shot.

Editing can also be used to tidy up the film generally to achieve a really professional looking product. You can, for example, insert cutaway shots to get rid of jump cuts, or insert long shots to set the scene. The editing process itself can greatly affect the overall impact of the film – the use of brief shots will give it pace, emphasising any desired impression of excitement, violence, gaiety, speed, etc., lengthy shots may suggest sadness, relaxation or contentment.

Editing can therefore be a very powerful and creative part of the film making process and should never be undervalued.

Time spent at the editing stage will **always** pay dividends. Of course, persuading young people that this is the case is an altogether different story, but why not arrange a trip to your local film of television studio to watch the professionals at work? This is guaranteed to produce some budding Oliver Stone or Steven Spielberg!

Story boards and Scripting

The planning and filming process has several different stages, and there is therefore plenty of opportunity for a division of responsibility amongst those involved. Using the professional method, the stages are roughly as follows:

- pick your subject
- define the film's purpose and the audience
- write an outline of the action
- expand this to include instructions on visuals and sound (if any)
- plan out any dialogue
- write out detailed planning cards
- arrange cards in shooting order
- shoot the film
- view the film
- arrange it in scenes
- edit the scenes and put back into story order
- record and add any additional soundtracks required.

It is important to organise this material into a format that will enable you to go ahead and shoot the film easily, and story boards can help you to do this. They can be used at several stages of the planning process, and in their simplest form, aim to gather together ideas for different scenes on planning cards which are then arranged in chronological order. Index cards are suitable and can be easily pinned on to a story board, e.g.

SCENE 1	ACTION	SCENE 2	ACTION
Outside the youth club- a number of young people are gathering.	General messing about, some of it on roller-skates.	Inside the youth club two workers are talking.	Animated discussion about the kids out-side- wondering why they won't come in to play table-tennis and football.

When you begin to discuss the detailed planning cards you get involved in the nitty gritty aspects like the kind of shot required, camera angles, props, etc.. There are further possibilities here for division of responsibility as a full film crew can comprise scriptwriter, director, camera person, sound person (if needed), editor and actors, and they can begin to psyche themselves into the skills or roles they will be using.

Detailed planning cards should contain all the information you need to proceed to the filming stage, e.g.

SHOT	DESCRIPTION	CAMERA POSITION	CAMERA ANGLE	DIALOGUE
1	Outside the youth club- half a dozen young people messing about- 2 of them on roller skates.	L.S. (long shot)	N.A. (normal angle)	Yells, screams, grunts, etc.

SHOT	DESCRIPTION	CAMERA POSITION	CAMERA ANGLE	DIALOGUE
2	Jim and Alec on roller skates begin to harrass the others by running rings round them.	M.S. (medium shot)	H.A. (high angle)	Yells, screams

Once completed, detailed planning cards can be arranged on the board in either chronological or shooting order, depending on the method of filming being used.

If you wish to use a script, (i.e. if you have a keen typist!), the headings on the detailed planning cards can be used, with the scenes and shots arranged in shooting order.

Producer's check list

Denis Mooney of Scottish Television gave us some helpful hints to make sure any video project runs smoothly.

Cost: Make sure you know *exactly* how much you have to spend on your project, and produce a budget for it.

Context: Decide *before* you start what the film is going to be about.

Presentation: With most films of a news, documentary or instructional nature, you really need to spell out your intentions to the viewers. You can do this easily by structuring your films like this:

- tell them what you're going to tell them
- tell them
- tell them what you've just told them.

This may seem very crude, but it's how the TV professionals do it, and it's the best way of making sure that you really get your message across.

Closing: Always make sure you've got a strong closing quote to finish with.

Timetable: Draw up a timetable for shooting your material. If location filming or interviewing is involved, leave plenty of time for setting up and travelling between locations (it always takes longer than you think).

Locations: Make sure you have permission to film on locations – don't assume it. If people do give you access, drop them a note of thanks – it works wonders when you want to use the same location again.

Editing: Make sure to leave enough time for editing before you plan to show the film, as editing is always very time-consuming. You can use an ordinary tape recorder to help you edit. If you record your video sound track onto audio tape, you can then get it typed up. From this typescript you can then decide which piece of video goes where; this cuts out the time-consuming process of watching the whole video through several times. Using this method also helps cut down the amount of time you have to spend in an editing suite.

Voice-overs : Remember that you can use 'voice-overs' to add to a 'head shot' or landscape etc..

Interviewer's Check List

Bob Tomlinson of Scottish Television recommends a few simple techniques to make sure that interviews work well.

- Make sure that the interviewees know why they are involved in the film.
- Tell them what you expect so that they have time to prepare.
- Don't keep them hanging around, e.g. when the equipment is being set up.
- Remember that to do a five minute interview on location will probably take at least half an hour (allowing for adjusting equipment, several 'takes' etc.)
- Make a point of seeing the interviewees and talking to them (on the phone if need be) before you do the shot. This gives them a chance to get to know you and find out why you are making the film.
- Ask the interviewee what they want to say and try to incorporate their comments.
- Always use strong eye contact when interviewing to stop folk gazing into the camera lens.
- Never switch the camera off at the end of the interview. Keep it running and ask if there's anything else they'd like to be asked, any comment they want to make, or anything they think has been missed. Check this out with the camera crew as well.You'll usually find that some of the best material is recorded at this point, after the 'official' interview has finished.

Filming

It's important that at least one person in the crew is completely conversant with all the equipment that is to be used and knows how to set it up. While this is likely to be an adult to begin with, every opportunity should be taken to enable the young people themselves to gain competence in using the various bits of hardware. This applies, also, to the planning process where their involvement is crucial in making sure that both adults and young people are committed to a particular project. Although workers do have a responsibility for creative input (especially with under-stimulated children whose ideas may be few and far between) most young people can come up with good ideas given encouragement.

Although in danger of stating the obvious, here are a few simple hints to help you on you way.

- Unless using a digital camera, always have plenty of spare videotape (and batteries) to hand.
- Always use a tripod when filming.
- Use titles and credits liberally as they make for polished production. Young people love to see their names in lights anyway!
- Experiment with different ways of making captions – e.g. by using film animation techniques you can make words appear one letter at a time.
- Simple computer graphics can be used to produce interesting titles and captions. More sophisticated effects, including digital still/video images, can be fully incorporated in the film using current technology.
- Never shoot into the light – always have the light source behind the camera, or to the side.
- Always set the scene by using a long shot of the place where the action happens, e.g. the outside of a building, the seaside, etc..

Film Animation (Cartoons)

Cartoon making, or film animation as it is more correctly called, is a fascinating aspect of the film medium. The authors have seen some really stroppy young people working in close harmony to produce their version of 'Popeye'! Although essentially a repetitive activity, the creative aspect of being able to make your own cartoon seems to exert a considerable fascination on young people. So much so that they are often prepared to spend quite long periods of time concentrating on the single frame filming that is necessary to produce good results. You'll probably find film animation best suited to work with small groups of two or three young people – one to work the camera and one or two to manipulate the objects being filmed.

In most cases, film animation requires that the camera is pointing down at the floor – the 'rostrum camera' position. It is relatively easy to build a wooden frame to support the camera in this position, and photoflood bulbs for illumination can be fixed to this as well. Underneath this, within the limits of the camera's viewfinder, you need to place a 'register board'. This can simply be a wooden batten fixed to the floor with a sheet of glass placed hard against it. Each time a change is made to the cartoon background or to the cut outs (e.g. of cartoon characters) which are placed on top of it, the sheet of glass is used to hold it flat and secure. A simple way to prepare a background for a story is to draw or paint it on a long roll of cartridge paper – and when a change of scene is needed the paper is simply moved along a bit.

Having said all this, workers in Dundee use an even simpler method which has been well tested with groups of young people.

For this you will need a:

- Camera capable of making single frame exposures.
- Cable release (remote control device for single frame exposure).
- Tripod.
- Simple floodlight (e.g. ES socket and lamp mounted on a pole or tripod).

Set the camera on the tripod and aim it down at the floor as near to vertical as the tripod will allow. Fix a piece of poster paper to the floor with drawing pins to create your picture area. Illuminate this with your photoflood lamp making certain that it is firmly fixed – any movement will create annoying changes in light intensity visible in the finished cartoon. Using the cable release take two or three frames for each segment of the animation.

This kind of set up can be used for animations like:

- A white sheet of paper upon which a picture gradually draws itself.
- A collage background to which cut-out figures with speech bubbles are added.
- Toys, dolls, tools, etc. in motion (e.g. scissors having a conversation).
- Patterns drawn in spilt salt.
- Card figures with jointed limbs moving around.
- Plasticine figures and objects.
- Liquorice Allsorts vs Smarties war.

It is also possible to film '3-D' animations from the side by setting them up on a table top. The same set-up should be used with tripod, cable release and photoflood. You may also want to hang up a large cloth or blanket as a background. With this arrangement you could have Lego structures building themselves, Bendy toys in action, a pool game playing away by itself or toy cars zooming around. The key to effective animation work is to let your imagination run riot.

SUPPLIERS' GUIDE

In compiling the *New Youth Arts and Crafts* book we have contacted over fifty suppliers across the UK. We have mostly met with courtesy and assistance and in a number of cases, literally hours of advice. Because we are keen that youth organisations should support local arts and crafts suppliers as well as national specialists, we would recommend that you try to visit your local shops and see what is available. Having said that, firms like Specialist Crafts can supply the materials and equipment for the majority of the activities listed in this book. A number of the national firms offer discounts for educational and youth groups, and may have special 'sampler' packs for the various crafts available.

General suppliers

Specialist Crafts Ltd (Dryad), PO Box 247, Leicester LE1 9QS. Tel. 0116 251 0405. *Arguably the biggest range of arts and crafts supplies in the UK. Happy to offer advice and assistance as well as selling their products.*

NES Arnold Ltd, Ludlow Hill Road, West Bridgford, Nottingham NG2 6HD. Tel. 0115 945 2200. *A specialist educational supplier whose catalogue range includes arts and crafts supplies for the whole school age range.*

Galt, Culvert Street, Oldham, Lancs. OL4 2ST. Tel. 0161 627 5086. *An educational supplier, with an educational games specialism. Their catalogue includes an art section.*

Fred Aldous, PO Box 135, 35 Lever Street, Manchester 1 M60 1UX. Tel. 0161 236 2477. *A craft supplier who covers many of the crafts in this book, plus traditional crafts such as embroidery, basket making and marquetry.*

Specialist suppliers

Badge making

London Emblem PLC, Emblem House, Blenheim Road, Longmead Industrial Estate, Epsom, Surrey KT19 9AP. Tel. 01372 745433. *We use their machines for metal button badge making and can vouchsafe their reliability.*

Enterprise Products, 36 Ridgeway Road, Redhill, Surrey EH1 6PH. Tel. 01737 772185. *A similar type of range to London Emblem.*

Circus and juggling skills

Jugglemania, 119 Chiltern Drive, Surbiton, Surrey KT5 8LS. Tel. 0181 390 6855. *An interesting array of circus, juggling and magic products, including books.*

The Big Top, 45-49 King Street, Glasgow G1 5RA. Tel. 0141 552 7763. *Special friends to youth and playworkers. They stock a good range of circus, juggling and playwork equipment including face paints from Grimas.*

The Boggle Brothers, 3 Jubilee Cottages, Herrington, Bath. *Circus and juggling skill tutors and performers.*

Design and Technology supplies

Trylon Ltd, Wollaston, Northants NN29 7QJ. Tel. 01933 664275. *Suppliers of candle making materials and many other CDT materials. A co-operative who want to help!*

Dyes
Dylon International, Worsley Bridge Road, Lower Sydenham, London SE26 5HD. Tel. 0181 663 4801. *The UK's main supplier of dyes for use on all sorts materials.*

Fabric and glass paints
Marabu, through Edding Ltd, Edding House, Merlin Centre, Acrewood Way, St Albans, Herts AL4 0JY. Tel. 01727 846688. *Includes Marabu silk, decorglass and textile ranges of paints and dyes, plus the Edding pen selection.*

Jewellery suppliers
Manchester Minerals, Rooth Street, Heaton Norris, Stockport, Cheshire SK4 1DJ. Tel. 0161 477 0435. *One of the best ranges of supplies for jewellery making.*

H.S. Walsh, 243 Beckenham Road, Beckenham, Kent BR3 4TS. Tel. 0181 778 7061. *Highly specialist suppliers of clock making, silversmithing and casting.*

Fimo, through Inscribe Ltd, Woolmer Industrial Estate, Bordon, Hants GU35 9QE. Tel. 01420 475747. *Suppliers of the Fimo range of modelling and jewellery making materials.*

Modelling, carving and sculpting
Alec Tiranti Ltd, 70 High Street, Theale, Reading, Berks RG7 5AR. Tel. 01734 302775. *A substantial catalogue of specialist resources, including how-to-do-it books on various aspects of carving and moulding.*

Leatherwork
Le Prevo Leathers, Blackfriars, Stowell Street, Newcastle upon Tyne NE1 4XN. Tel. 0191 232 4179. *Extremely helpful specialist leather suppliers.*

S. Glassner, 476 Kingston Road, Raynes Park, London SW20 8DX. Tel. 0181 543 1666. *A good range of special leather working supplies.*

Pyrography
Janik Enterprises Ltd, Brickfield Lane, Ruthin, Clwyd LL15 2TN. Tel. 01824 702096.*Specialist suppliers of pyrography materials and equipment plus wooden and leather products*

BIBLIOGRAPHY

This bibliography is a fair indication of some of the books and resources which we have used to inform and improve our own arts and crafts work. The age of some of the books (and their likely availability) are indicative of the number of years we have been working with young people! We do not know the date of publication of a few of the books – sorry! In addition to the books listed in this section, we would strongly recommend readers to get hold of current catalogues and resource books produced by suppliers such as Specialist Crafts, Galt, NES Arnold, Le Prevo Leathers, London Emblem and others listed in the Suppliers' section.

GENERAL GUIDES

Anderson, Enid, 'Crafts and the Disabled', Batsford, 1982
Caket, Colin, 'Infant Crafts', Blandford Press, 1983
Harlow Eve, 'The Book of Handicrafts', Sundial Books, 1975
Hawes, Sonia, 'Simply Art', NAYC Publications, 1981
Jenkins and Morris, 'Crafts from your microwave', Quintet Publishing, 1994
Make It Easy Cards, Hamlyn Publishing Group, 1978
NES Arnold, 'Introducing Art' series (includes drawing, painting, printing, clay and 3-D construction) NES Arnold, 1996
NFPA/Play Train, 'Play Ideas Bank', Play-Train, Birmingham, undated
Paget, Dawn, 'The Art of Craft', Cassell, 1990
Park, Louise, 'Art Attack', Ashton Scholastic
Readers Digest Manual of Handicrafts, Readers Digest, 1980
Simmons, Rosemary, 'Printmaking in Easy Steps', Cassell and Collier Macmillan, 1977
Specialist Crafts, '500 series' Arts booklets (16 page booklets – a variety of titles on enamelling through to braid weaving)

AIRBRUSHING

Breckon, Brett, 'Airbrushing and photo-retouching', Apple Press, 1987
Leek, Michael, 'Encyclopedia of Airbrush techniques', Headline, 1995
Tombs Curtis and Hunt, 'The Airbrush Book', Orbis, 1980

CALLIGRAPHY

Goffe and Ravenscroft, ' Calligraphy step-by-step', Harper Collins, 1994
Martin, Judy, 'The Complete Guide to Calligraphy', Phaidon, 1984
Pearce, Charles, 'Little Manual of Calligraphy', Harper Collins, 1982
Thomson, George, 'The Art of Calligraphy', Treasure Press, 1985

CANDLE MAKING

Carey, Mary,'Candle Making', Evans Brothers Ltd, 1974
Millington, Deborah, 'Traditional Candlemaking: simple methods of manufacture', Intermediate Technology Publications, 1992
Strose, Susanne, 'Candle Making', Sterling Publishing Co Inc, 1968

COLLAGE

Beaney, Jan, 'Fun with Collage', Kaye and Ward, 1979
Cooper, Graham & Sargent, Douglas, 'Painting the Town', Phaidon, 1979
Korstad, Mueller Mar, 'Murals: Creating an Environment', Davis Publications Inc, 1979
Nuttall, Prudence, 'Make a Collage', Evans, 1974
Pluckrose, Henry, 'Collage Ideas', Evans, 1979
Steele, Philip 'Collage', Kingfisher Books, 1993

COOKING AND BAKING

Coles, Angela, 'The Reluctant Cook', Whittet Books Ltd, 1980

Holloway, Malcolm ,'The "How to" Book of Bread and Bread making', Blandford Press, 1981

McCallum, Cass, 'The Real Food Guide: Pulses, Seeds and Grains', Richard Drew Publishing, 1981

NPFA, in 'Towards a Safer Adventure Playground', NPFA, 1985

Pay, Joanna, 'Cooking for kids the healthy way', Dunitz, 1986

Queen's College Glasgow, 'The Glasgow Cookery Book', John Smith & Son, 1975

Richardson, Rosamund, 'Vegetarian cooking for children', Piatkus, 1986

COSTUMES AND DRESSING UP

Asher, Jane, 'Jane Asher's Fancy Dress', Pelham, 1983

Beaton, Claire et al, 'Let's Dress Up', Merehurst, 1995

Caudron, C, 'Usborne Book of Dressing-up' Usborne, 1993

CYCLING

Ballantine, Richard, 'Richard's New Bicycle Book', Pan, 1989

Plas, Rob vander, 'The Mountain Bike Book', San Francisco Bicycle Books, 1993

DÉCOUPAGE

Anaya Publishers, 'Creative Papercrafts', Anaya, 1994

Moxley, Juliet, 'Découpage', Letts

Thomas and Fox, 'Practical Découpage', Anaya, 1993

ENAMELLING

McGrath, Jinks, 'First Steps in Enamelling', Apple Publishing, 1994

Untracht, Oppi, 'Enamelling on Metal', Pitman, 1977

FACE PAINTING AND MAKE-UP

Alkema, Chester J, 'Mask-Making', Oak Tree Press, 1976

Beaton, Clare, 'Face painting', Kingfisher, 1990

Grimas, Face Painting for professional and hobby', Grimas, 1992

Quant, Mary, 'Mary Quant on Make-Up', Century Hutchins, 1986

Snazaroo, 'Fantastic Faces', 'First Faces' and 'Five minute faces'. Snazaroo, various dates

FLOWERCRAFT

Berry et al, 'Flowercraft', Collins and Brown, 1995

Westland, Pamela, 'Glorious Flowercraft', Apple Press

JEWELLERY MAKING

Bagley, Peter, 'The Encyclopedia of Jewellery Techniques', B.T. Batsford, 1986

Bagley, Peter, 'Making Silver Jewellery', B.T. Batsford, 1982

Budwig and Coles, 'Book of Beads'

Case, Barbara, 'World of Beads', David and Charles, 1995

Hutton, Helen, 'Practical Gemstone Craft', Studio Vista, 1972

Wicks, Sally, 'Jewellery Making Manual'

KITES

Denyer, Miles, 'Making Kites', Apple Publishing, 1993

Gallot, Phillipe, 'Making and Flying Fighting Kites', Batsford, 1990

Pelham, David, 'The Penguin Book of Kites', Penguin, 1976

Lloyd, Ambrose et al, 'Making and Flying Kites', Hamlyn, 1977

LEATHERWORK
Cope, A and J, 'Leatherwork', Pan
Grainger, Sylvia, 'Leatherwork', Kestrel Books, 1978
Hayes and Vincent, 'Making it in Leather', David and Charles, 1973
Michael, Valerie, 'Leatherworking Handbook', Cassell, 1994

LINO PRINTING
Palmer, Frederick, 'Monoprint Techniques', Batsford, 1975
Simmons, Rosemary, 'Printmaking in Easy Steps', Cassell and Collier, Macmillan, 1977

MAGAZINES AND NEWSPAPERS
Bjelland, Harley, 'Create your own Desktop Publishing System', Windcrest, 1994
InterAction, 'Make-it-Yourself Handbook', InterAction, 1982
Parker, Roger C, 'Desktop Publishing and Design for Dummies', IDG Books, 1995
Zeitlyn, Jonathan, 'Print: how you can do it yourself', InterAction, 1980

MASKS
Baranski, Matthew, 'Mask Making', Worcester, 1972
Peters, J, 'Make a Mask', Batsford
Wright, Lyndie, 'Masks', Franklin Watts, 1991

MOBILES
Mytton-Davis, Peter, 'Mobiles', Ward Lock, 1971
Pointney, Kate, 'Make a Mobile', Faber and Faber, 1974

MURALS
Bamett, Alan W, 'Community Murals', Cornwall Books, 1984
Directory of Social Change, 'The Mural Kit', undated
Mueller, Mary Korstad, 'Murals', Davis Publications, 1979
Pavey, Don, 'Art-based Games', Methuen, 1979

PAINTING, DRAWING AND VARIATIONS
Edwards, Betty, 'Drawing on the Right Side of the Brain', Souvenir Press, 1979
Miura, Einen, 'The art of marbled paper', Zaehnsdorf, 1990

PAPIER MÂCHÉ
Anaya Publishers, 'Creative Papercrafts', Anaya, 1994
Elliot, Marion, 'Papier Mâché Project Book
Robins, Deri, 'Papier Mâché', Kingfisher Books, 1993
Usborne How to make series, 'Papier Mâché', Usborne, 1993

PEBBLE POLISHING
'How to Polish Gemstones', available through Manchester Minerals
Fletcher, Edward, 'Pebble Polishing', Blandford Press, 1972
Jarrard, Reginald Arthur, 'The Amateur Lapidary', Barton, 1969

PERFORMANCE ARTS
Bolton, Reg, 'Circus in a Suitcase', New Plays Incorporated, 1982
Finnegan, Dave, 'The Complete Juggler', Butterfingers, 1982

Kostelanetz, Richard, 'The Theatre of Mixed Means', Pitman, 1970

PHOTOGRAPHY
Ilford Book of Classroom Photography, Ilford
Davenport, David, 'A Practical Guide to prize winning photography', Oxford Illustrated Press, 1987
Peach and Butterfield, 'Photography', Usborne Guide, 1987
Pickering, John, 'Photography for Children', Batsford, 1976

PUPPETS
Currell, David, 'Puppet Making'
Fraser, Peter, 'Puppets and Puppetry', Batsford, 1980

PYROGRAPHY
Grainger, Stuart, 'An Introduction to Pyrography'
Havez, Bernard, 'Pyrography', Evans Brothers, 1978

RUBBINGS
Busby, Richard J, 'Beginners Guide to Brass Rubbing', Pelman Books, 1969
Bodor, John J, 'Rubbings and Textures: A Graphic Technique', Chapman Reinhold, 1968

SCREEN PRINTING
Bristow, Nicholas, 'Screenprinting', Batsford, 1990
Hollebone, Sarah, 'Screen Printing: The Beginners Guide', A & C Black Ltd, 1980
Kinsey, Anthony, 'The Art of Screen Printing', Batsford, 1979
Stellabrass, Anne, 'Fabric Screeprinting'
Treweek and Zeitlyn, 'Alternative Printing Book', Penguin 1983

SPRAY CAN ART
Chalfont and Prigoff, 'Spraycan Art', Thames and Hudson, 1987

STAINED GLASS
Bier, Barry, 'The Art of Stained Glass',
Metcalf, Robert, 'Making Stained Glass', David and Charles, 1972
Shedenhelm, W, 'Stained Glass', Tab Books, 1987

TIE DYE AND FABRIC PRINTING
Ball, Kazz, 'Learn Fabric Painting', Harper Collins, 1989
Buckanan, Celia, 'Tie-Dyeing'
Campbell, Joy, 'Batik', Apple Publishing, 1994
Meilach, Dona, 'Contemporary Batik and Tie-dye', Allen and Unwin, 1973
Williams, Melanie, 'Fabric Painting

VIDEO FILM MAKING
Dowmunt, Terry, 'Video with Young People', InterAction, 1980
Hannen, Foss, 'How to Make your own Video Programmes', Elm Tree Books, 1982
Hedgecoe, John, 'Complete Guide to Video', Collins and Brown, 1992
Lewis, Roland, 'Video Maker's Handbook', Macmillan, new edition, 1995